Twayne's United States Authors Series

Sylvia E. Bowman, *Editor*

INDIANA UNIVERSITY

Thomas Wolfe

 50

THOMAS WOLFE

by B. R. McELDERRY, Jr.
University of Southern California

TWAYNE PUBLISHERS
A DIVISION OF G. K. HALL & CO., BOSTON

FOR FRANCES

Contents

Chronology   13

1. Introduction: 1900-1926.   17

2. Thomas Wolfe: Dramatist   34

3. 1926-1929 *Look Homeward Angel*   45

4. 1929-1938 *Of Time and the River*   67

5. The Webber Novels   88

6. Wolfe's Shorter Fiction   104

7. The Man   126

8. The Writer   153

Notes and References   174

Selected Bibliography   184

Index   198

Preface

RECONSIDERATION of Thomas Wolfe is timely. It is now twenty-five years since his death, and thirty-four years since his greatest novel, *Look Homeward, Angel,* appeared. Since World War II, most readers who grew up with Wolfe have naturally moved on to other interests, and now associate Wolfe with the remote prewar past. A whole new generation has appeared to whom Wolfe is not a contemporary but part of the enormous literary inheritance which must be sorted out. There is some feeling that Wolfe can be dispensed with. Younger readers are likely to be told that Wolfe's fiction was "mere" autobiography, that he was "adolescent" and "lyrical," that he was deficient in social insights, and that he was too uncritical ever to achieve "form."

There is truth in these charges, but not the whole truth. By a fresh survey of Wolfe's career and his achievement, this book seeks to establish a more just perspective on Wolfe's qualities and defects. Wolfe's material was autobiographical; but his method was far more selective than has been recognized. In treating each novel I have shown not only the parallels between Wolfe's life and the fiction based upon it, but also the omissions and the shifts of emphasis. For example, the Carolina Playmakers gave great encouragement to Wolfe by producing two of his short plays and by providing him association with a lively group excited about regional writing. Nothing whatever is said about this activity in *Look Homeward, Angel,* though he might have satirized the Playmakers as he did almost all phases of college life that he treated.

The impression that Wolfe was "adolescent" and "lyrical" is much modified by giving due credit to his humor. It seems presumptuous to say that Wolfe as a humorist was more versatile and more subtle than Mark Twain, but the evidence is in the books, if they are rightly read. Wolfe's reputation for "formlessness" rests on his failure to perfect his long works. His failure in this respect is relative, in any case, and it should not obscure his conspicuous success with episodes, both short and long. It is unreasonable to praise the episodes of *Huckleberry Finn* and to reject those of *Of Time and the River.*

Critics, following Wolfe's own comments, have regarded his years of dramatic apprenticeship at the University of North Carolina and at Harvard as a great mistake. The fact is that Wolfe came very close to success with the New York Theatre Guild when he was only twenty-three. Many of Wolfe's best pages of fiction are dramatic, rather than lyrical, and they owe something to the apprenticeship he served. Attention to his two full-length plays—*Mannerhouse* and *Welcome to Our City*—reveals that the social awareness in Wolfe's posthumous novels, supposedly so "new," was actually a return to earlier preoccupations. There is, therefore, greater inner coherence and more evidence of growth in Wolfe's career than has usually been supposed.

My attempt has been to emphasize that inner coherence without denying the inconsistencies and failures in Wolfe's life and works. For many interesting topics I have not found space: a detailed examination of Wolfe's revision of short fiction published in magazines and later included in his novels: similarities and differences between Wolfe and other Southern writers; and Wolfe's reputation abroad. Though privileged to have access to much manuscript material at the University of North Carolina, at the Pack Memorial Library in Asheville, N.C., and at Harvard University, I have based my account primarily on published sources. Richard S. Kennedy's *The Window of Memory*, a thorough study of the Wolfe manuscripts, appeared after my book was completed; in my notes I have added a few references to his discussion.

In reviewing so large a body of fiction and in disentangling the fiction from the biography, I have derived much help from previous writers, particularly from Elizabeth Nowell's edition of Wolfe's *Letters* (1956) and from her biography *Thomas Wolfe* (1960). Specific indebtedness is indicated in the notes and bibliography. I should like to acknowledge particularly the pleasure and profit of long conversations about Wolfe with Professor C. Hugh Holman of the University of North Carolina; with Miss Myra Champion, Curator of the Wolfe Collection in the Pack Memorial Library in Asheville, N.C.; and, on a memorable afternoon, with Fred Wolfe, the only surviving member of the Wolfe family.

B. R. McELDERRY, JR.

University of Southern California
Los Angeles, California

Acknowledgments

The author wishes to thank editors and publishers for the use of various materials. Quotations from the following works are made with the permission of Charles Scribner's Sons:

A Stone, A Leaf, A Door by Thomas Wolfe. Copyright 1945 Maxwell Perkins, Executor.

Editor to Author: The Letters of Maxwell E. Perkins edited by John Hall Wheelock. Copyright 1950 Charles Scribner's Sons.

The Face of a Nation by Thomas Wolfe. Introduction by John Hall Wheelock. Copyright 1939 Charles Scribner's Sons.

From Death to Morning by Thomas Wolfe. Copyright 1935 Charles Scribner's Sons.

The Letters of Thomas Wolfe collected and edited by Elizabeth Nowell. Copyright 1956 Edward C. Aswell, Administrator C.T.A. of the Estate of Thomas Wolfe, and/or Fred W. Wolfe.

Look Homeward, Angel by Thomas Wolfe. Copyright 1929 Charles Scribner's Sons; renewal copyright 1957 Edward C. Aswell as Administrator C.T.A. of the estate of Thomas Wolfe, and/or Fred W. Wolfe.

The Marble Man's Wife: Thomas Wolfe's Mother by Hayden Norwood. Copyright 1947 Charles Scribner's Sons.

Of Time and the River by Thomas Wolfe. Copyright 1935 Charles Scribner's Sons.

The Story of a Novel by Thomas Wolfe. Copyright 1936 Charles Scribner's Sons.

Thomas Wolfe's Letters to His Mother edited by John Skally Terry. Copyright 1943 Charles Scribner's Sons.
Letter dated October 29, 1945. Maxwell E. Perkins to J. S. Terry.

Quotations from the following works are made with the permission of Doubleday & Company, Inc.:

Thomas Wolfe by Elizabeth Nowell. Copyright 1960 by Doubleday & Company, Inc.

To Albert F. Gegenheimer, Editor of *Arizona Quarterly*, thanks are due for permission to use parts of essays previously published in that journal: "The Autobiographical Problem in Thomas Wolfe's Earlier Novels" (Winter, 1948); and "The Durable Humor in *Look Homeward, Angel*" (Summer, 1955).

To Walter J. Meserve, Associate Editor of *Modern Drama*, thanks are due for permission to adapt as Chapter II of the present work my essay, "Thomas Wolfe: Dramatist," which first appeared in the journal (May, 1963).

Chronology

1900 Thomas Wolfe born in Asheville, North Carolina, October 3. Youngest of eight children born to William Oliver Wolfe and Julia Elizabeth Westall Wolfe.

1904 Accompanied mother and several of the other children to St. Louis for the World's Fair. Grover Cleveland Wolfe, Ben's twin, died there.

1905 Attended Orange Street Public School.

1912 Transferred to North State School, private school established by Mr. and Mrs. J. M. Roberts.

1916 Entered the University of North Carolina, Chapel Hill.

1918 Did civilian war work at Norfolk, Va., in summer. Enrolled in Professor Koch's playwriting course in fall. Favorite brother Ben died, October 19.

1919 *The Return of Buck Gavin*, presented by the Carolina Playmakers, with Wolfe in the title role, March 14, 15. Won the Worth Prize for essay in philosophy, "The Crisis in Industry." Became editor of *Tar Heel*, the student paper. "The Third Night, A Mountain Play of the Supernatural," presented by the Playmakers, December 12, 13.

1920 Graduated from the University of North Carolina. Rejected offers of various newspaper positions, and an opportunity to teach at Bingham School, near Asheville. Entered the Harvard Graduate School and the 47 Workshop in September.

1921 Wolfe's short play *The Mountains* produced by the Workshop. Completed in May three of the four courses required for the M.A. Remained in Cambridge for summer course. Brief visit to Asheville. Continued graduate work and 47 Workshop in September. *The Mountains* produced as full-length play October 21, 22.

1922 Completed requirements for the M.A. at Harvard. Father died, June 20. Wolfe returned to 47 Workshop in September.

1923   *Welcome to Our City* presented May 11. Play submitted to the New York Theatre Guild; rejected in November or December, with suggestions for revision.

1924   Began teaching English at Washington Square College of New York University in February. Taught summer term. Sailed for England, October 25. Manuscript of *Mannerhouse* stolen in a Paris hotel.

1925   Returned to New York in August. Met Mrs. Aline Bernstein at end of voyage. Brief trip to Asheville. Resumed teaching at Washington Square in September.

1926   Left June 23 on second trip to Europe. Joined Mrs. Bernstein in the English Lake Country in July. Having failed to sell his two plays, turned to the writing of fiction. Traveled in England and on the Continent. Returned to New York, December 29.

1927   Worked on his novel during the spring. Third trip abroad in the summer. Resumed teaching at Washington Square in September.

1928   Finished his novel, *Look Homeward, Angel,* in March. Fourth trip to Europe in summer. Injured in a fight at the Munich Oktoberfest. Scribner's wrote, October 22, that it was interested in his novel. Sailed for New York, December 21.

1929   Scribner's accepted the novel. Wolfe taught half-time at Washington Square in the spring semester, full-time in the fall. Spent part of the summer in Maine, reading proofs. "An Angel on the Porch" published in the August *Scribner's Magazine. Look Homeward, Angel* published October 18.

1930   Was awarded Guggenheim Fellowship in March. Sailed for Europe, his fifth trip, May 10. Met Fitzgerald several times. Wolfe was mentioned favorably in Sinclair Lewis' Nobel Prize Speech, December 12.

1931   Met Sinclair Lewis in London. Returned to New York in late February and settled in Brooklyn.

1932   "A Portrait of Bascom Hawke" tied for a *Scribner's Magazine* prize; published in April issue.

1933 Delivered to Maxwell Perkins, Scribner's editor, the manuscript then called "The October Fair," part of which was published as *Of Time and the River.*

1934 *Of Time and the River* sent to the printer in July.

1935 Sailed for Europe, sixth trip, March 2. *Of Time and the River* published March 8. Entertained in Germany. Returned to New York, July 4. Guest lecturer at the Colorado Writers' Conference, July 22 to August 9. Trip to the Grand Canyon, Los Angeles, San Francisco. *From Death to Morning,* collection of short stories, published November 14.

1936 *The Story of a Novel,* the lecture delivered in Colorado, published April 21. Quarrel with Scribner's over royalties on this book and over other matters. Seventh trip to Europe: in Berlin for the Olympic Games in August. Sued for libel in "No Door," a story in *From Death to Morning.* Trip to New Orleans in December.

1937 Settlement out of court of Dorman suit for libel. Visit to Asheville. Break with Scribner's became publicly known in September. Contract with Harper's signed December 31.

1938 Lecture at Purdue University, May 19. Western journey through National Parks, June 21 to July 2. Illness in Seattle. Left for Johns Hopkins hospital September 6. Operation performed on September 12 revealed incurable miliary tuberculosis of the brain. Died September 15.

1939 *The Web and the Rock* published June 22, 1939.

1940 *You Can't Go Home Again* published September 18, 1940.

1941 *The Hills Beyond,* collection of short stories, published October 15.

1943 *Thomas Wolfe's Letters to His Mother* published May 5.

1948 *Mannerhouse: A play.*

1951 *A Western Journal.*

1956 *The Letters of Thomas Wolfe,* ed. Elizabeth Nowell, published in September.

1957 "Welcome to Our City," *Esquire,* October.

CHAPTER 1

Introduction: 1900-26

AMONG THE MANY fine novels appearing in 1929 were two which in their contrast represented major attitudes of the time—attitudes still significant to us. In the spring came Ernest Hemingway's *A Farewell to Arms,* a tale of fruitless war and fated love. At the end, Lieutenant Henry stands at the bedside of the dead mother of his dead child: "It was like saying goodbye to a statue. After a while I went out and left the hospital and walked back to the hotel in the rain." In those concluding sentences is all the shell-shocked numbness which was so important a heritage of World War I, a numbness that was to be powerfully reinforced by the stock market crash of October, 1929. But in that same October appeared a novel of different temper: Thomas Wolfe's *Look Homeward, Angel.* A key scene is the death of Eugene Gant's favorite brother Ben:

Filled with a terrible vision of all life in the one moment, he seemed to rise forward bodilessly from his pillows without support—a flame, a light, a glory—joined at length in death to the dark spirit who had brooded upon each footstep of his lonely adventure on earth; and, casting the fierce sword of his glance with utter and final comprehension upon the room haunted with its gray pageantry of cheap loves and dull consciences and on all those uncertain mummers of waste and confusion fading now from the bright window of his eyes, he passed instantly, scornful and unafraid, as he had lived, into the shades of death.

We can believe in the nothingness of life, we can believe in the nothingness of death and of life after death—but who can believe in the nothingness of Ben? Like Apollo, who did his penance to the high god in the sad house of King Admetus, he came, a god with broken feet, into the gray hovel of this world. And he lived here a stranger, trying to recapture the music of the lost world, trying to recall the great forgotten language, the lost faces, the stone, the leaf, the door.

O Artemidorus, farewell! [1]

There is no numbness here. In the presence of death, there is a vibrant sense of life. It is this vitality that is the central quality of Wolfe's work. Readers who demand artistic perfection will find his novels disappointing. Others, who appreciate the struggle between the artistic impulse and overwhelming human experience, will find them rewarding.

I *Wolfe's Career in Brief*

When he published *Look Homeward, Angel* Wolfe was virtually unknown. He had grown up in Asheville, North Carolina, graduated from the State University at Chapel Hill, attended Harvard Graduate School for three years, taught English at New York University for five years, and made four trips to Europe. While at Harvard, he had worked hard to make himself a dramatist. Despite encouragement from George Pierce Baker and serious consideration from the Theatre Guild, Wolfe had been unable to sell a play for commercial production. Turning to fiction in the summer of 1926, he put all his energy into the huge manuscript which later became his first novel. Aside from student contributions to University of North Carolina publications and a single travel article in an Asheville paper in 1925, Wolfe had published nothing when, at the age of twenty-eight, his novel was accepted by Scribner's. "An Angel on the Porch," a version of Chapter XIX of the novel, was published in the August issue of *Scribner's,* partly to give advance publicity to a hitherto unpublished novelist.

The success of *Look Homeward, Angel,* though moderate, was sufficient to allow Wolfe to give up his teaching position at New York University early in 1930. Scribner's offered an advance of $4,500 on his second novel, to be paid $250 a month; and Wolfe seemed well launched toward the literary fame he so desperately desired. The first novel which had been closely based upon his youthful experience in Asheville and his college years at Chapel Hill, closed with his departure for Harvard. It was natural that he continue the story. In March of 1935 *Of Time and the River* chronicled his impressions of Harvard, New York University,

New York City, and Europe in approximately 400,000 words (as compared with the 250,000 words of *Look Homeward, Angel*). The second novel closed with the meeting of Eugene Gant and Esther, the fictional counterpart of Mrs. Aline Bernstein, whom Wolfe met in August, 1925, on his return voyage from his first trip to Europe.

The prolonged and tempestuous negotiations with Maxwell Perkins, Scribner's editor, over the preparation of these two novels put a great strain on what had begun as a very friendly association early in 1929. The difficulties were aggravated by Wolfe's relationship with Mrs. Bernstein and by a long series of petty but annoying legal problems. There was also the growing opinion that Maxwell Perkins' services as editor were so great that much of the credit for Wolfe's book really belonged to Perkins. Inadvertently, Wolfe gave support to this idea in *The Story of a Novel*, first given as a long lecture, then published in *The Saturday Review of Literature*, and later in book form. In this account Wolfe gives generous praise to Perkins for his sympathetic help. Between editor and author, however, there were sharp differences of opinion about the manuscript designed as Wolfe's third novel. In January, 1937, Wolfe formally severed connections with Scribner's, and the following December signed a contract with Harper's.

After several months of hard work in the spring of 1938, Wolfe delivered a lecture at Purdue University, and continued west to Denver, Portland, and Seattle. On July 11 he was taken to the hospital with a high fever. After some improvement, he complained of severe headaches, and he was advised to go to Johns Hopkins for treatment. On September 12 he submitted to a brain operation which revealed miliary tuberculosis in so advanced a stage that no cure was possible. He died early in the morning of September 15, his thirty-eighth birthday a little over two weeks away.

From the great mass of manuscript that remained, Edward Aswell of Harper's published two novels posthumously: *The Web and the Rock* in June, 1939, and *You Can't Go Home Again* in September, 1940. A collection of short pieces, *The Hills Beyond*, followed in October, 1941, supplementing a collection published in November, 1935, and entitled *From Death to Morning*. The two posthumous novels showed a certain parallel to the earlier novels which tell the life story of Eugene Gant. The new hero, George "Monk" Webber, like Eugene Gant, grew up in a small Southern town, attended a state university, and came north to New York City. Major differences from the Gant story are the full account of Monk Webber's affair with Esther Jack (the "Esther" whom Eugene met at the end of *Of Time and the River*), and the preoccupation with social ideas, notably the significance of the rising Nazi power in Germany.

Such, in brief, is the exterior pattern of Wolfe's career. It is a pattern typical of his time and one still common in American experience: youth in a small provincial town, college years in a university far from the actual centers of power and creativity, young manhood in a great Eastern university and in the infinite variety of New York City. For thousands of readers there are a dozen points of contact, of identification. The very fact that Wolfe's fiction is "autobiographical" makes it accessible and immediate, just as, in a sense, Fitzgerald's fiction is accessible and immediate only to the limited number of readers who have always been rich, or who have intimately known rich people.

Yet the autobiographical nature of Wolfe's fiction can be misleading. Normally we read a novel and then later learn something about the writer's life that illuminates his choice of situations and his treatment of them. It is worth knowing, for example, that Sinclair Lewis did indeed grow up in Sauk Centre, Minnesota, which bears some resemblance to the Gopher Prairie of his fiction. But we sense a difference between Sinclair Lewis and Dr. Kennicott: we accept the doctor as a fictional character, soundly based on Lewis' experience and observation. With Wolfe, our experience is likely to be different. He has been so prominently tagged as an "autobiographical" writer that the reader is likely to come to his work forearmed with the knowledge that W. O. Gant was in fact Wolfe's father; that Eliza is really Julia Wolfe, his mother, the shrewd real estate speculator; that every one of the bickering Gant family has his counterpart in Wolfe's brothers and sisters. The Pulpit Hill of fiction is transparently Chapel Hill, the actual University of North Carolina; and Professor Hatcher of the famous playwriting course at Harvard is none other than the renowned George Pierce Baker, exposed, for once, in all his Cambridge snobbery. Esther Jack is indeed Aline Bernstein, and Foxhall Edwards, the editor with Yankee inhibitions in *You Can't Go Home Again,* is surely Maxwell Perkins, from whom Wolfe rightly "liberated" himself.

There is truth in all these similarities, and we cannot ignore it. But the truth in the novels is not the whole truth or the literal truth, and to assume that it is, is to distort our experience of the novels. Closely as Wolfe used events and observations of his personal life, he was selective; and he shaped the emphasis of his material for fictional effect. If Wolfe's representation of his family, of his beloved Asheville teacher, Mrs. Roberts, or of Professor Baker of Harvard seems ungenerous to the point of bad manners or even bad morals, we are still unwise in using the man to damn the book or the book to damn the man. We must perform a difficult critical act. We must see book and man together, for in a sense they are inseparable; but we must also view book and man separately. It is necessary to use what knowledge we have of the man to understand the experience out of which the fiction came. It is even more necessary to understand the fictional process by which the experience was turned into fiction. In this book, therefore, we shall first describe as accurately as possible the various stages of Wolfe's experience on the evidence of his letters and the accounts left by his associates. Then, turning to the novel in question, we shall illustrate not only some of the similarities but some of the differences, attempting in the end a judgment of the fictional or artistic validity of the novel irrespective of its "autobiographical" quality.

By this time a great deal of objective biographical evidence has accumulated. Besides a number of short reminiscences by classmates and colleagues, there are Wolfe's letters to his mother (1943), to Mrs. Roberts (1946-47), and the comprehensive selection published by Elizabeth Nowell (1956). There is a circumstantial account of Wolfe's mother (1947), and one dictated by his sister, Mabel Wolfe Wheaton (1961). Two books document Wolfe's experience at New York University. Many of Maxwell Perkins' letters to Wolfe appear in *Editor to Author* (1950). Finally, there is Elizabeth Nowell's fine biography (1960) in which she, as former Scribner's staff member and later as literary agent for Wolfe, has meticulously sorted out fact from rumor.

II *Youth in Asheville*

Asheville, North Carolina, was a quiet Southern town of fifteen thousand inhabitants when Thomas Clayton Wolfe was born there, October 3, 1900. It was the horse and buggy era, and, when Wolfe went off to college in 1916, teams were still more common than automobiles. As a winter resort, Asheville was beginning to enjoy a modest fame, and boarding houses like the "Old Kentucky Home" of Wolfe's novel were common. A few miles out of Asheville was "Biltmore House," the famous Vanderbilt mansion built in the style of a French chateau, which guaranteed to Asheville occasional notice in metropolitan society columns. Asheville itself had none of the grandeur of "Biltmore." Like so many old American towns, it was built around a square, and W. O. Wolfe's marble shop was on the southwest corner. Everyone knew everyone else, and Mrs. Wolfe's conversation, even in her old age, was full of stories about people of the town.

William Oliver Wolfe, the author's father, was born in Pennsylvania in 1851. He was the fifth of a family of six children. After the Civil War he learned the stonecutter's trade in Baltimore, and in 1871 moved south to Raleigh, North Carolina. Divorced by his first wife, he married again, bringing his wife Cynthia to Asheville. After the death of Cynthia, her mother kept house for Wolfe until he married Julia Elizabeth Westall in 1885. Julia herself tells how, as a book agent, she called on the stonecutter, and how the acquaintance led to marriage— an incident used with comic effect in *Look Homeward, Angel*.

W. O. Wolfe was a tall, powerful man, better able than his helpers to manage the heavy blocks of stone. He was a great reader, fond of Shakespeare and the poems in a Golden Treasury edited by Stoddard and Browne. Sentimental pieces like Gray's "Elegy" and Hood's "The Bridge of Sighs" appealed to him. In Mrs. Wolfe's words, he was "a spree drinker," and she seems to have recognized in him a physical compulsion that was beyond any control. His appetite for food was gargantuan, as his children testified. Toward his children he was generous in an easygoing way, but only Tom and Fred were sent to college. Tom's obvious bent toward learning convinced his father that he should go into law and politics, and therefore should attend the state university. With Tom's desire to transfer to Princeton in 1917 the father had no sympathy. By the time Tom left for Harvard in 1920, W. O. Wolfe was already very ill with cancer. He died in May, 1922, before Tom could reach home.

Two passages in letters to his mother show Tom's special affection for his father. In January, 1923, he wrote:

I think often of my childhood lately: of those warm hours in bed of winter mornings; of the first ringing of the Orange St. bell; of Papa's big voice shouting from the foot of the stair "Get up, boy," then of the rush down stairs like a cold rabbit with all my clothes and underwear in my arms. As I go through the cold dining room I can hear the cheerful roar of the big fire he always had kindled in the sitting room. And we dressed by the warmth of that fire. Then breakfast—oatmeal, and sausages, eggs, hot coffee, and you putting away a couple of thick meat sandwiches in a paper bag. Then the final rush for school with Ben or Fred, and the long run up the Central Avenue hill with one of them pulling or pushing me along.[2]

That Wolfe recognized literary material in his memories of his father is evident from this comment in March, 1923, when he was still intent on becoming a dramatist:

Mama, in the name of God, guard Papa's letters to me with your life. Get them all together and watch them like a hawk. I don't know why I saved them but I thank my stars now that I did. There has never been anybody like Papa. I mean to say that all in all, he is the most unique human being I have ever known. I am convinced there is nobody in America today anywhere like him. . . . He is headed straight not for one of my plays, but for a series. He dramatized his emotions to a greater extent than anyone I have ever known—consider his expression of "merciful God"—his habit of talking to himself *at* or *against* an imaginary opponent. Save those letters. They are written in his exact conversational tone: I won't have to create imaginary language out of my own brain—I verily believe I can re-create a character that will knock the hearts out of people by its reality.[3]

Like her husband, Julia Elizabeth Westall Wolfe came from a large family, the fourth of eleven children. Her father, Thomas Casey Westall, and her mother, a Pentland, were descended from families identified with Virginia and North Carolina since colonial days. Julia grew up fond of music, and for three years before she married, she taught school. When Mr. Wolfe—she always referred to him thus—refused to allow her to continue teaching school, she took in boarders. Even before her marriage she had begun to see possibilities in real estate, and she persuaded her husband to make some investments. Financial loss through a bank failure in 1896, Mrs. Wolfe thought, led to Mr.

Wolfe's excessive drinking. Partly because of the drinking, she took five of her seven children to St. Louis in 1904 and set up a boarding house in connection with the World's Fair. It was then that Grover, Ben's twin, died suddenly of typhoid.

Returning to Asheville, Mrs. Wolfe in 1906 bought the large house at 48 Spruce Street, which she named "The Old Kentucky Home" (the Dixieland boarding house in *Look Homeward, Angel*). Her husband, incensed at her action, remained at 92 Woodfin, a few blocks away, where Mabel kept house for him. The children went back and forth between the two establishments despite their father's maledictions on the boarding house as "a murderous and bloody barn." It was in "The Old Kentucky Home" that Ben died in 1918, and, until Tom's death in 1938, Mrs. Wolfe continued to run the boarding house. In her later years, Mrs. Wolfe traveled much, relished the attention paid to her by Tom's friends and readers, and willingly collaborated in a book which allowed her to gossip about her life to her heart's content. She died in 1945, aged eighty-five.[4]

To W. O. and Julia Wolfe eight children were born. The first, a girl named Leslie, died in infancy. Effie, the next child, was enough older than Tom so that she figures only in a minor way as Daisy in *Look Homeward, Angel*. Frank (Steve), Mabel (Helen), and Fred (Luke) are all important fictional characters; the twins, Grover Cleveland and Benjamin Harrison, appear under their own given names. Though the correspondence of the real life characters to the fictional characters is unmistakable, Mabel comments: "We deny, as a matter of fact, being characters in the book. We know that the reading world so regards us, and readers who know us, as they did in the days immediately following the book's coming out, make a game of pairing off the real persons with the fictional counterparts."[5]

From 1905 to 1912 Tom attended Orange Street Public School, where his precociousness in reading attracted attention. Outside of school hours he could go about the small town pretty much at will—to his father's marble shop, to "the other house" at 92 Woodfin, and to the homes of his schoolmates. For a time he sold *The Saturday Evening Post* under the direction of his older brother Fred, boasting happily of his success in an early letter to his sister Effie: "I am selling Post and won a prize last month and think i am going to win one this month."[6] His schooling was often interrupted, as he accompanied his mother on trips to

New Orleans; to St. Petersburg, Jacksonville, St. Augustine, Daytona, and Palm Beach, Florida; to Hot Springs, Arkansas; and even in 1913 to Washington, D.C., for the inauguration of President Wilson. Mrs. Wolfe, preoccupied with finding relief for her rheumatism, sometimes put the boy in a local school, and sometimes not.

The major event of his childhood, however, was his transfer in 1912 to a new private school (North State School) established by J. M. Roberts, who had been principal of the Orange Street Public School. Tom wrote an essay which attracted the attention of Roberts and his wife, and they urged upon his parents the advantages they expected to provide in the new school. From Mabel and his brothers, Tom encountered some teasing and a mild resentment that he was being sent to a private school. Tom's letters to Mrs. Roberts are eloquent testimony that the transfer was fortunate. In 1927 he confided to her:

> I was without a home—a vagabond since I was seven—with two roofs and no home. I moved inward on that house of death and tumult from room to little room, as the boarders came with their dollar a day, and their constant rocking on the porch. My overloaded heart was bursting with its packed weight of loneliness and terror; I was strangling, without speech, without articulation, in my own secretions—groping like a blind sea-thing with no eyes and a thousand feelers toward light, toward life, toward beauty and order, out of that hell of chaos, greed, and cheap ugliness—and then I found you, when else I should have died, you mother of my spirit who fed me with light.[7]

In June, 1916, Tom completed the college preparatory course. He distinguished himself in his last term by winning a prize for his essay on Shakespeare, and another prize for delivering it as an oration.

III *University of North Carolina*

Having failed to persuade his father to send him to the University of Virginia, Tom set off in the fall of 1916 for Chapel Hill, a village of fewer than fifteen hundred people, about two hundred miles northeast of Asheville. That fall the University had about eleven hundred students. As a conspicuously tall freshman not quite sixteen years old, Tom came in for all the customary college pranks. Years later he wrote a classmate: "I don't suppose you remember me very well my first year at Chapel Hill, but I made history. It was I who made the speech of acceptance when elected to the Literary Society, I took the catalogue exam, went to Chapel Saturday and let a Sophomore lead me in prayer at noon." [8]

Despite such gags he was elected vice-president of the Freshman Debating Society, and was never quite the neglected student pictured in Eugene Gant. Though he tried to persuade his father to allow him to transfer to Princeton at the end of his first year, he seems to have returned to Chapel Hill willingly. In his second year he joined Pi Kappa Phi, a social fraternity; hoped to win his letter in track (but did not); and at the end of the year was elected managing editor of *Tar Heel*, the campus paper. In his junior year, Tom began to submit poems and stories to *The Carolina Magazine;* in the spring he won the Worth Prize for an essay, "The Crisis in Industry." He was also active in the newly organized Carolina Playmakers directed by Professor Fred Koch. In his last year, Tom was Editor of *Tar Heel* and contributed to the humor magazine *Tar Baby*.

In addition to all these activities, he made a good though not brilliant record as a student. His ten A's were chiefly in English, with one in Greek and two in philosophy; his two D's were in mathematics and chemistry. Just over half of his grades were B's. The two professors who impressed him most were Horace Williams, a Hegelian philosopher, and Edwin Greenlaw, a hard-driving research man who taught English literature and composition with energy and resourcefulness. In the year 1918-19 he set the class up as a Peace Conference to motivate student discussion and writing. Later on he converted the class into a typical city group for the exploration of the conflict between capital and labor.[9] Young Wolfe, separated for the first time from a family which could not share his emotional and intellectual interests, found a great deal to make his college years bright. To the classmate quoted above he wrote: "you stand as a symbol of that happy and wonderful life I knew during 1916-1920."

Wolfe's life at this period was not all happiness, however. In the summer of 1917 he had a love affair with a girl who lived for a time at "The Old Kentucky Home." His mother and his sister say that the Laura James episode in *Look Homeward,*

Angel, based on this affair, is much exaggerated, but as late as 1924 Tom wrote Mrs. Roberts: "Did you know I fell in love when I was sixteen with a girl who was twenty-one? Yes, honestly—desperately in love. And I've never quite got over it. The girl married, you know: she died of influenza a year or two later." [10] In the spring of his second year in college Tom's roommate, an Asheville boy who was managing editor of *Tar Heel,* died suddenly of a heart attack. Tom was so much affected that he never slept in their room again, staying instead with other friends. The following summer (1918) Tom worked near Norfolk, Virginia, as time checker for a gang of laborers and later as checker of supplies at the docks. His brother Fred, then in the navy, saw him at this time, and he confirms the temporary joblessness and near-starvation described as part of Eugene's experience in *Look Homeward, Angel.*

In October, shortly after the beginning of his junior year, Tom was called home by his brother Ben's fatal illness. Ben, a competent young newspaperman and a moody but devoted elder brother, was closer to Tom than any other member of the family. The description of Ben's death in *Look Homeward, Angel*—quoted in part at the beginning of this chapter—is generally considered one of Wolfe's best passages. It is a literary expression of the literally overwhelming grief felt at the time. Years later Tom said: "Life at home practically ceased to be possible for me when Ben died." [11] It was Ben who had urged Tom to take all the education he could get, but when Tom graduated in June, 1920, Ben was not there. Neither was Tom's father, who by this time was seriously ill with cancer. The elation Tom felt in the "happy and wonderful life" of college triumphs was thus mingled with personal griefs and anxieties.

A major impact on all college students of this period was "the Great War," as it was then called. Wolfe was only thirteen when the war began in August, 1914. In North Carolina and the South generally there was almost no pro-German sentiment. As an impressionable boy, Wolfe would have seen the Anglo-French cause as a remote, romantic crusade against the savage Huns. He would have thought very little about the Russians, Italians, and Turks. In the fall of his freshman year, months before America's formal entry into the war, Frederick Palmer, the famed war correspondent, spoke on the campus. With his graphic descriptions of trench warfare he brought the combat close enough to induce Paul Green, Wolfe's twenty-two-year-old classmate (later the playwright), to enlist immediately.

In April, 1917, America formally declared war, and Wolfe envied the students old enough "to go." In September enrollment had dropped from eleven hundred students to seven hundred. Military drill was introduced, and Tom wrote to his brother Ben: "They're giving us blazes in this military stuff. Military engineering, bomb throwing, trench warfare, bayonet fighting are a few of the things we are doing." [12] By the summer of 1918 the war had created feverish activity in hundreds of places like Norfolk, Virginia, where during his vacation Wolfe did "war work" as a civilian. In September, 1918, Chapel Hill, like most college towns, was turned into a military camp by the Students Army Training Corps, a device to induce young men to continue their education before active participation in a war that then looked interminable. Wolfe, still under eighteen, was not eligible to join the unit. In November came the Armistice. Like almost all boys just too young for military service, Wolfe had a sharp sense that he had missed a great experience. He could read about Rupert Brooke and worship from afar; he could never emulate that romantic martyrdom. An indirect result of the war was Wolfe's availability for campus positions which in normal times would have attracted greater competition. Four years earlier or four years later, the pattern of his college years might have been somewhat different.

Wolfe's undergraduate writing seems today to show little beyond energy and facility. Much of the journalism is unsigned and not positively identifiable, but leafing through the files of *Tar Heel* when Wolfe was editor does not lead one to suspect a genius on the staff. Editorials on winning the war and getting behind the football team have the same conventional pep. "The Creative Movement in Writing," a signed piece at the end of his junior year, comments with serious enthusiasm on the emphasis of native, local material in the efforts of the Carolina Playmakers as representative of a new national impulse in literature. The burlesque of the Raleigh *News and Observer* (Josephus Daniels' newspaper) was doubtless amusing in the 1920 issue of *Tar Baby*, but the sparkle has vanished.

Of Wolfe's ten contributions to the *Carolina Magazine*, five were inspired by the war. He wrote of Flanders: "A war-ripped field,—with what a tale to tell!" He wrote a tribute to France:

"And still brave France kept fighting / Until it seemed that France must die." His poem "The Challenge" was acclaimed by his father as a masterpiece and reprinted in the Asheville paper: "You have given us your mandates,—we have made our purpose clear, / We will buy the prize with red blood and no price will be too dear. . . ." Of Rupert Brooke he proclaimed: "His name will live. I would I could express / His beauty, truth and loveliness." In much the same strain of sentiment and melodrama, Wolfe's short story explains how Roger Cullenden recovers from a fit of cowardice to die a hero's death: " 'Well, boys,' he smiled, 'they got me—got me good. But'—almost inaudible—'I am going out a Cullenden—of—Virginia.' " The brief quotations do not misrepresent these pieces. There is hardly a phrase to redeem them from mediocrity. Wolfe's other contributions to the *Magazine* show no greater skill. "The Drammer," is a verse satire on melodrama. "An Appreciation" is an odd comment on springtime in Japan. "Russian Folksong" is a satire on the Bolshevik revolution. Two short plays, hardly more inspired, will be discussed in the next chapter.[13]

Wolfe's most impressive writing as an undergraduate is to be found not in his verse, his dramas, or his short story about Roger Cullenden, but in the essay "The Crisis in Industry," which won the Worth Prize in 1919. Wolfe's idea—that civil war could be avoided only by recognition of labor as something more than a commodity—was hardly a new one. His statement and development of the idea, however, is literate and well reasoned. If Wolfe's essay is nebulous as to how the conflict can be resolved, the past forty years of social development have supplied some of the particulars. Reading the essay today, one is inclined to feel that Wolfe in 1919 was much closer to a successful career in law and politics than he was to a career in literature. These sentences are typical:

> Labor today is in active revolt against the whole system whereby its labor, the product of its blood, bone, sinew, and brain is treated as a commodity—something to be bought at will, the price of which to be forced up or down, just as the price of flour or sugar. . . .
> The principle of self-determination, intended primarily for the small nation, which our democracy now advocates, must finally, I think, be used industrially, as well as politically. And—government must recognize and promote this.[14]

In this prize essay Wolfe showed a clear sense not only of the basic issues but of the direction which would be followed by government in the period of his own maturity. Moreover, he seemed at home with the rhythms of language adapted to political discussion.

Weak as most of Wolfe's undergraduate literary efforts may seem today, they were not mediocre in the eyes of Wolfe's classmates and teachers. The writings were inseparable from the writer, a tall, slender, rather awkward, and often unkempt boy of boundless energy. It is not the moody, self-pitying Eugene Gant that Chapel Hill remembers, but the hero of the composition class story so many times retold. Asked by Professor Greenlaw to read his composition aloud, Wolfe fumbled in various pockets for scraps of paper on which parts of his essay were scribbled and finally concluded by reading a portion written on toilet paper. "Mr. Wolfe," said Professor Greenlaw, "are we to judge the quality of your essay by the paper on which it is written?" [15] The student capable of this gag was naturally in demand for impromptu speeches and burlesques.

Wolfe was a nonpareil who so impressed everyone with his potential that his actual accomplishments seemed larger than they were. The legend was already at work. Professor Horace Williams thought him one of the six ablest students he had encountered in thirty years of teaching. Professor Greenlaw, a man of very different temperament, thought Wolfe "an exceedingly able writer . . . and a man of interesting personality." [16] Jonathan Daniels, a fellow student, spoke of him as "the big dominating mountain boy who had all the honors and practically all the friends." [17]

IV *Harvard, New York University, Europe*

On graduation Wolfe rejected several newspaper offers and an opportunity to teach in Bingham School, an Asheville military academy. He thought vaguely of "journalism" as a career, but Professor Williams and others had encouraged him to go on to Harvard for graduate study. Wolfe's father was not sympathetic to this idea, but eventually Mrs. Wolfe agreed to send him for a year. It was not until mid-August that Wolfe wrote for permission to register. On September 13 he was accepted by the Harvard Graduate School, and a few days later he left

Asheville for Cambridge, stopping briefly in Baltimore to see
his father, who was once more in the Johns Hopkins hospital.
Arrived in Cambridge, he found a room with Professor N. A.
Walker, a North Carolina professor then studying at Harvard.

Wolfe's great ambition was to join Professor George Pierce
Baker's 47 Workshop. Mrs. Baker has recorded her astonishment on answering the doorbell one morning to find Tom Wolfe
towering over her and asking to see her husband. She ushered
the young man in to the professor, and immediately Wolfe
explained that he had been one of Koch's students at North
Carolina.[18] Koch was a former student in the Workshop, and
Baker gave his consent at once. Wolfe also registered for Baker's
course in drama from the Greeks to modern times, Greenough's
course in American literature, and Lowes's course in the Romantic poets. He audited Kittredge's Shakespeare. By the following
May he had completed three of the four courses required for
the M.A., but he had failed the examination in French (later
passed).

Fearing he would not be allowed to return to Harvard for
a second year, he did not go home in the summer of 1921, but
remained in Cambridge except for a short visit to his father,
still in Baltimore. For six weeks he stayed on in the house
vacated by his friend Professor Walker, and was kept alive by
food given him by the two old maids who were the next occu-
pants. At this time Wolfe tried unsuccessfully to rewrite his
play *The Mountains.* In July he registered for a course in English history. He had already been urged by Professor Lowes to
become a teacher, but in his second year he devoted himself
almost exclusively to his plays. In March of 1922 he registered
with the Harvard Appointments Bureau for a position as a
teacher of English, and he received an offer from Northwestern
University. While he was considering this offer, he was called
home by the fatal illness of his father, who died before his son
reached Asheville.

During the summer of 1922, Wolfe's mother was persuaded
to send him back to Harvard for a third year. Later, Wolfe
signed a paper agreeing to consider the expense of his three
years at Harvard as his fair share of the estate, now much
depleted by W. O. Wolfe's long illness. Having now completed
the requirements for his M.A., Wolfe devoted himself wholly to
the Workshop. He began the year by submitting first acts for

six different plays, finally settling down to one called *Nigger-town*, which was later retitled *Welcome to Our City*. Though this play failed to win the coveted Belmont Prize, Baker still had faith in it, and recommended it to the New York Theatre Guild.[19] Wolfe spent the summer and early autumn in Cambridge and New York, anxiously waiting word about his play. Then he went to Asheville for a time. Returning to New York in November, he learned that the Guild had rejected his play, although suggestions for its revision and an offer to reconsider it had been made.

It was then that Wolfe decided he must turn to teaching, despite Baker's vigorous opposition. A vacancy occurred at Washington Square College of New York University, and immediately after application to Professor Homer A. Watt, Wolfe accepted an instructorship in English at eighteen hundred dollars a year.[20] His duties began in February, and by teaching through the summer he could afford to make his first trip to Europe in October, 1924. Wolfe sailed for England with about four hundred dollars and apparently no fixed plan. He had been offered two thousand dollars to return to New York University the following February, but he did not commit himself. He actually did not return until the fall term of 1925.

On the voyage to England he wrote much about his fellow passengers, hoping to develop some travel sketches; but little came of this. He spent a month in England, and in December went to Paris. In a small hotel there, a suitcase containing his only copy of the play *Mannerhouse* was stolen, and Wolfe, who plunged into a desperate effort to rewrite it, finished the script by January 3. Meanwhile he had met various Chapel Hill and Harvard friends, among them Kenneth Raisbeck, a Workshop associate. Through Raisbeck Wolfe met two young women from Boston. Wolfe fell in love with one of these girls, then quarreled with her and with Raisbeck. By this time Wolfe was out of money, and was forced to write his mother for help. Apparently checks from her, with some money from his brother Fred, kept him going and paid his passage back in August.

For the ten months abroad, Wolfe had only the rewritten *Mannerhouse* to show, plus a brief travel article published in the Asheville paper. Shortly before he left Europe, Wolfe wrote his mother: "I have come alone, wandered alone, almost without plan—indeed, in an insane fashion—but it has been right *for me.*" [21] As the boat was landing, he met by accident Mrs. Aline Bernstein, who had known his name through her association with the Neighborhood Playhouse; she was a stage designer and a director of the Playhouse, in which capacity she had read *Welcome to Our City.*

Up to this time, despite discouragements, Wolfe had considered himself a dramatist. A year later—in 1926—he began work on the novel published as *Look Homeward, Angel.* Wolfe's fiction has so frequently been characterized as "formless" that his early devotion to drama has seemed a youthful error, hardly worth examination. Error or not, Wolfe's dramatic work was a five-year apprenticeship in his development as a professional writer. That it is worth examination will be shown in the next chapter.

CHAPTER 2

Thomas Wolfe: Dramatist

IN THE FALL of 1918 Dr. Frederick H. Koch came to the University of North Carolina from the University of North Dakota, where he had had considerable success in developing an interest in folk drama.[1] A former student at George Pierce Baker's 47 Workshop, Koch was a man with a mission; he believed passionately in the future of native American drama, and his enthusiasm was infectious. For the first meeting of his course in English Dramatic Composition that fall, Tom Wolfe and seven coeds appeared, and the class was immediately dubbed the Ladies Aid Society. Wolfe recruited a few other men, and interested students soon formed The Carolina Playmakers. With the end of the war in November, a number of somewhat older and more mature men were available. One of these was Paul Green, who had left Chapel Hill in 1916 to enlist. By 1927 he had developed from a Carolina Playmaker to a Pulitzer prize-winner with the play *In Abraham's Bosom*; in the same year his play *The Field God* opened both in New York and London.

In the four series of published *Carolina Folk Plays*, one encounters a dozen or so names whose local success aroused the hope that more than one Paul Green would be discovered. Green's plays brilliantly illustrate the possibilities of regional realism, with occasional imaginative touches through the use of superstition, which Koch set out to develop. Under his leadership between 1918 and 1941, nine full-length plays were produced, and fifty-four bills of short plays, usually three in each program. Productions were given in six other universities and in many towns throughout North Carolina. Thick scrapbooks still preserved at the University testify to the constant flow of favorable publicity given the efforts of the Playmakers. Wolfe was extremely fortunate to come in contact with a man of Koch's energy and to participate in a group enthusiastically writing, acting, and producing their own plays. This kind of experience was available to very few college students before 1920.

For the Playmakers Wolfe wrote four plays, two of which were produced. All are simple and undistinguished, even when compared with the work of his contemporaries in the group. *The Return of Buck Gavin,* best known of the four, is an implausible story about an outlaw who risks his life to go back home to place flowers on the grave of his dead partner. Koch gave Wolfe a newspaper clipping which provided the idea for the play, and Koch insisted that Wolfe act the title role. A picture of Wolfe as Buck Gavin appeared in a national magazine at the time, and has been frequently reprinted. In *The Third Night,* Wolfe played "Captain Richard Hankins, a degenerate Southern gentleman," whose guilty conscience is roused by the ghost of the man he has robbed and murdered. *Deferred Payment,* printed in *The Carolina Magazine,* but not produced, is a slightly more complex play about a convict's return to the man actually guilty of the crime; the convict gets no revenge, and is in fact killed by his unscrupulous enemy; but in his dying speech he prophesies that the villain "will pay." These three plays are written in a strained, theatrical dialect reminiscent of John Fox, Jr., but they were exciting to the Playmakers. The fourth play, *Concerning Honest Bob,* also published in the *Magazine,* is a slight satirical piece exposing the hypocrisy of a campus politician.[2]

By 1924 Wolfe was a little ashamed of his "juvenile one-acts," as his letter to Margaret Roberts shows; and in 1933 he asked Koch not to produce them any longer. In doing so, however, he acknowledged generously his debt to Koch and the Playmakers:

> I am very proud to call myself one of the Playmakers and to remember that I belonged to the first group you ever taught at Chapel Hill, and had a part in writing and producing some of the first plays. I want to tell you also that no one is prouder than I of the great success the Playmakers have achieved and of the distinguished work which has been done by them. The fact that I was associated with that work at its very beginning, even in an obscure and unimportant fashion, is another fact I am proud of. I am also proud to remember that two little one-act plays that I

wrote were among the first plays put on by the Playmakers and that I acted in them and helped produce them. I was a boy of eighteen years when I wrote those plays, and I wrote each of them in a few hours because I did not then understand what heart-breaking and agonizing work writing is, and I think those plays show this and are fair samples of the work of a boy who did not know what hard work was and who wrote them in a few hours. But I do not think they are fair samples of the best which the Playmakers can do and have done, nor of the best in me. I therefore want to ask you, as my old friend who will not misunderstand my plain and sincere feeling in this matter, that you do not allow either of these plays to be used again for production. I should like to be remembered as a Playmaker and as one who had the honor to be a member of that pioneer first group, but I do not want to be remembered for the work which a careless boy did.[3]

I *The 47 Workshop*

The most important result of Wolfe's experience with the Carolina Playmakers was Professor George Pierce Baker's willingness to admit him to the 47 Workshop in the fall of 1920. By this time the Workshop was solidly established. Following experiments with student dramatic composition as early as 1903 (at Radcliffe), Baker had begun a Workshop with that title in January, 1913. O'Neill was enrolled as a special student in 1914-15, and he later wrote Baker that only lack of money prevented him from returning for a second year. In 1920, when Wolfe arrived, Baker's list of former students was impressive: among them were such dramatists as Edward Sheldon, Cleves Kinkead (author of *Common Clay*), S. N. Behrman, Sidney Howard, and Philip Barry (author of the then current success *You and I*); and other men of the theatre, such as Kenneth MacGowan, Robert Benchley, Heywood Broun, Hiram Moderwell, and John Mason Brown. It is perhaps more than coincidental that of the eight persons most influential in forming the Theatre Guild in 1919, three had been former students at the Workshop: Theresa Helburn, Lee Simonson, and Maurice Wertheim.[4]

Wolfe participated in the Workshop for three years, from the autumn of 1920 through the spring of 1923. During his first term he worked on a one-act play, *The Mountains,* which was given a trial performance January 25, 1921, and was produced at Radcliffe's Agassiz Theatre on October 21 and 22 of the same year. Though it has never been published, Wolfe gave an outline of the play in a letter to his mother: ". . . it is the real thing and deals with a great tragedy, the tragedy of a fine young man who returns to his mountains with fine dreams and ideals of serving his people. It is not a feud play, although the feud is used. The tragedy of the play is the tragedy of this fine young man fighting against conditions that overcome him and destroy him in the end. When you read this play, I hope you will be aware of this tragedy, and the tragedy of the lot of those poor oppressed mountain people, old and worn-out at middle age by their terrific hopeless battle with the mountain." [5]

More specifically, the fine young man is Richard Weaver, who has just completed his medical studies and come home to take over his father's practice among the mountain people. Richard confides to his sister that he will not participate in the senseless old family feud. When the feud breaks out again, however, family pressure is too strong. Throughout the play the mountain Baldpate symbolizes the dominating restrictions of mountain life. That the melodramatic tone of Wolfe's undergraduate plays was carried over into *The Mountains* is suggested by the one line recalled years later by John Mason Brown, who played the part of the doctor. The line that stuck in Brown's memory was this: "Goddam you Baldpate, yuh hemmin' me in!" [6] There is, however, a good deal of realism in the minor mountain characters who represent the erosion of human values by the narrow, grinding mountain life. In May, Baker read the prologue to the class, and Wolfe wrote excitedly to his mother: "To my great joy he pronounced it the best prolog ever written here." [7] The class production, however, was not well received.

Wolfe's two full-length plays, *Mannerhouse* and *Welcome to Our City*, were composed concurrently between 1920 and 1924. *Mannerhouse* was begun in the fall of 1920, but was not considered by the Theatre Guild until early 1926. The manuscript of this play is the one that disappeared in Paris early in 1925. Meanwhile Wolfe's trip home in 1922 had exposed him to the real estate boom, and the play *Welcome to Our City* was written that fall. It was produced at Harvard on May 11 and 12, 1923, but it failed to win the Belmont Prize that Wolfe hoped for. Baker, nevertheless, still had faith in the play, and he persuaded the Theatre Guild to consider it. The Guild rejected the play in December, made specific suggestions for revision, and was willing to reconsider the revised script. Wolfe agreed that revision was necessary, but by April, 1924, he had lost interest in the attempt to revise the play. In the winter of 1925-26 both *Mannerhouse* and *Welcome to Our City* were considered by the Theatre Guild, the Provincetown Theatre, and the Neighborhood Playhouse.

What was the Theatre Guild like in 1923 and 1924, when Wolfe hoped it would produce one or both of his plays? The Guild, like the Workshop, was solidly established. From an initial subscription list of 135 in 1919, support had grown to 12,000 subscribers in 1923. The following year $600,000 worth of bonds were sold to finance a new building. The Guild Theatre was begun that year, and it opened on April 5, 1925. Of thirty-nine plays produced from the spring of 1919 to the summer of 1925, the following fourteen had runs of over a hundred performances: St. John Ervine's *John Ferguson* (the second play produced); *Jane Clegg* by the same author; Shaw's *Heartbreak House* (a world premiere); Arthur Richman's *Ambush;* Andreyev's *He Who Gets Slapped;* Karl Capek's *R.U.R.;* Ibsen's *Peer Gynt;* Shaw's *Saint Joan* (another world premiere); Ernest Vajda's *Fata Morgana;* Molnar's *The Guardsman;* Sidney Howard's *They Knew What They Wanted;* Shaw's *Arms and the Man.* These successes and the variety of experiment illustrated by the whole roster of Guild plays indicate that Wolfe's dramas faced extremely strong competition. Literally, rejection was failure; but to have received serious consideration at such a time from such a group was substantial recognition of talent and promise.[8]

Despite their defects as plays, both *Mannerhouse* and *Welcome to Our City* show a capacity to visualize objectively and to focus in a single scene a variety of dramatic contrasts. Neither play is autobiographical. Both are in some degree melodramatic, but both display an authentic talent for humor and satire.

II *Mannerhouse*

Mannerhouse is a play about the Ramsay family. A prologue shows the building of a house in the eighteenth century, and the aristocratic strength of the founder is demonstrated through his subjugation of a giant slave, a native African king. The play itself traces the disintegration of the family through the Civil War. Young Eugene Ramsay (who only faintly foreshadows Eugene Gant) dominates most of the scenes. Early in the play he satirically exposes the romantic illusion of his father's devotion to the Confederacy, but he concludes: "I admire your courage. I respect your character. . . . I follow the man and not the cause." The Negro servant Tod (a reincarnation of the giant slave-king of the prologue) imparts a sense of aristocratic tradition. Following a brief interlude suggesting the course of the war, Eugene and his father return home.

The postwar scenes provide opportunity to satirize the local military historian who insists that "we were defeated but not beaten"; the adherence to Walter Scott chivalry; the fantasies which General Ramsay indulges in with respect to the servants, all of whom, except Tod, have long since departed. At the end, General Ramsay is dead, the house has been sold to an ignorant lumberman, and Eugene returns unrecognized as a workman to help tear down the house. He cries out at the final curtain: "Tod! Tod! Oh I have failed. Here was a house. It was by you begun; by you it must be ended." Like Samson, Tod pulls down the supporting pillar, and the house collapses.[9]

Besides some skillful satire, there is in the key scenes a very real sense of doom, a sense that agreeable, well-bred people are somehow unable to carry on the power they have inherited. Less successful are the abortive and unclear romance between Eugene and Margaret; Eugene's hostility toward his mother; the patent Shakespearean parallels with Falstaff's speech on honor and the ghost in Hamlet; and the over-literary stage directions.

Wolfe's own opinion of the play is set down at length in Chapter LXII of *Of Time and the River* (1935). Eugene Gant is represented as reading *Mannerhouse* aloud to his wealthy young friends, Joel and Rosalind Pierce. Through author-comment Wolfe points out the influence of *The Cherry Orchard, Cyrano, Hamlet,* and the Samson story. Nevertheless "there was good stuff in the play, dramatic conflict, moving pageantry. . . . But the scenes between the hero and the girl were less successful. . . ." In the scenes between Eugene and the Major (the military historian of local fame), "a great deal of the falseness, hypocrisy and sentimentality of the South was polished off . . .

and 'the War'—the Civil War—was used effectively as a stalking horse to satirize the Great World War of modern times." Most effective of all, thought Wolfe in retrospect, was the prologue showing the building of the great house: "really splendid, thrilling in its dramatic pageantry, and undoubtedly would have been a good and moving one upon a stage." The play as a whole, Wolfe thought, showed not only the influence of the young author's reading, but "how he had also already begun to use some of the materials of his own life and feeling and experience, how even in this groping and uncertain play, some of the real grandeur, beauty, terror, and unuttered loveliness of America was apparent" (544-49).

Publication of the play in book form (1948) led to its production the following spring by the Yale Dramatic Society. Explaining the choice of *Mannerhouse* a spokesman for the society said in the program: "It is the story of an idea. Thomas Wolfe has said that it is the distillation of his philosophy of life. It combines many of the important theses of his later novels, and, as the only major play by one of America's ranking novelists, we feel proud to give *Mannerhouse* its initial production." Impressions published in the *Yale Daily News* were mixed. One reviewer thought the play demonstrated Wolfe's "potential Shakespearean ability." Another thought the play "a conglomeration of Wolfe's ideas thrown together in his most undisciplined manner, with a few effective moments. . . ." Professor Norman Holmes Pearson commented favorably on the acting and the sets, and on the play as a whole, "All in all, it was a very good job." [10]

III *Welcome to Our City*

Wolfe's other full-length play is a loosely constructed but more original play about real-estate greed and racial prejudice.[11] Realistic, satiric, and in some scenes melodramatic, the play also has an element of fantasy, as is suggested by Baker's comment that he thought it had a better chance of success than Elmer Rice's *The Adding Machine*, a notable hit of 1923.[12] The first scene of *Welcome to Our City* gives an impressionistic panorama of "Darktown," the Negro quarter of Altamont. The life of the Negroes is presented entirely without dialogue: a cheap restaurant, a poolroom, young men pitching horseshoes and ogling the girls, the dignified Negro preacher walking by, the return of the workmen to their homes after the six o'clock whistle blows. Against this visible background, a small group of white men cryptically discuss some kind of real-estate promotion. Later we learn that these men want to move the Negroes out and to develop this now central part of the city for their own profit.

The specific story begins in scene two, in the offices of the Altamont Development Company. A stranger, Jordan, comes in to purchase a house he had been shown the previous day. While he waits for the manager, Mr. Sorrel, a number of persons come in and go out in a natural way, and in a sequence that permits development of several themes: Jordan's outside, unsympathetic view of "progress"; the community prejudice against Johnson, a Negro doctor who lives in the old Rutledge home; the commercial hollowness of the slogan "Welcome to Our City" when it is revealed that Jordan, the stranger, is a "lunger." These themes are dramatized, not merely explained, and suspense is aroused. Dialogue is lively, and includes a variety of effects: Miss Neely, the unquestioning office secretary; Joe Bailey, the loquacious chamber of commerce booster; Sorrel, the efficient maneuverer; Rutledge, the aristocrat whose ancestral home is now owned by the Negro doctor.

Later a country club scene advances the action by reporting that Dr. Johnson is now willing to sell the Rutledge home, but the scene is more memorable for some excellent burlesque. The candidate for governor is introduced and heavily flattered by Sorrel and Bailey; after these older men move off-stage, their speech and manner are parodied by two young men, one of whom is Lee Rutledge. At the close of this scene, Lee, who is drunk, insists on driving over to see the old house. There he meets Annie Johnson, whom he has long known. Lee and Annie are alternately affectionate and quarrelsome, pointing up the anomaly of their relationship. Johnson enters, rebukes his daughter, and struggles with young Rutledge.

Following young Rutledge home, Johnson makes clear to the boy's father that he will not sell his home after all. A "Darktown" scene then shows the resentment of the Negroes at being ordered to vacate their homes. Johnson joins the group, and with very solid realism tells the Negroes they will continue to be pushed around for the simple reason that the white men know the Negroes will not effectively resist. The Negroes are persuaded, and vow they will stand with Johnson; but, on hearing the first strains of music from a minstrel show parade, they rush off to look and listen. Nevertheless, enough resistance develops to create a race riot. The National Guard is called out; and, as a lieutenant in the Guard, young Rutledge kills the Negro doctor. As Johnson dies, the elder Rutledge talks with him, pronouncing as the curtain line: "Poor fool! So still! So still! Why did you choose to become a man?"

The production of *Welcome to Our City* at Harvard was considered a failure, but two student comments [13] praise the play for its boldness and fresh dramatic quality. Oliver M. Sayler, in a survey of the contemporary theatre in 1923, hailed it as "a play as radical in form and treatment as the contemporary stage has yet acquired." [14] Even now *Welcome to Our City* would justify production, at least by some of our experimental theatres. There is unusual opportunity for skilled direction in the "Darktown" scenes. The satirical treatment of the real-estate people still has thrust. The Negroes are shown as exploited and victimized by racial prejudice, yet they are not sentimentally idealized. There are many roles worthy of good acting talent.

IV *Dramatic Manuscripts*

Wolfe's published plays, whatever their merits, represent only a small part of the energy he devoted to dramatic experiment between 1918 and 1925. About three thousand pages of dramatic manuscript and typescript survive, most of it in the Wisdom Collection at Harvard. Besides manuscripts and drafts of the two full-length plays, there are complete and partial drafts of *The Mountains*, produced by the 47 Workshop in 1921. Several fragments of a play about "Professor Weldon" seem to derive from Wolfe's acquaintance with Professor Horace Williams, the Hegelian idealist whose classes in philosophy so impressed Wolfe at Chapel Hill. In one scene Professor Weldon is dismissed from the university for his liberal views. In another he discovers he has incurable cancer. Another play, *The Strikers*, deals with a cotton mill strike in terms reminiscent of Galsworthy's *Strife* (1909). There are several fragments, one titled *The Batesons* and one *The Family*, in which Wolfe tried to use his own family as dramatic material. An important side of

Wolfe's nature is illustrated by numerous experiments in fantasy. He noted ideas for a play about Satan, and an adaptation of *Six Characters in Search of an Author*. He drafted twenty pages of *Interstellar Interlude;* he wrote an extended prologue to *Mycerinus (A Satire of Kingship and Priesthood)*, which contains some very passable Shavian touches.

V *Wolfe's Dramatic Talent*

It is evident that in the seven years of his dramatic apprenticeship, Wolfe was using themes natural and reasonable for a young man from the South. Increasingly he blended realism with imaginative experiment. He attempted to present ideas without propaganda, to avoid oversimplification by stressing the complexity of human situations. In *Mannerhouse* the Ramsays go down to destruction, partly through the accident of war, partly through their own incompetence. Yet, foreshadowing Faulkner's Snopeses, the rising white man who replaces them seems made of poorer clay. In *Welcome to Our City* the aristocratic Rutledges are exposed as hollow men, as are the real-estate crowd and the politicians. In the presentation of the Negroes there is a touch of the Catfish Row humor and pathos so successfully created in Du Bose Heyward's *Porgy* (1925) and dramatized two years later by Heyward's wife, who had been one of Wolfe's classmates in the Workshop of 1923. The manuscript plays about "Professor Weldon" and the cotton-mill strike show a search for vital reality as the necessary basis for good drama.

With characteristic exaggeration, Wolfe said in his 1938 Purdue speech that his youthful conviction that he must be a playwright was "not only wrong—it was as fantastically wrong as anything could be. Whatever other talents I had for playwriting—and I think I had some—the specific requirements of the theatre for condensation, limited characterization, and selected focus were really not especially for me." [15] This judgment is misleading, for like many other novelists who have never written a successful play, Wolfe did achieve in his best passages "scenes" of condensation, limited characterization, and selected focus. The town madam's purchase of a tombstone for one of her girls, the return of Gant from his Western travels, and the death of Ben—to mention only three scenes from his first novel—are all sharply visualized and dramatically paced. Wolfe's youthful conviction that he must be a playwright had considerable wisdom in it; the dramatic quality of his novels derives very largely from his early efforts to write plays and from his vital association with people of the theatre such as Paul Green and George Pierce Baker. Without the discipline of objective dramatization, Wolfe could never have handled the autobiographical material of his fiction so skillfully as he did.

CHAPTER 3

1926-29: *Look Homeward, Angel*

WOLFE'S ATTACHMENT to Mrs. Aline Bernstein, whom he met at the end of his first trip to Europe, was immediate and intense. It was the major factor in his personal life during the academic year 1925-26, his second year at New York University. By June of 1926 he was convinced that he could not sell either of his two full-length plays, and he had little inclination to go ahead with any of his other dramatic ideas. Therefore he sailed for England at the end of the academic year, and was shortly joined by Mrs. Bernstein at Ilkley, a small town in the Lake Country. There he outlined the novel which eventually became *Look Homeward, Angel,* and when Mrs. Bernstein returned to New York, Wolfe remained in England to work on it. After a short trip to Belgium in September, he took a room at Hilltop Farm, near Oxford. By November he had gone "dead and flat." On money sent him by Mrs. Bernstein, he went to Germany and Switzerland, sailing for home in late December. Mrs. Bernstein had taken a loft at 13 East 8th Street, where Wolfe was to live and write, and where Mrs. Bernstein was to do part of the stage and costume designing for which she was in great demand. She persuaded him not to teach during the spring semester, though he was urged to return at $2,200 a year ($400 above his starting salary in 1924). In July, 1927, he went abroad again with Mrs. Bernstein, and in September returned to teach at the University.

By March of 1928 he had finished the huge manuscript of some 300,000 words. He gave friendly notice to Professor Watt that he would not teach in the fall, and was assured that he was welcome to return if he later changed his mind. While the novel was being read by various publishers, Wolfe considered the possibility of writing for radio, and finally refused a definite offer from the J. Walter Thompson advertising agency. In June he made a brief visit to Asheville before sailing once more to Europe—his fourth trip. He and Mrs. Bernstein had quarreled frequently during the past year, and though she too was abroad during the summer of 1928, they did not see each other.

I *Acceptance and Publication*

In Munich Wolfe greatly enjoyed the Oktoberfest, but became involved—innocently, by his own account—in a drunken fight. While in the hospital, recovering from head wounds and a broken nose, and in fear lest he had killed one of his assailants, he suffered pangs of remorse, and wrote a penitent letter to Mrs. Bernstein. It was in this mood that he received her cable that Scribner's was interested in his novel. This news was borne out by a letter from Mrs. Ernest Boyd, Wolfe's first literary agent; and, after some delay, Wolfe received a cordial note from Maxwell Perkins, senior editor at Scribner's:

Dear Mr. Wolfe:
    Mrs. Ernest Boyd left with us, some weeks ago, the manuscript of your novel, "O, Lost!" I do not know whether it would be possible to work out a plan by which it might be worked into a form publishable by us, but I do know that, setting the practical aspects of the matter aside, it is a very remarkable thing, and that no editor could read it without being excited by it and filled with admiration by many passages in it and sections of it.
    Your letter, that came with it, shows that you realize what difficulties it presents, so that I need not enlarge upon this side of the question. What we should like to know is whether you will be in New York in a fairly near future, when we can see you and discuss the manuscript. We should certainly look forward to such an interview with very great interest.[1]

Wolfe acknowledged this letter cordially, but he continued his travels until late December. Soon after arriving in New York, he went to see Perkins. They agreed so well, that on January 7, 1929, Wolfe had a contract and an advance check for five hundred dollars.

During the spring term, Wolfe taught half-time at New York University, but most of his energy went into "the book." He began with a clear recognition that the manuscript required drastic revision, but he found it hard to accept specific omissions. Nevertheless, following Perkins' suggestion, a ninety-page introductory passage elaborating old man Gant's boyhood in Pennsylvania was omitted on the ground that it was unnecessary to the basic theme of young Eugene's development. To carry out this theme, other omissions and some rearrangement of material were necessary. As he worked over the manuscript, Wolfe had some misgivings about the autobiographical nature of the novel and his use of easily recognizable Asheville people and situations. To eliminate such material, however, would have been to eliminate the novel. By summer, proofs began to come in, and these Wolfe read at Ocean Point, Maine. In August, one chapter of the novel, revised for separate publication, appeared in *Scribner's Magazine*. In September Wolfe resumed his teaching at New York University, remaining there until near the end of the term in January, 1930.

On October 18, *Look Homeward, Angel* was published. Harry Hansen's review in the New York *World* acknowledged "strength and promise" in the novel, but he ridiculed its adolescent quality. Two women—Margaret Wallace in the New York *Times* and Margery Latimer in the *Herald-Tribune*—were enthusiastic in welcoming a new American writer of major stature. By November 6, Scribner's had sold 2,600 copies; and, though *Look Homeward, Angel* never became a best-seller, it continued to have a substantial sale. Scribner's considered that Maxwell Perkins' editorial judgment was vindicated. Wolfe was well launched on his literary career—but at some cost. Asheville became excited and indignant, despite a favorable review in the local paper. Mrs. Roberts, Wolfe's favorite teacher, was deeply hurt at the portrayal of her husband as stupid and inept in the classroom. Jonathan Daniels, who had known Wolfe at the University of North Carolina, felt that Wolfe had also betrayed his friends there.[2]

II *The Gants*

To those who knew nothing about Wolfe's personal life, all this hubbub was beside the point. The typical readers of 1929 took the book as a novel and enjoyed it as such. After the gritty realism of Dreiser, the tired sophistication of Fitzgerald, the waspish satire of Sinclair Lewis, and the feverish brooding of Eugene O'Neill, *Look Homeward, Angel* was like going home again, if only for a visit. The simple pattern of the novel—a small town, a large family, school, and college—was one that thousands of readers had lived and could identify with. Yet the sentimentality usually associated with the pattern was transformed by an intensity, a richness of impression, a sense of vaultless ambition, that the home one revisited was something larger than life.

The first reading of *Look Homeward, Angel* is a strange, moving, and memorable experience. That incredible, yet extraordinarily vivid family of Gants! Seen from the point of view of Eugene, the sensitive youngest child, they are like characters in a nightmare. W. O. Gant, the father, by trade a maker of tombstones, a man of huge and uncontrollable appetites, lurches drunkenly through the narrative, roaring, weeping, howling: "Merciful God! it's fearful, it's awful, it's croo-el. What have I ever done that God should punish me like this in my old age?" [3] Eliza, his wife, is a practical woman who puts up with her husband's vagaries as the pioneers accepted acts of God:

> What Eliza endured in pain and fear and glory no one knew. He breathed over them all his hot lion-breath of desire and fury: when he was drunk, her white pursed face, and all the slow octopal movements of her temper, stirred him to red madness. She was at such times in real danger from his assault: she had to lock herself away from him. For from the first, deeper than love, deeper than hate, as deep as the unfleshed bones of life, an obscure and final warfare was being waged between them. Eliza wept or was silent to his curse, nagged briefly in retort to his rhetoric, gave like a punched pillow to his lunging drive—and slowly, implacably had her way. Year by year, above his howl of protest, he did not know how, they gathered in small bits of earth, paid the hated taxes, and put the money that remained into more land. Over the wife, over the mother, the woman of property, who was like a man, walked slowly forth. (18)

Of the ten children born to this ill-assorted pair, seven lived to figure in the novel; and of these Steve, Helen, Ben, and Luke are important in the developing life of Eugene, the central character. Steve, the oldest, was expelled from school at fourteen, sampled all the vices early and found them all congenial. Eliza once defended her son:

"Well, maybe if he hadn't been sent to every dive in town to pull his daddy out, he would turn out better."

"You lie, Woman! By God, you lie!"[Gant] thundered magnificently but illogically. (48)

Inevitably, Steve left home, but just as inevitably he returned, boasting, bullying, and whining his way into general disfavor. Ben, in contrast, was the solid, dependable boy who left school early and supported himself by miscellaneous tasks at the newspaper. "Ben, sullen, silent, alone, had withdrawn more closely than ever into his heart: in the brawling house he came and went, and was remembered, like a phantom" (112). He did what he could for everyone except Steve, but bitterly resented any interference. It was Ben's loneliness that established a special bond with young Eugene: "He was a stranger, and as he sought through the house, he was always aprowl to find some entrance into life, some secret undiscovered door—a stone, a leaf,—that might admit him into light and fellowship" (113). Luke, too, was dependable, but in a hard-driving, money-grubbing way.

And it was as the smiling hustler that he wanted to be known. He read piously all the circulars the Curtis Publishing Company sent to its agents: he posed himself in the various descriptive attitudes that were supposed to promote business—the proper manner of "approach," the most persuasive manner of drawing the journal from the bag, the animated description of its contents, in which he was supposed to be steeped as a result of his faithful reading. . . .

"Yes, sir. Yes, sir," he would begin in a sonorous voice, dropping wide-leggedly into the "prospect's" stride. "This week's edition of *The Saturday Evening Post,* five cents, only a nickel, p-p-p-purchased weekly by t-t-two million readers. In this week's issue you have eighty-six pages of f-f-fact and fiction, to say n-n-nothing of the advertisements. If you c-c-c-can't read you'll get m-m-more than your money's worth out of the p-p-pictures" (119-20).

Helen, the more important of Eugene's two sisters, was ten years older than he. There was a special bond between Helen and her father, and even as a child she could do more with the drunken Gant than anyone else. "She adored him. He had begun to suspect that this devotion, and his own response to it, was a cause more and more of annoyance to Eliza, and he was inclined to exaggerate and emphasize it, particularly when he was drunk, when his furious distaste for his wife, his obscene complaint against her, was crudely balanced by his maudlin docility to the girl" (67). It was little Helen who gave the drunken Gant hot soup, slapping her father with her small hand to make him pay attention: "You *drink* this! You better!" (25). And it was Helen who kept house for her father after Eliza bought "Dixieland," moved into it, and operated it as a boarding house.

III *Structure*

Look Homeward, Angel is divided into three parts: the first and shortest deals with Eugene's childhood, to his twelfth year; the second, with his schooldays in Altamont; and the third, with his college years, marked at the end by his brother Ben's death, and his mother's reluctant agreement to finance Eugene's further education at Harvard. Through all this period of childhood and adolescence, the unifying force in the story is the conflict between Eugene's passionate love for the emotional satisfactions of his growth and the even more passionate hatred for its frustrations. The death of his brother Grover (Ben's twin) left upon the young child Eugene a sharp sense of the utter loneliness of death, caught in the refrain, "O lost, and by the wind grieved, ghost, come back again."

But there was also a sense of family solidarity, confirmed by common grief. Later, when Eugene's father returned to Altamont from his wanderings in California, Eugene shrieked happily with the other children, "Papa's home!"—a joyful admission that in this jangling household there was a fierce, indestructible unity. Yet when Eliza moved into "Dixieland," leaving Helen to keep house for Gant, Eugene wandered back and forth between the two establishments. Helen's possessive affection only partly bridged the gap. All through the story the pride of Eugene in his brother Ben's dogged independence is a family tie as pervasive as the theme of a symphony.

Meanwhile the thrust of Eugene's own individuality becomes more and more decisive. In the crude daydreams of early reading he sees himself as the young missionary bound for the Far West, exalted by the love of Grace, the beautiful parishioner; or again as Bruce, the heroic vagabond, saving the endangered

Veronica from wild natives. Later still, there is the opportunity to go to the Leonards' private school, where his taste for books is fed, and his isolation from his unintellectual family increased. Then comes college; the groping toward some recognition for his mind and wit; the rebellious feelings against an unappreciative faculty; the escapades and pranks; the vacation love affair with Laura James; and a summer of war work in Norfolk. These are the elements of Eugene's experience.

The climax of the novel, however, is the death of Ben, which cuts the last real tie with the family. Gant, Eliza, Helen, Luke, and Steve all remain vibrant strands of his past, but Eugene has gone beyond them now. On his graduation from college his ambition is vaguely fixed on writing as a career. Whatever reservations the reader may make about the "adolescent" qualities of the novel, it powerfully represents the American struggle to go beyond the limitations of home and home town. In a sense, the very weaknesses of individual passages make the total effect more comprehensive and convincing. Such passages are usually better in their context than when they are detached for ironic critical comment.

IV *Lyric Elements*

The "lyrical" quality of *Look Homeward, Angel* has been much exaggerated, partly because the refrain "O lost and by the wind grieved, ghost" struck a note conspicuously absent from most fiction of the 1920's. Actually, variations on this lyrical motif take up little space in the novel. The half-page epigraph placed before the first chapter sets the tone:

> . . . a stone, a leaf, an unfound door; of a stone, a leaf, a door. And of all the forgotten faces.
>
> Naked and alone we came into exile. In her dark womb we did not know our mother's face; from the prison of her flesh have we come into the unspeakable and incommunicable prison of this earth.
>
> Which of us has known his brother? Which of us has looked into his father's heart? Which of us has not remained forever prison-pent? Which of us is not forever a stranger and alone?
>
> O waste of loss, in the hot mazes, lost, among bright stars on this most weary unbright cinder, lost! Remembering speechlessly

we seek the great forgotten language, the lost lane-end into
heaven, a stone, a leaf, an unfound door. Where? When?
O lost, and by the wind grieved, ghost, come back again.

Of the more than twenty echoes of this passage, most are not
more than three or four lines long, sometimes merely the phrase
"O lost!" (58, 60, 81, 269, 526). A half-page variation, an
apostrophe to Eugene, is placed in Chapter XXII, describing
the Niggertown paper route. Another long paragraph occurs
when Eugene, home on vacation, first becomes drunk. A third
long passage occurs in the description of Eugene's experiences
on the docks at Norfolk. Best known are the page-long passage
at Ben's grave and the last lines of the last chapter. All told,
such passages do not fill more than six pages of the six-hundred-
page novel. The fact that every reader remembers them is evidence that in some degree they do create a poetic resonance for
the often brutal realism. If one adds to this recurrent motif such
descriptive tours de force as the catalogues of food (68) and
the enumeration of varied smells—"the smell of whittled wood,
of all young lumber, of sawdust and shavings" (85)—there are
perhaps a dozen more pages of obtrusive lyrical fervor. So
distinctive were these passages, so fresh to the first readers, that
they somewhat obscured more basic qualities of the novel.

V *Drama*

The real power of the novel is in the nearly two hundred
sequences of dialogue, linked by highly charged exposition and
narrative, with a moderate use of interior monologues (there
being little stream-of-consciousness in the exaggerated, incoher-
ent sense). Chapter VIII, for example, describes Eugene at six,
just starting to school. Two pages explain his isolation at the
time, his mother's reluctance to let him go, the preoccupations
of his brothers and sisters, and his father's plan to make a
lawyer of the boy for the simple reason that he is a great
reader. Then comes half a page of argument between Gant and
Eliza. Eugene's reading of Stoddard's *Lectures* and *With Stan-
ley in Africa* is described, and the exotic recollections of the
World's Fair in St. Louis lead into the two-page passage on
smells. Eugene's difficulties in learning to write, the big boys

who tease him into giving them most of his lunch, the delights of Christmas, the boy's first awareness of sex are all given in exposition that suggests the boy's responses. Of the fourteen pages in the chapter, only five are unbroken by dialogue. Sometimes the spoken words will be a brief interjection, like Eliza's "Why, say—you can't grow up yet. You're my baby."

Or in a brief episode there is the effect of conversation even when dialogue is not given. Eugene and a small playmate think they see a huge serpent. "Shaken with fear they went away, they talked about it then and later in hushed voices, but they never revealed it." Though this chapter might be labeled "descriptive" or "lyrical," the adjectives would be misleading. Eugene's developing awareness is not static. Things described are experience, and the language is dynamic. As Eugene grows older, the dramatic method is increasingly available and is well used. Chapter XVIII tells in twelve pages of Eugene's departure for college and his first impressions there. Included are dialogues between Eugene and Margaret Leonard, the parting advice of Ben, Eugene's interview with Dr. Torrington, his English professor, and two classroom encounters with his classics professors. It would indeed be surprising if Wolfe's apprenticeship in drama were not reflected in his first novel. Because that apprenticeship has been so casually considered, Wolfe has never been given sufficient credit for the dramatic quality of his fiction.

VI *Autobiography?*

That Wolfe's Eugene Gant is a fictional representation of his own character and experience seems self-evident. On the other hand, Wolfe repeatedly denied that his novels were autobiographical in a literal sense. He wrote to Margaret Roberts the summer before *Look Homeward, Angel* appeared: "I can only assure you that my book is a work of fiction, and that no person, act, or event has been deliberately and consciously described." [4] In a broader sense, his note "To the Reader" concedes that the book is autobiographical: "If any reader . . . should say that the book is 'autobiographical' the writer has no answer for him: it seems to him that all serious work in fiction is autobiographical—that, for instance, a more autobiographical work than 'Gulliver's Travels' cannot easily be imagined." This pronouncement confuses rather than clarifies the issue, for Swift's book and Wolfe's novel are not autobiographical in the same way.

Obvious as it is that both Thomas Wolfe and Eugene Gant grew up in a North Carolina resort town, were present at the death of a beloved older brother, and attended the state university, the autobiographical problem remains. In Wolfe's letters to Mrs. Roberts and to his mother, in conversations with his friends, and in *The Story of a Novel*, he shows that he was haunted by the recognizably direct relation between his experience and his fiction. He felt a difference, but could never clearly articulate what that difference was. A partial answer can be found by turning to the factual accounts left by his mother and his sister Mabel.

Though *The Marble Man's Wife* is largely concerned with Mrs. Wolfe's early life, there are many details that differentiate her from the fictional Eliza. Mrs. Wolfe tells us, for example, that when Mr. Wolfe first proposed to her, she explained that she had already been in love and did not think she could love again. He was incredulous, and persuaded her that love would come. On the tensions that developed between them, this detail throws some light not found in *Look Homeward, Angel*. The accounts of her learning to play the fiddle, her playful masquerade in men's clothes, and her success in teaching present a more attractive woman than the virtually sexless Eliza. The picture of W. O. Wolfe and Julia reading aloud to each other *When Knighthood Was in Flower* is hard to associate with the feuding Gants of the novel. Julia's practical courage in the presence of the supposed burglar (who turned out to be a cat), her presence of mind in setting Tom's dislocated finger when he was twelve, and W. O. Wolfe's agreement to at least one of her real-estate deals suggest a competence and family acceptance not reflected in *Look Homeward, Angel*. Ben's brief apprenticeship to his father is a family detail not suggested in the fiction. Another is Julia's tears over Tom's failure to let the family know when he was out of money and nearly starving in Norfolk.[5]

Conspicuous in showing the difference between Wolfe's treatment of incident and his mother's are the two accounts of how the young woman sold books to the man in the marble shop. As Wolfe tells it in the novel, Eliza finds Gant drawing on his coat after a rest on an old sofa in the shop. To his explanatory complaint that he has been in bad health:

"Pshaw!" said Eliza briskly and contemptuously. "There's nothing wrong with you in my opinion. You're a big strapping fellow, in the prime of life. Half of it's only imagination."

In a long paragraph Eliza elaborates the deceptive powers of imagination, with no opportunity for Gant to interrupt.

Merciful God! he thought, with an anguished inner grin. How long is this to keep up? But she's a pippin as sure as you're born.

Then Eliza gets down to business.

"My name," she said portentously, with slow emphasis, "is Eliza Pentland, and I represent the Larkin Publishing Company."

She spoke the words proudly, with dignified gusto. Merciful God! A book-agent! thought Gant.

"We are offering," said Eliza, opening a huge yellow book with a fancy design of spears and flags and laurel wreaths, "a book of poems called *Gems of Verse for Hearth and Fireside* as well as *Larkin's Domestic Doctor and Book of Household Remedies,* giving directions for the cure and prevention of over five hundred diseases."

"Well," said Gant, with a faint grin, wetting his big thumb briefly, "I ought to find one that I've got out of that."

"Why, yes," said Eliza, nodding smartly, "as the fellow says, you can read poetry for the good of your soul and Larkin for the good of your body" (10-12).

So Gant bought the books, and as Eliza departed with hearty good humor, Gant "turned back among his marbles again with a stirring in him that he thought he had lost forever."

Following, in full, is Mrs. Wolfe's account of the transaction.

"I was one of those dread book agents at that time, after Mr. Wolfe's wife died. I had an agency; I took the orders during vacations and in the afternoons and Saturdays. I didn't go into all the business places. I was very particular. I was prissy, you know, didn't go just anywhere. I went into the tailor shop next door to Mr. Wolfe's place. It was Mr. Shartle's shop. He was a very fine man, and after he had bought a book I asked if any of his tailors might like to see my book. He said, oh no, they didn't read.

" 'But,' he said, 'you go in next door. Mr. Wolfe will buy

your book.' And I said, 'Do ladies go in there?' He laughed and said, 'You go in and tell him I said to buy this book.' So I went. I stood in the room outside his office. He was working on a stone, and I saw he had his apron on. I can see him now, throw that apron off and grab his coat when he saw me. I was pretending I didn't see him. When he opened the glass door I said, 'Don't get excited. I'm not a customer. I don't need a stone today.'

"And he was all smiles. I said, 'I am one of those dread book agents. Your neighbor sent me in here. I'm not going through the regular sales talk. I'll just show you the book and you can look through it and put your name down here.' Well, he thumbed through it and put his name down like I said. Then he asked me, 'Do you ever read novels?' 'Oh,' I said, 'I read most anything. Not the Bible as much as I should, though.'

"He said, 'I have a set of books; they are fine, too—love stories. Did you ever read "St. Elmo"?' 'No,' I said, 'but a friend of mine said he had the book and would bring it to me.' 'Well,' he said, 'I have it.' And he went on to say what a fine book it was. I said, 'I have got a prospectus coming—a book called "Thorns in the Flesh"—I'll bring that around. It's a historical novel of the Civil War.' He said, oh yes, he liked history. I thought, here's a customer before the book comes.

"Well, he sent a colored man with 'St. Elmo' for me to read. Two days after that I started out to sell 'Thorns in the Flesh.' It was a book that was written from the Southern point of view, but I didn't stop to think that Mr. Wolfe was from the North, a Yankee—I guess they called him a damn Yankee in Raleigh—but he changed his views and sided with the people in the South when he saw how they were treated in the Reconstruction Days. He was bitter against the North when he saw how they were treated.

"Well, I came across the Square to Mr. Wolfe's place of business. When I came across, the door was closed and I thought, 'He may not stay up here every day.' But I was bent on showing him that book because he said he was interested in history. I wasn't thinking about him being a Northerner, and of course, as I say, that book told the Southern side of it.

"Well, I knew where he lived on Woodfin Street. It was a little out of my way, but anyhow it was time to go home to dinner, nearly one o'clock, and I thought, 'I'll just go by there, and if he is home I'll show him the book.' He answered the door, and I told him that I was on my way home to dinner and I saw his shop door closed and didn't suppose he went up there every day, not thinking it was dinnertime for him, too.

"He said, 'We are at dinner; I'll tell Mrs. Allen.' Mrs. Allen was his mother-in-law, Cynthia's mother, and she lived there and took care of him, and he said, 'I'll tell Mrs. Allen,' and he called her and spoke to her. Of course, I know now that he was telling Mrs. Allen to make another place at dinner. They were about finished, and so she appeared at the door and said, 'Oh, how do you do?' She knew me; was already acquainted with me. She said, 'Come right on in. I've brought in a fresh bowl of soup.'

"I said, 'I was just going on home.' 'No, you come on in.' And Mr. Wolfe, he was the same way. I don't know whether I ate much or not, I talked so much. After we had finished, I said, 'I'll show you this book.' Mrs. Allen said, 'I'll come in the parlor just as soon as I put my things away and wash up the dishes.' " [6]

As might be expected, the parlor scene leads into Mr. Wolfe's proposal of marriage. One suspects that Mrs. Wolfe's account is more literally accurate than the incident in the novel, but it is rambling, discursive, and gossipy. The two meetings with Mr. Wolfe are run together so that neither gets maximum emphasis. The novelist, having heard this story countless times, focused on the first encounter, changed details—introducing the sofa and the ill health, for instance—and shifted the point of view from Eliza to Gant. This is precisely what a young man with experience in writing drama might be expected to do. Because the raw material of Wolfe's experience has so often been used to "account" for his novels, too little attention has been paid to the treatment by which he enriched the literary effect of that material.

Mabel Wolfe Wheaton's book aimed to present the Wolfe family "as we really were." She comments:

Many persons, including a great proportion of Tom's readers, no doubt, must picture us as a quarrelsome, often fighting, usually unhappy, generally uncouth group of individuals. But as I turn the pages of flooding memories and examine each of us individually and then study us collectively, I know that we Wolfes were not like that. Though there was conflict at times— what family doesn't have it?—our battles were never long waged. Furious words were often spoken, and I think we inherited from Papa our proclivity for shouting angry epithets, but we, like Papa, never meant what we were saying or screaming, and when the thunder and lightning of our quick anger had subsided, we were happy again and our love for each other had not been impaired.[7]

That there was more than quarreling between W. O. Wolfe and Julia is illustrated by the story of what happened after Effie, emulating her absent father, threw kerosene on the fire and set the house ablaze. Immediately after the fire was put out, Julia set about rebuilding, and when W. O. returned home several weeks later he saw the rebuilt house and heard the story. He himself told it repeatedly with admiration: " 'Julia's the most resourceful woman I ever saw,' he would invariably end his recital. 'Merciful God, that little woman can do anything, and do it right.' " Of W. O. himself an episode unused in *Look Homeward, Angel* is Mabel's story of being awakened on a winter night and taken to a window from which she and her father watched a woman and a boy stealing coal from the Wolfe basement. Her father whispered: "Don't say a word. . . . Let the poor devils have whatever they can carry, and welcome to it. Anyone who would come out on a night like this, Baby, is sorely in need—freezing, no doubt."

Along with the tempestuous "spree drinker," as Julia called him, W. O. was a man of dignity and character. Frank Wolfe's misbehavior at school led the principal to send the boy home for the rest of the day. That afternoon the principal, with some apprehension, saw W. O. Wolfe come into his office. After being told the particulars, Mr. Wolfe bowed and said, "Thank you. And I believe your story, Mr. Schultz." W. O. was, too, the generous father who at Christmas time gave Mabel fifty dollars— a large sum for those days—to spend on presents for the family. In the light of such incidents, it is possible to accept Mabel's assertion that her father's epithets—he called his children "miserable scoundrels" and "fiends from hell" and the boarding house "a murderous and bloody barn"—were not so seriously meant as they seem in the novel. In Mabel's opinion, W. O. Wolfe was "a born actor," to whom exuberance and exaggeration were natural. Papa always "made the grass greener," she says.[8]

A pervasive change in the novel is the social status of the family. Mabel is at pains to emphasize that the Wolfes were highly respected in Asheville. She speaks of the parlor at Woodfin Street as a room "of grandeur, attesting to the family's affluence and culture." There were Haviland china and a silver tea service. The description of Effie's wedding in 1908, and Mabel's own wedding in 1916, supported by a photograph showing the men in formal dress, certainly suggests a family in the upper middle class. Through the successful marble business and through Julia's accumulation of property, the family would naturally have been regarded as "substantial."

Mabel insists that the neighbors were fond of the Wolfes. She specifies that one of the Cromwells later married Doris Duke, and a Cromwell daughter married Douglas MacArthur. There were also the Perkinsons, the Browns, the Colvins, and the Hazzards, whom Mabel recalls as being very friendly. Julia's brother, Will Westall, was in the early 1900's a wealthy man with an imposing brick residence.

From Mabel's account it is not possible to tell how much the status of the family was affected by Mr. Wolfe's sprees, the frequent family quarrels, Frank's scrapes, Mabel's touring as a vaudeville singer, and especially the establishment of the "Old Kentucky Home" as a boarding house. In general, the keeping of a boarding house, in those days before the small apartment, was quite respectable. Yet Mr. Wolfe seems to have resented the idea from the beginning. Mabel concedes that Tom himself was quite self-conscious about the boarding house, for he asked his university friends to let him out of their car some distance away. Church affiliation, usually of social importance in a small town, seems rather indefinite. For several years after their marriage, Mr. and Mrs. Wolfe attended the Baptist Church. Later they seem not to have attended any church, but pastors of the Presbyterian Church (where Tom attended Sunday School) presided at family weddings and funerals.[9]

In the novel, Wolfe says of Ben and Eugene, when the two boys were twenty and twelve, that they were "by nature aristocrats." Eugene had just begun to feel his lack of social status. Ben had felt it for years. After Ben rages at his mother for not providing his little brother with clean clothes and for not having his hair cut, he moodily comments: "The rest of us never had anything, but I don't want to see the kid made into a little tramp." Shortly afterward, when Eugene goes to a private school, the older children (except Ben), think he is putting on airs. Eugene's attachment to Margaret Leonard, his new-found teacher, is specifically accounted for by "the misery, drunkenness, and disorder of his life at home."[10] Luke and Helen are represented as opposed to their mother's side of the family:

> In spite of this violent dislike for the Pentlands, both Helen and Luke had inherited all Gant's social hypocrisy. They wanted above all else to put a good face on before the world, to be well liked and to have many friends. They were profuse in their thanks, extravagant in their praise, cloying in their flattery. They slathered it on. They kept their ill-temper, their nervousness, and their irritability for exhibition at home. And in the presence of any members of Jim or Will Pentland's family their manner was not only friendly, it was even touched slightly with servility. Money impressed them (238-39).

Helen is represented as highly conscious of the questionable nature of some of the guests at the "Old Kentucky Home," just before her wedding: "Mama, in heaven's name! What do you mean by allowing such goings-on right in the face of Hugh and his people?" When Eliza visits Eugene at college, she embarrasses him by giving some of his friends several advertising cards for the boarding house and asking them to send people to her.[11] From such passages it is evident that Wolfe desired to emphasize the isolation of Eugene by suggesting that the family had something less than solid self-respect and social position. This is fictionally appropriate for a situation constantly disorganized by Gant's drinking and his unpredictable absences from home.

VII *Fictional Intention*

Upon turning back to the novel after reading the books of Mrs. Wolfe and Mabel, one sees more clearly Wolfe's literary intention. It was not to present a literal or "fair" autobiography. It was to take the framework of his early life and develop the theme of a sensitive boy pitted against a family whose boisterous affection never included a real understanding of him. To carry out this intention, Wolfe carefully selected detail and intensified it. W. O. Gant is chiefly the comic, violent, and irrational side of W. O. Wolfe, subject to insane bouts of drinking which upset the household. Eliza is the avaricious side of Julia, forced by a difficult marriage to get what comfort she could by satisfying her greed. Luke is the comic side of Fred, his stuttering unmercifully underlined in every scene. Mabel's affection for Tom and the family is trimmed down to Helen's rasping irritability, and her coarse teasing of Eugene: "Your girl went and got married, didn't she? She fooled you. You got left." Worse yet was "the poisonous hatred of her tongue." [12] Frank, the undisciplined and irresponsible boy, becomes Steve, of unrelieved petty vice. The only strong affection Eugene has is for Ben, who intensifies Eugene's sense of opposition to the rest of the family.

A similar selection and intensification is observable when one turns to Eugene's experience at Pulpit Hill. Arriving there as a boy just under sixteen, Eugene's first year "was filled for him with loneliness, pain, and failure." The students played pranks on him and jeered at him. His English teacher was an insufferable prig; his Latin teacher irritated him into deceptively—and successfully—riding a pony; only his Greek teacher taught him something worth learning. Sophomore year began in the autumn after America's entry into World War I, but the campus was little changed. Eugene began to be aware of college politics. Unpromising as his start had been, he began to be accepted. Winning a place on the college paper and magazine, he soon became a universal joiner. Eugene's third and fourth years at college are not clearly distinguished. In fact, the death of Ben appears to be in the October of his senior year instead of the third year (1918) as it actually was. The fall of 1918, the year of the Students Army Training Corps, found Eugene in a fervor of patriotism, but just under age for a uniform. He "did his bit" by turning out the school paper, filled with crusading editorials. When peace came, he remained "a big man on the campus," but not without interludes of gloom. He brooded because other students thought he was not clean; or because an aching tooth made him fear that he would soon lose all his teeth; or because a sore on his neck would not heal; or because other students thought him queer. In the philosophy class he turned realistic, and cynically contradicted the conventional approval of Galileo's heroism. And he resorted to solitary pranks such as ringing a doorbell and soberly asking for Mr. Coleridge—Mr. Samuel Taylor Coleridge. At commencement, however, "his face grew dark with pride and joy" (599) as he graduated with honors. In all this there is a heavy weighting of Eugene's isolation from his fellows.

Impressions of Wolfe at this period as recorded in a few published letters and in the comments of friends are at variance with the fictional portrait. Writing to his mother in December of 1919, his senior year, Wolfe said:

> I have never been so horribly busy. Have not a moment to call my own. Exams are here and I am divided between studying for them and getting out a feature edition of the Tar Heel of which I am now Editor in Chief—highest honor in college, I believe. Everyone runs to me with this and that and I am busy not part of the time but all of it—sleeping five hours is essential but I can't spare any more. I have my last examination tomorrow but will be forced to stay around when all the rest are gone getting out Tar Heel to send to students all over the state. It's hard, I know, but you must pay dearly for college honors.
>
> I get lots of praise: faculty say Tar Heel's editorials which I write have been steadying influences on campus this unsettled year, but you get tired of praise when you're too tired to think, almost.[13]

The notable feature of this letter is its dead serious tone, the complete absence of humorous exaggeration. The writer is clearly well pleased with his college honors, responsibilities, and reputation. For this impression of Wolfe as a successful undergraduate, well pleased with himself, there is strong support in the sketches of Jonathan Daniels and Legette Blythe, two men who knew him in undergraduate days. "If anybody enjoyed companionship and college associations, it was Tom," says Blythe. "He belonged to about everything on the Hill."[14] Jonathan Daniels, some time before Wolfe's death, was quoted as follows: "Tom's classmates voted him the ablest writer, the wittiest and most original of them all. They liked him at Chapel Hill. They still like him. And they wonder, still a little bewildered, why the big dominating mountain boy who had all the honors and practically all the friends looks back at Chapel Hill with the sad eyes of a baffled boy far from home on a strange, cruel campus."[15]

In the novel, of course, Wolfe may have emphasized discontents and frustrations not apparent to his classmates and unlikely to turn up in an isolated letter to his mother to whom he was always justifying himself. Perhaps in this respect the novel tells more of "the petrified truth" than the letter or the sketches of college friends. A more important point, however, is that such satisfaction as Wolfe got from his college experience is minimized and satirized. For example, here is a paragraph of interpretation regarding campus organizations:

> The yokels, of course, were in the saddle—they composed nine-tenths of the student body: the proud titles were in their gift, and they took good care that their world should be kept safe for yokelry and the homespun virtues. Usually, these dignities—the presidencies of student bodies, classes, Y.M.C.A.'s, and the managerships of athletic teams—were given to some honest serf who had established his greatness behind a plough before working in the college commons, or to some industrious hack who had shown a satisfactory mediocrity in all directions. . . . If he did not go into the law or the ministry, he was appointed a Rhodes Scholar (487).

Why is this paragraph inserted? It represents not the feeling of Eugene at the time he was happily collecting campus jewelry, but the later judgment of Thomas Wolfe on the triviality of campus honors. The effect of such a passage is to present not a literal autobiographical record, but an interpretation. To Jonathan Daniels the interpretation was something of a betrayal of the record.

If it was a betrayal of the record, a distortion of Wolfe's real college experience, several explanations may be suggested. The 1920's saw a violent reaction against sentiment of all kinds, particularly the "college spirit" sort. So far as intellectual values were concerned, it was highly unfashionable to admit that they existed in colleges. And perhaps by the mid-1920's, when he began *Look Homeward, Angel,* Wolfe's Northern experience had made him a trifle ashamed of the provincial university he had attended. Perhaps by 1926 or 1927 he wished he had been a little more dissatisfied with the University of North Carolina than he had actually been when he was there.

Certainly, the man who wrote the college chapters of the novel differs from the loyal alumnus who wrote his mother from Cambridge in 1920: "I recognize the greatness of Harvard but more and more every day I have borne to me the greatness of Chapel Hill. . . . Of course my love and affection will always be first with the University, with its unpaved streets which become pools of mud when it rains, and its brown dirty old buildings. The *spirit* of Carolina is just as great as that of Harvard." [16]

Of Wolfe's "two great teachers" at Chapel Hill—Williams and

Greenlaw—only Williams appears in *Look Homeward, Angel,* and there is no largeness in the scene. Even more notable is the complete omission of the Carolina Playmakers. This group had been so important a part of his college experience, that one can only conclude that he was unwilling to treat it in the satiric pattern which dominates the presentation of Eugene's college years.

VIII *Wolfe and Twain*

Thus the Pulpit Hill episodes underline the inference previously made that Wolfe worked over his actual experience by the customary literary processes of selection, emphasis, and development of a unifying point of view. In short, he operated much as Mark Twain did, and a brief comparison is relevant. Twain's best books are largely autobiographical: *Innocents Abroad* (1869), *Roughing It* (1872), *The Adventures of Tom Sawyer* (1876), *Life on the Mississippi* (1883), and *Adventures of Huckleberry Finn* (1884). Had Twain set out to write his autobiography, of course, he would have written the books in this order: *Tom Sawyer, Huckleberry Finn, Life on the Mississippi, Roughing It,* and *Innocents Abroad.* Twain never made any secret of the fact that he felt free to make use of his own experience, and to modify it for literary effect. There really was a character named Injun Joe, he explains, and in *Tom Sawyer* "I starved him entirely to death . . . in the interest of art." [17] *Huckleberry Finn* begins the accounts of his adventures with a reference to Mr. Mark Twain's book about Tom Sawyer: "There was things which he stretched, but mainly he told the truth." In *Life on the Mississippi* it pleases Twain's fancy—and his readers—to present himself as one of the stupidest cub pilots ever to turn up for lessons, a greenhorn who acts no more than sixteen years old and makes every possible mistake. Now in life, the young Sam Clemens who learned piloting from Horace Bixby was twenty-three, had learned the printer's trade, and had practiced it in such faraway places as Philadelphia and New York. It is reasonable to doubt that he was the complete greenhorn pictured in the book. Twain made the cub pilot amusing and memorable by literary exaggeration.

If it is reasonable to regard both Twain and Wolfe as "autobiographical" writers, why is it that customarily we find tolerance of Twain's practice but condemnation of Wolfe as "adolescent" and "unfair"? The answer is easy to find. Twain restricted himself to boyhood and to those adult episodes which were more or less stock situations: the lazy man in *Roughing It,* the skeptical tourist in *Innocents Abroad.* The painful years of adolescence he almost never touched, and a serious treatment of intimate personal relationships he never attempted in his successful books. Wolfe's extension of the autobiographical method, his intensity and his willingness to go beyond conventional limits of taste, have aroused antipathies. "Autobiographical" has too long been used as a club to beat him with. It is time to be more discriminating.

The autobiographical method, like any other, will yield good results when it is guided by insight and judgment. In his best passages, Wolfe's insight and judgment are superb. Like Mark Twain, Wolfe was an episodic writer, and his poorest passages are far below his best. Overconcern with the autobiographical nature of his fiction results in searching for a one-for-one relationship between Wolfe's experience and his fiction. Though the relationship between Wolfe's experience and his fiction will always have a strong interest for many of his readers, it is his frequent capacity to concentrate and to transcend experience that makes him an important writer.

Wolfe's capacity to transform a family story into dramatically humorous effect has already been illustrated by a comparison of the meeting of W. O. Gant and Eliza as presented in the novel, and the amusing but essentially commonplace narrative of Mrs. Wolfe. Another episode, we suspect, was similarly heightened. On one of his sprees, Gant falls in a stupor on the floor. Young Ben turns to Eliza in real fright:

> "Well," she said, picking her language with deliberate choosiness, "the pitcher went to the well once too often. I knew it would happen sooner or later."
> Through a slotted eye he glared murderously at her. Judicially, with placid folded hands, she studied him. Her calm eye caught the slow movement of a stealthy inhalation.
> "You get his purse, son, and any papers he may have," she directed. "I'll call the undertaker."
> With an infuriate scream the dead awakened.
> "I thought that would bring you to," she said complacently.
> He scrambled to his feet.

"You hell-hound!" he yelled. "You would drink my heart's blood. You are without mercy and without pity—inhuman and bloody monster that you are" (280).

Subtler, however, is the remarkable scene in which "Queen" Elizabeth, the town madam, orders from Gant a tombstone for one of her girls. " 'And she was such a fine girl, Mr. Gant,' said Elizabeth, weeping softly. 'She had such a bright future before her. She had more opportunities than I ever had, and I suppose you know'—she spoke modestly—'what I've done' " (266). Elizabeth insists on purchasing the stone angel, Gant's favorite piece of statuary, and together they select a suitable verse:

> She went away in beauty's flower,
> Before her youth was spent;
> Ere life and love had lived their hour
> God called her, and she went.
> (268)

No excerpt can convey the delicate balance that prevents this scene from falling into burlesque. Gant, the town drunkard, and Elizabeth, the town madam, are far from respectability, and they have no secrets from each other. Yet the obvious sincerity of their mutual human respect for each other enriches the scene and saves it from farce. Wolfe is wise enough to refrain from satirical interjections. It is doubtful that Twain could have done so, had he attempted such a scene.

Look Homeward, Angel is Wolfe's best novel. It has structure, dramatic episodes of great variety, and lyric intensity. In 1926, when he began it, he had served an apprenticeship in "objective" writing for the theater. Turning inward to his own story, he found a perspective on an important pattern in American life: the struggle of the individual against family and home town, the conflict between the academic and the real. As he worked to convert his experience into fiction, he was sustained by the love affair with Mrs. Aline Bernstein, to whom he dedicated the novel. Despite the quarrels which had begun even before *Look Homeward, Angel* was published, Wolfe never minimized what her unfailing faith in his talent meant to him at this crucial time. Of special importance was the fact that, as their acquaintance grew, Mrs. Bernstein's own very different childhood and youth—a city girl, an actor's daughter with a natural affinity for European culture—helped Wolfe to come to himself.

CHAPTER *4*

1929-38: *Of Time and the River*

THE SUCCESS of *Look Homeward, Angel* led Scribner's to make an advance of $4,500 on Wolfe's second novel, payable in monthly installments of $250. Thus, for the next eighteen months, he had more than his New York University salary would have been, and he was completely free to devote himself to writing. He therefore resigned from his instructorship in January, 1930, just before the end of the first semester. In March he received a Guggenheim award of $2,500, and on May 10 he sailed for Europe. In the seven months since the publication of *Look Homeward, Angel* Wolfe had accomplished little. He was much upset by adverse criticism from Asheville. He was hypersensitive to all critical discussion of his book. And Mrs. Bernstein, who had passionately devoted herself to him for nearly six years, bitterly opposed his decision to break off with her and depart for Europe. A minor pleasure of this disorganized spring was a first visit to his father's kin in Pennsylvania.

Wolfe remained in Europe until February, 1931, but despite his financial security these months were troubled and unproductive. In Paris he was angered by what he considered an exorbitant dental bill, sent on from New York. He had an unpleasant encounter with a woman friend of Mrs. Bernstein, and later with Mrs. Bernstein's sister. He met Scott Fitzgerald several times and suspected him of relaying reports about him to Mrs. Bernstein. From Mrs. Bernstein herself came a stream of cables and letters, with frightening threats of suicide.

When *Look Homeward, Angel* appeared in England in July, 1930, the English reviews were sufficiently unfavorable (though by no means wholly so) to make Wolfe tell Perkins that he would write no more books. In Montreux, Switzerland, Wolfe went on a tremendous spree, which he himself described in a letter to a New York University friend.[1] In December, Sinclair Lewis' praise of Wolfe in his Nobel Prize speech led to a meeting of the two writers in London; a drinking party developed, later to be described, with some exaggeration, in the Lloyd McHarg episode of *You Can't Go Home Again.*

Arriving in New York in February, 1931, Wolfe soon settled in Brooklyn. He was resolved not to resume his relationship with Mrs. Bernstein. For his nine months abroad "free for writing," Wolfe had only a jumble of manuscript to show. For the next four years he worked on "the book" during the day, and nearly every evening went to see Max Perkins at Scribner's. In the office, over dinner, or walking in Central Park, the two talked endlessly. Not until early 1933 did they agree that the second novel should start where *Look Homeward, Angel* left off.

Meanwhile Wolfe's "Portrait of Bascom Hawke" (later revised and included in *Of Time and the River*) tied for first place in the Scribner's contest for short fiction in 1932, bringing the author a welcome $2,500. On publication in the April *Scribner's Magazine* it was much praised, but it provoked bitter protest from Wolfe's Boston uncle and his two daughters. To one of them he wrote: "I do not consider the man in my story, for better or worse, to be even a close approximation of your father, although I would not deny that we both know where much of the clay that shaped that figure came from. . . ."[2] Less successful was a long work entitled "K 19," the title indicating the number of a pullman car, and serving as a device to put together travel episodes. As publication of a second novel was postponed by indecision, Wolfe tried with some success to publish shorter pieces in such magazines as *The American Mercury, The Redbook,* and *Scribner's.*

The long manuscript then called *October Fair* was delivered to Perkins on December 23, 1933, and the debate over revision continued until the following July. Perkins then overruled Wolfe's objections and sent the manuscript off to the typesetter. Printing and proofreading of the huge book (about 400,000 words) occupied several months. Wolfe continued to propose major revisions, but was unwilling to make necessary minor corrections; for example, parts of the story still had to be shifted from first person to third person. As a result of Wolfe's failure to read the proofs systematically, numerous errors had to be corrected in later editions. The bill for $1,180.60 for corrections in the plates, he bitterly resented, though it was in strict accordance with his contract. When *Of Time and the River* was published on March 8, 1935, Wolfe had arrived in Paris. In disbelief, he received from Perkins cables reporting favorable reviews.

I *Structure*

The nine hundred pages of *Of Time and the River* are arranged in eight books of unequal length, each given a title drawn from traditional myths. These titles, perhaps a result of Joyce's influence, are ornamental and metaphorical rather than precise and structural. "Orestes: Flight Before Fury" seems an inflated way of referring to the frustrations, greed, and blind impulses of Altamont, the world Eugene Gant leaves behind as he sets out for Harvard. The opening twenty-three pages, filled with Eliza's gossip, her inept greeting of Eugene's college friend, Robert Weaver, and the pointless bickering of Helen are long drawn out. The folksiness—"Gene! ain't one college enough for you, boy?"—is as far as possible from Greek tragedy, and any ironic intent is too loose to be impressive. On the train, the smoking-car conversation of the older men from Altamont, with the unthinking, casual questions about Eugene's brother Ben, dead now for two years, has a Sinclair Lewis quality. The drinking scene and quarrel with young Robert Weaver possesses a witless frenzy. The visit to Eugene's father in the Baltimore hospital signals his irrelevance to Eugene's future: "'Be a good boy, son,' Gant said gently. 'Do the best you can. If you need anything let your mother know,' he said wearily and indifferently, and turned his dead eyes away across the city." [3]

There is more appropriateness in "Young Faustus" as the title of Eugene's invasion of Harvard, but it has no relation to the long and powerful episode of Gant's death (210-73). And the juxtaposition of Faustus with Orestes seems haphazard. "Telemachus" tells of Eugene's return home to await the verdict on his play and of his involvement in a drunken spree that lands him in a South Carolina jail, from which his brother rescues him. "Proteus: the City" depicts the variety of New York: the harsh, banal street talk; the university classes; the quarrel and later friendship with Abe Jones, a Jewish student; the wonder of a weekend at Joel Pierce's luxurious Hudson River estate. "Jason's Voyage" describes Oxford, and the life of the Rhodes scholars there; first impressions of Paris; the hectic month with Francis Starwick, a Harvard friend, and the two young women who were with him. This association ends in a violent quarrel when Eugene's love for one of the girls is not returned, and he discovers that Starwick is a homosexual.

"Anteus: Earth Again" chronicles minor episodes in provincial France, including meetings with a countess who runs a cheap boarding house and a marquise to whom Eugene is unwillingly introduced as a correspondent for the New York *Times*. "Kronos and Rhea: The Dream of Time" does not parallel the story of the Titans; but in terms of Eugene's ramblings through Tours, Marseille, Dijon, and Arles there are suggestions of all periods of time since Homer, together with contrasts of Europe and America. "Faust and Helen," the ten-page concluding chapter and book, briefly sums up the voyage home and, at the dock in France, the meeting with Esther: "He turned, and saw her then, and so finding her, was lost, and so losing self, was found, and so seeing her, saw for a fading moment only the pleasant image of the woman that perhaps she was, and that life saw. He never knew: he only knew that from that moment his spirit was impaled upon the knife of love" (911).

Except for vague poetic suggestions in the myths of these subtitles, the sequence of development would be more clearly rendered by the bare geography of the huge novel: Altamont, Harvard, New York, England, Paris, Southern France, the voyage home. In a sense, the book is all middle. In the Altamont section one is reminded at length of the banalities Eugene is fleeing from, but they would hardly be clear without previous knowledge of *Look Homeward, Angel*. Harvard and New York represent a fuller knowledge of the world, and the conflict between the academic approach to reality and reality itself. Europe in its various regions and human types constitutes the perspective through which America is more searchingly felt and seen. The final episode, the coming of love (anticipated in the abortive affection for one of Starwick's friends), implies a fulfillment that brings an end to youthful, aimless searching; but it forms no real conclusion. There is organization of a kind, but it is obscured by overelaborate development of many episodes. Moreover, the heavy dependence on non-dramatic interpretation

and description makes this novel seem a far more static work
than *Look Homeward, Angel.*

II *Selective Autobiography*

Of Time and the River follows the main sequence of Wolfe's
life from September, 1920, when he went to Harvard, until
August, 1925, when he met Mrs. Bernstein at the end of his
homeward voyage from his first trip to Europe. There are, however, many omissions and shifts of emphasis. Wolfe's experiences
at Harvard and at New York University are of special interest
and are well documented. We can, therefore, compare the fictional treatment with the facts. The Harvard period occupies
the whole of Book II, "Young Faustus," two hundred and thirty-
five pages of the nine-hundred-page novel. Only a third of this
space is devoted to Eugene's university life, which is represented by these episodes: his mad delight in the library (Chapter VII); his meeting with Starwick, Professor Hatcher's assistant in the playwriting course (Chapter VIII); five chapters
satirizing Hatcher and his students (chapters X, XII, XVI,
XXXV, XXXVI); and a final chapter narrating a quarrel between
Eugene and Starwick (Chapter XXXVIII). Interpolated with
this material are several chapters on Eugene's uncle, Bascom
Pentland; the episode of Eugene's insincere friendship with the
girl Genevieve; a sketch of the Murphys, with whom Eugene
rooms; and the long sequence on the death of Eugene's father.
This organization of Book II has the effect of making a rather
conventional contrast between the hollowness of academic life
and the rich energy and anguish of life "outside."

In order to strengthen the contrast, Wolfe omitted almost
every favorable aspect of his university experience. George
Pierce Baker may have had something of Hatcher's snobbery:
"You know, Barrie was saying the same thing to me the last
time I saw him" (133); but Baker was also the man who welcomed the gangling boy from North Carolina, and of whom
Wolfe wrote in 1923: "He is a wonderful friend and he believes
in me." [4] After the presentation of *Welcome to Our City* in May,
1923, Baker took Wolfe to his summer home for the weekend.
This side of Wolfe's acquaintance with Baker, apparently, did
not fit in with the fictional scheme which governed *Of Time and*

the River. The troubled friendship with Kenneth Raisbeck was strongly emphasized in this part of the novel because of its sequel in Europe. The concentration on Raisbeck (Starwick) led Wolfe to omit friendships which seem to have been genial: Henry Carlton, Frederic L. Day, Robert Dow, Olin Dows, George Wallace.[5] Of Wolfe's academic courses and professors no details whatever are given in the novel; yet his academic experience was almost wholly satisfying and stimulating. Professor Lowes was then in the midst of writing *The Road to Xanadu,* a seminal book on the ways of the imagination; Wolfe did well in the two courses (Romantic Poets, the Renaissance) with Lowes, and wrote appreciatively of him to a North Carolina friend.[6] Even Kittredge, whose Shakespeare course Wolfe audited, was not turned into a fictional character. Harvard gave Wolfe a considerably greater respect for intellectual values, to judge from casual references in his letters; but emphasis on them did not fit the plan of the novel.

In a similar way, Wolfe's treatment of his experience at New York University is fragmentary and highly selective. The period of the novel included only the spring and summer terms of 1924 as a basis for Eugene's life as a teacher. Yet, since the novel was largely written between 1930 and 1934, one might expect those early terms to be fictionally enriched by the perspective of Wolfe's six-year association with the university. Actually, the reverse is true. After Book II, "Young Faustus," there follows "Telemachus," a section of nearly a hundred pages occupied with Eugene's anxious waiting for the acceptance of his play and with the aimless episode of being jailed in a South Carolina town with three drunken companions. Book IV, "Proteus," combines Eugene's teaching experience with his impressions of New York; the chaotic affairs of Robert Weaver, a college friend; and trips away from New York, especially a visit to the palatial home on the Hudson of a wealthy young friend. This latter episode occupies nearly a hundred pages.

Only five chapters (XLVII, XLIX, LI, LIII, LV) deal directly with his teaching, and more than half of the forty pages are devoted to Eugene's relation with a single student of his first term. This student, Abe Jones, focuses the aggressive, alien, hostile attitudes which Eugene senses in his students. From the instructor's rostrum Eugene looks down on "dark, ugly, grinning faces in their seats below him." As he reads a Shakespearean sonnet, "almost every one in the class of thirty people, in fact, was either engaged in conversation, or preparing to engage in conversation." Of one attentive student, Wolfe writes: "Mr. Boris Gorewitz always remained faithful. He sat on the front row close, very close, ah fragrantly, odorously close, too, too close to his teacher! He took notes. When beauty was revealed he smiled murkily, showing large white wet-looking teeth" (426).

Abe Jones was also attentive. After class he waits for Eugene with questions and complaints. When Eugene can stand it no longer, he tells Abe that he will have him transferred to another section: "I've had all I can stand from you. . . . Why you damned dull fellow. . . . Sitting there and sneering at me day after day with your damned Jew's face." Abe protests: "Say! you've got the wrong idea! . . . I don't want to leave your class. . . . Why, that's the best class I've got!" Respect and friendship then follow. Eugene had not dreamed to find such a young man in New York, but he concludes that "Abe was made of better stuff than most dreams are made of" (447). Later Eugene even goes to Abe's home and acquires a certain puzzled interest in Abe's tempestuous family.

The treatment of Abe has been objected to as a "smear."[7] Judged as a literal and typical representative of the student body, Abe Jones may be "a smear," but as a fictional episode combining the repulsions and attractions possible between a teacher and student of antithetic backgrounds, the passage is memorable. Wolfe's generalized charge of sexual aggressiveness in the women students has also been objected to: "they pressed upon him, breathing, soft and warm and full, as they cajoled, teased, seduced with look or gesture, questioned trivially, aggressively, uselessly. . . ."[8] One man's impressions of such students may differ from another man's; moreover, the emphasis in this passage may be intended as much to characterize Eugene— which it does—as to impart the literal truth about the coeds.

Wolfe's letters and the recollections of his friends suggest a much more complex and, on the whole, more satisfactory experience with students than was allotted to Eugene. "My little devils like me," he confided to Mrs. Roberts in May, 1924. "I tell them every week that I'm no teacher."[9] Henry Volkening, a colleague whom Wolfe liked and knew well, says that Wolfe "enjoyed hugely" the classroom work.[10] In conducting his classes, he was apparently haphazard, depending a great deal on reading aloud and floods of enthusiastic comment which students hesitated to interrupt. He also assigned oral book reports, which gave him opportunity for impromptu comment. One colleague says that Wolfe came to New York University, despite his achievements at North Carolina and at Harvard, with no real discipline: "he lacked both method and substance when he began to teach." Even at the end, according to the teacher who replaced him, he depended greatly on the sheer force of his personality to hold his students: "God! men, that is poetry! That *is poetry!*" he said after reading aloud Ben Jonson's apostrophe to Shakespeare. Nevertheless, Wolfe was a severe marker, giving only three A's to classes totaling over a hundred students in his first term. Moreover, he customarily appended long, elaborate comments to the themes he returned.[11]

In offering Wolfe a position at New York University, Professor Homer A. Watt told him he would find his students "rough but eager." To Mrs. Roberts, Wolfe wrote his satisfaction at the prospect of teaching in an institution where he would be given great liberty, and he added: "The students, moreover, mainly Jewish and Italian, have come up from the East Side; many are making sacrifices of a very considerable nature in order to get an education. They are, accordingly, not at all the conventional type of college student. I expect to establish contacts here, to get material in my seven months' stay that may prove invaluable." [12]

In similar vein he wrote to a Harvard friend, commenting: "I came without racial sentimentality—indeed with strong racial prejudice concerning the Jew, which I still retain." There is some reflection of this prejudice in the treatment of Abe Jones, but one actual student is emphatic in denying that he ever saw a trace of anti-Semitism in Wolfe's classes.[13] He was sufficiently well liked by his summer students in 1924 that they gave him a Dunhill pipe at the end of the course. At various times Wolfe could write of teaching as "work for which I had no affection" and of being "forced back into teaching," yet when he resigned in 1928 he said, "I think one of the chief reasons for my leaving now is not that I dislike teaching, and find it dull, but that I may like it too well." [14] From such comments, one concludes that, like most teachers—and many other people—Wolfe sometimes liked his job and sometimes loathed it. In particular, he made no secret that writing was his primary interest, and he quite naturally begrudged the time he devoted to reading themes and doing other routine chores. There were real satisfactions, however, even if they are hardly suggested in *Of Time and the River.*

Wolfe's relationships with his colleagues are also little treated in the novel. Eugene's securing of his position is briefly and impersonally noted. His fear of being discharged gives no hint of the cordiality and personal interest which Professor Watt, head of the department, manifested in Wolfe himself from the first. The "creature employed to oversee the work and methods of the instructors" is caricatured as having "a mind of the most obscene puritanism." [15] Other colleagues are represented only as a group consumed with envy and fear. Hardly two pages are devoted to them.

Wolfe's actual experience was quite different. He was offered a position three days after he applied, for his academic record and references were excellent. Most of the twenty or so members of the department were young, and at various times during Wolfe's stay there were a number of others with recognized literary talent: Léonie Adams, E. B. Burgum, Vardis Fisher, Frederick Prokosch, Margaret Schlauch, William Troy. Of these, Wolfe became well acquainted only with Fisher. He also knew well John Terry, a North Carolina friend, and Henry Volkening, whose reminiscences best supplement the negative impressions gained of the Wolfe of this period from the novel. Though Wolfe seems usually to have held himself aloof, he introduced himself to Volkening and talked until three in the morning after their first meeting. With Fisher he was often similarly loquacious.

After Wolfe's first teaching, in 1924, he was repeatedly offered the opportunity to teach, being virtually told that whenever he needed a job there would be one for him. His salary increased from $1,800 a year (two terms) in 1924, to $2,400 in 1929-30. Due consideration was given to his teaching schedule by Professor Watt, and during his absence in 1925-26 Professor James B. Munn showed similar interest. Later Munn read a draft of *Look Homeward, Angel* and made encouraging comments. In January, 1929, when Wolfe's novel had been accepted, and he needed some employment to keep him going during the spring, Munn found some teaching for Wolfe in the College of Fine Arts. Just after the publication of the novel, Watt arranged for

Wolfe to give a woman's club lecture in New Jersey and later supported his application for a Guggenheim fellowship. That Wolfe recognized he was something of a privileged person in the department is indicated by his defense against such an opinion, which he believed was current. In his letter of resignation to Watt written April 1, 1928, he apologizes for having been "surly, ill-tempered, unable to join happily with other people" during the weeks of his final work on his novel, but insists that he has always done his work conscientiously. In the same letter he expresses appreciation for the humane consideration of a colleague stricken with tuberculosis. He concludes: "Let me assure you that I will never forget your kindness, and your generous comprehension, and that if any *good* distinction ever attaches to my name, I shall be proud to acknowledge my connection with this place—if any *bad* one, I shall keep silent." [16]

In the light of all this mutual good will during six years, it is not surprising that the publication of *Of Time and the River* in 1935 dismayed Wolfe's friends: "It was received with incredulity, astonishment, anger, and grief at Washington Square. How could he who had broken bread amongst us, who had shared our limited fare and small rewards, treat us as he had done? Had he no sense of the betrayal of an enterprise to which he had committed so much of himself—a measure, at least, of others' commitment?" [17] Allowances were made by many for the vagaries of genius, but for some, such allowances were cold comfort.

The Harvard and Washington Square episodes of *Of Time and the River* illustrate the same principle already demonstrated in *Look Homeward, Angel*. Autobiographical in source these novels are. Autobiographical in treatment they are not, in any full sense. In neither book did Wolfe set down a "fair" or literal account of his experience. He selected those scenes and characters which would be useful in developing fictional themes. In *Of Time and the River* he was dealing with more recent experience, experience which in 1935 was still not fully assimilated. The fictional themes were therefore less easy to define. The conflict between the provincial boy and the life of Cambridge and New York is a valid pattern. The conflict between the sensitive, creative mind and the great university on one hand and metropolitan life on the other, is another valid pattern. Wolfe tried to combine the two, and in doing so seems to have oversimplified his own experience. Despite the floods of words, the patterns remain too geometrical to be convincingly human. Academic life has been caricatured so long that a stereotype has been created. Wolfe gave too much credence to the stereotype. The first part of his second novel would be better if he had made bolder and richer use of his own unique passage through Harvard and New York University. Significantly, when George Webber looks back on his first novel he finds it "not autobiographical enough" (*You Can't Go Home Again,* p. 384).

Lacking the opportunity to make such close comparisons between Wolfe's European experience and the latter part of *Of Time and the River,* we suspect that there, too, he was somewhat betrayed by his anxiety to convert his raw material into the approved modes of melodrama and sentiment. Striking as are many of the European episodes—the Oxford romance, the abortive love affair with Ann, the quarrel with Starwick, the impoverished countess—they do not lead to the kind of self-knowledge in Eugene that betokens thorough understanding on the part of the author.

III *Drama and Rhetoric*

Though part of *Of Time and the River* was written before the publication of *Look Homeward, Angel,* the book as we have it was largely written between July, 1932, and July, 1934. Perkins, not Mrs. Bernstein, was now the adviser. The solitude of Wolfe's Brooklyn apartment was not interrupted by classes at Washington Square. These changed conditions and a desire to "develop" as a writer led to a novel very different in kind from *Look Homeward, Angel,* despite the fact that it continued the story of Eugene Gant. An important difference was less dependence on the dramatic method. In the nine hundred pages of *Of Time and the River,* three hundred are solid type unbroken by a line of dialogue. This is nearly twice the proportion of lyrical, expository, rhetorical matter appearing in the earlier novel.

Both novels open with minimum reliance on dramatic scenes, but it is interesting to see how much more rapidly the earlier novel moves. *Look Homeward, Angel* gives in six pages a dynamic narrative of W. O. Gant's early life: the migration of the Englishman Gilbert Gaunt to Pennsylvania in 1837, Oliver's

boyhood recollection of rebel soldiers on their way to Gettys-
burg, his move to the South, his first marriage, and his arrival
in Altamont. Without the aid of dialogue, a strong focus of
interest is created. By page ninety-four the whole Gant family
has been introduced, Grover has died in St. Louis, Gant himself
is back from his Western journey, and the child Eugene is filling
out his sensory impressions of a wonderful world of food, play,
school, and family life. In *Of Time and the River* eighty-six
pages (and they are larger pages) are used to get Eugene from
Altamont to Baltimore. Harvard lies on beyond. There is a good
deal of interest in the smoking-car scenes, but very little comes
of them in later parts of the novel. Robert Weaver, the reckless
friend from Altamont, does appear later in the novel—notably in
the South Carolina jail episode of "Telemachus," and as an
unwelcome guest in Eugene's New York hotel—but, though
Eugene is involved in Weaver's affairs, he is little affected by
them. Wolfe seems almost to distrust his basic story and to spin
out the preliminaries as a means of postponing the main action.

It is interesting also to consider some of the extended rhetorical passages. In *Look Homeward, Angel*, Eugene's experience
in private school is described: "But the school had become the
center of his heart and life—Margaret Leonard his spiritual
mother. He liked to be there most in the afternoons when the
crowd of boys had gone, and when he was free to wander about
the old house, under the singing majesty of great trees, exultant
in the proud solitude of that fine hill, the clean windy rain of
the acorns, the tang of burning leaves" (231). Such a passage
fills out the sense of Eugene's content in perhaps the only way it
could be done.

In another passage, Gant, after selling the stone angel to
Elizabeth, stands on the porch of his shop looking out on all the
familiar sights of Altamont Square as reminders of his vanished
youth. Eugene's experience of poetry is effectively summoned
up in titles and phrases: "Tam O'Shanter," "Fear no more the
heat o' the sun," and "Too much of water hast thou, poor
Ophelia." The feel of 1917 is conjured up: "War is not death
to young men; war is life. The earth had never worn raiment of
such color as it did that year. The war seemed to unearth pockets
of ore that had never been known in the nation: there was a
vast unfolding and exposure of wealth and power."[18] Such
passages cannot really be objected to as padding. They supply

an echo of character or situation in the way that the spoken voice would transform lines of dialogue on the page of a play script. They help to realize; they blend with the narrative.

There is less defense for such a passage as Chapter XIII of *Of Time and the River.* The chapter is just over fourteen pages long, and on only four of them are there representative scraps of Bascom Pentland's conversation. It is spring of Eugene's first year at Harvard:

> Suddenly spring came, and he felt at once exultant certainty and joy. Outside his uncle's dirty window he could see the edge of Faneuil Hall, and hear the swarming and abundant activity of the markets. The deep roar of the markets reached them across the singing and lyrical air, and he drank into his lungs a thousand proud, potent, and mysterious odors which came to him like the breath of certainty, like the proof of magic, and like the revelation that all confusion had been banished—the world that he longed for won, the word that he sought for spoken, the hunger that devoured him fed and ended (137).

This is the first half of the paragraph. There follows a reminiscent contrast of spring in Old Catawba. Then Eugene senses from the docks the varied smells of warehouses, bakeries, and butcher shops, and the smell of the sea, so strong for a boy from inland Catawba. Uncle Bascom interrupts to renew his invitation for Sunday, and to satirize women in a matchless paragraph. Eugene suggests something of the story of Bascom's early life: "He wanted to know what the old man's youth beyond its grim weather of poverty, loneliness, and desperation had been like." But the chapter closes with Eugene's own insatiable lust for life: "He had a tongue for agony, a food for hunger, a door for exile, and a surfeit for insatiate desire: exultant certainty welled up in him, he thought he could possess it all, and he cried: 'Yes! It will be mine.'"

In this chapter Uncle Bascom is seen to advantage in comic focus. Eugene is hardly in focus at all, but is evoked by generalized rhetoric. The enumeration of smells is an extraordinary tour de force, and is of interest in itself; but it is hardly integrated with the drama or the narrative of the scene. Similar examples of rhetorical elaboration may be found in the account of Wolfe's teaching (chapters XLVII and LIII), in parts of the visit to the Joel Pierce mansion, the meeting with the Rhodes scholars (Chapter LXXI), the twenty-page sequence of note-book excerpts (661-80), the Starwick association (680-794), and the descriptions of provincial France.

The great length of the book does not come from the fullness of its representation of Eugene's experience. We have seen how much richer and more complex Wolfe's own experience was, but the selection for the novel of incident and emphasis was so narrowly based, so emphatic of black-and-white contrasts, that Wolfe gave way to his instinctive capacity for rhetorical elaboration. This capacity had been checked by his apprenticeship in drama, and was still reasonably under control in the writing of *Look Homeward, Angel.* The reliance on rhetoric is never more conspicuous than at the end of *Of Time and the River;* the meeting with Esther is neither narrated nor dramatized—it is rhapsodized.

The heavy reliance on rhetoric in *Of Time and the River* results in part from Wolfe's desire that his second novel be "different" and in part from his failure to develop his central character in young manhood as effectively as he had managed to do in the earlier novel. A comparison with Somerset Maugham's *Of Human Bondage* is illuminating. At the end of this novel—a favorite of Wolfe's—Philip does seem to have learned something through his experiences. A sensitive, intelligent young man, handicapped from boyhood by lameness, poverty, and a tyrannical guardian, Philip has passed through many follies. His love affair with the crude and worthless Mildred, for example, had no justification in anyone's eyes but his own. He fails in his ambition to become an artist. At the end, without pretension and without unction, he faces the future with a believable confidence. At the end of *Of Time and the River*, Eugene is twenty-five. He has failed at playwriting, and he is largely contemptuous of his life as a teacher. He has been disappointed in Professor Hatcher; in Starwick ("my best friend"); in Ann, who did not return his love; and in himself. If Eugene is as intelligent as one has been led to believe, ought there not—at least might there not—be more evidence that experience has had some effect on him? Would he not be a more interesting and convincing character if this were true?

And yet, if *Of Time and the River* is not so finished and satisfying a novel as *Look Homeward, Angel*, it does show greater writing power. And though Maugham's *Of Human Bondage* has

just been cited as possessing a more convincing central character, most readers would agree that Wolfe's novel has greater
verve. The best episodes have an emotional depth and fresh-
ness that persuades readers to be tolerant of the inferior pages.
In such a work, to be sure, what is a dull digression to one
reader may be a favorite beauty of another; but there is general
agreement that the death of W. O. Gant is one of Wolfe's most
notable successes. For this particular passage it is important to
realize that Wolfe was not present at his father's death, as he
had been at his brother Ben's; in the strict sense, this long
passage is neither autobiographical nor "mere memory." Wolfe
was sent for, but arrived from Cambridge several hours after
his father died. The account of the death, therefore, had to be
"imagined" in the sense of taking the facts he could gather from
his loquacious family and fitting them together, guided by his
sense of "this is the way it must have been." Woven into the
narrative is the sub-action of Dr. McGuire's adulterous affair
and his death the morning of the funeral.

In Chapter XXI the episode begins by shifting abruptly from
Eugene in Cambridge to his sister Helen in Altamont. She asks
Dr. McGuire about her father. He assures her that Gant is dying,
and that nothing more can be done. How long before death will
come is beyond human knowledge. In her overwrought state,
McGuire gives her advice: "Don't die the rotten, lousy, dirty
death-in-life—the only death that's really horrible!" McGuire's
own trouble with an unfaithful mistress comes into the next
chapter, and he is almost hopelessly drunk when Gant's hemorrhage necessitates an emergency call. Helen's unhappiness in
her own childless marriage aggravates her anxiety about her
father. Gant recovers from one hemorrhage only to have another
one a few weeks later. Eliza, nevertheless, keeps talking about
indications of recovery no one else can see, thus creating a
grotesque perspective on Gant's fatal illness.

Eugene's receipt of the telegram in Cambridge is a brief
interlude, and the scene shifts back to the sickroom, and the
hall outside, where Gant's friends of many years gather to ask
about his condition and to comfort the family. Gant himself,
"knowing that often he had lived badly, was now determined to
die well." He even compliments Eliza on how well she cooks
chicken, reducing the unsentimental woman to tears. Later,
when they are alone, he says quietly: "Eliza, you have had a

hard life with me, a hard time. I want to tell you that I'm sorry." She goes to get him some water, and, when she returns, he is gone. At the funeral, it was his father's hands that Eugene remembered: "Yet, even in his death, his father's hands seemed to live, and would not die. . . . The great hands had a stony, sculptured and yet living strength and vitality, as if Michelangelo had carved them." [19]

As an episode by itself, for those readers who have known Gant in *Look Homeward, Angel,* the death of Gant is peculiarly poignant. It is remarkable what variety of perspective Wolfe creates and blends together. The old man, with all his sins and violence behind him, still seems to dominate; and no memory is sufficient to mar the affection that everyone feels, the awe at the sheer power of the man, and the love for his generous nature which seemed to belie so many of his acts. And yet, the death of Gant does remain an episode. Omit it from the book, and the novel would still be over eight hundred pages long. Eugene would still be the same Eugene in the end.

IV *The Last Three Years*

Six days before the publication of *Of Time and the River,* Wolfe sailed for England on his sixth trip abroad. Arrived in London, he received with disbelief Perkins' enthusiastic cables about the book's success. In the first few weeks twenty thousand copies were sold; and reviews, though mixed, were on the whole favorable. Characteristically, Wolfe agonized over the unfavorable comments. His English publisher, A. S. Frere, saw that Wolfe met literary people in London; but Wolfe was ill at ease and, through over-drinking, was rude to Frere and his wife on at least two occasions. Late in April, Wolfe went to Holland, and in May he was in Germany. Publication of a German translation of *Look Homeward, Angel* in 1932 had built up a substantial money credit for the author, and had also made him well and favorably known. Ernest Rowohlt, his publisher, arranged interviews and parties in his honor. The American ambassador, William E. Dodd, and his daughter Martha, also extended hospitality. Wolfe had a strong romantic appreciation of Germany's artistic past, and a special interest in Goethe. Despite the rise of the Nazis, which Wolfe did not take seriously at this time, Wolfe thought the German people "the cleanest, the kindest, the warmest-hearted, and the most honorable people I have met in Europe." [20]

Illness and the threat of a suit by his former literary agent, Mrs. Madeleine Boyd, led Wolfe to return to New York early in July. Perkins met him at the dock, with news that Mrs. Bernstein also threatened suit if Wolfe carried out his intention to publish *October Fair*, now the title of a manuscript which narrated in fictional guise the affair between Wolfe and Mrs. Bernstein. Wolfe was happy to be home, however, and he and Perkins had a convivial evening together. The next day Wolfe started to plough through stacks of reviews and a great accumulation of mail at the Scribner's office. Included was a letter from Mrs. Bernstein, and a few days later there was a chance meeting. A temporary reconciliation occurred, but the long separation was too much to overcome.

Later in July, Wolfe accepted an invitation to lecture at the Writers Conference at Boulder, Colorado. A long preface intended for *Of Time and the River*, and dropped on Perkins' advice, became the basis for the Boulder lecture, which Wolfe says lasted one hour and forty minutes. He remained at Boulder for twelve days of enthusiastic acclaim and entertainment. An old New York University friend, Desmond Powell, met him in Denver and took him by car to Santa Fe. From there he went on to the Grand Canyon and to Hollywood, where he met Jean Harlow and received an offer to work for the M-G-M studios. In San Francisco he was entertained by Dr. Russel Lee, whom he had met on shipboard. Chinatown and a trip to the big trees in Big Basin delighted him. Finally, in mid-September he headed East, stopping off in St. Louis to revisit the house where his brother Grover had died in 1904.

Returning to New York in late September, Wolfe took an apartment at 865 Fifth Avenue, two blocks from Perkins' home. In November, *From Death to Morning*, a collection of Wolfe's short stories, appeared. Despite the sale of forty thousand copies of *Of Time and the River*, the volume of short stories was not well received. Various plans for further books were discussed with Perkins, but *October Fair* was temporarily shelved because of Mrs. Bernstein's continued threat to prevent its publication by legal means. Meanwhile Wolfe decided to publish the Writers' Conference speech. It was accepted by *The Atlantic Monthly*, but proved too long. In three installments it then appeared in *The Saturday Review of Literature* (December 14, 21, 28). In April, 1936, the long essay, *The Story of a Novel*, was published as a small book. Bernard De Voto's essay, "Genius is Not Enough," was ostensibly a review of this volume, but it actually was an attack on Wolfe's whole career.[21] Wolfe was not overexcited by this attack, but De Voto's exaggerated emphasis on Perkins' part in the shaping of Wolfe's two novels rankled. Besides the old quarrel over Perkins' sending the manuscript of *Of Time and the River* to the printer without Wolfe's permission, there had been disputes about *October Fair*, about Wolfe's other plans for future writing, and about *The Story of a Novel* itself. De Voto's attack on April 23, in fact, came just two days after Wolfe had made peace with Perkins. A variety of disputes and distractions thus complicated Wolfe's relations with Perkins in the spring of 1936, and Wolfe was beginning to think of changing publishers before he left in July on his seventh and last trip to Europe.

In August he attended the Olympics in Berlin, and was most enthusiastic about the exploits of Jesse Owen, the Negro athlete on the American team. At this time Thea Voelcker was assigned to make a sketch of Wolfe for the *Berliner Tageblatt*. He did not like the sketch, but he fell in love with the artist. The affair continued until his return home in October. More importantly, this 1936 visit to Germany forced Wolfe to alter his opinions of the Nazi movement. Awareness of the power and cruelty of the Nazis crystallized as Wolfe saw a little Jewish man taken from his train compartment at the German border by Nazi officials. The method of arrest and the man's obvious terror resulted in Wolfe's sketch, "I Have a Thing to Tell You," which appeared in *The New Republic* (March 10, 17, 24, 1937). Later it was incorporated in *You Can't Go Home Again*.

On his return to New York in October, 1936, the quarrels between Wolfe and Perkins were renewed. Wolfe was exasperated by the Scribner's lawyer, who handled a libel suit over "No Door," a sketch based on a Brooklyn family. He quarreled with Perkins over the presidential campaign, and over Perkins' lack of interest in "No More Rivers," a story about a publishing house, revised to conceal the most obvious traces of satire against Scribner's. On November 16, Wolfe asked for a definite release from his connection with Scribner's. To Perkins' three replies, partly formal and partly friendly, Wolfe wrote a long answer—but did not mail it. After having Christmas dinner with the Perkins family, he left for New Orleans, taking his long, unmailed letter to Perkins with him. As usual, Wolfe was lavishly entertained by friends in New Orleans. In a confused state, he received a letter in connection with a minor lawsuit, and immediately blamed Perkins for giving out his address. The letter he then sent Perkins was a new one, composed out of drunken bitterness instead of the reasoned consideration of their differences he had written in New York. A few days later he mailed the earlier letter with a postscript making the break final. To this Perkins made three replies, all conciliatory.

Leaving New Orleans, Wolfe went to Chapel Hill for his first visit to the University since his graduation in 1920. Faculty friends and undergraduate worshipers welcomed him. All was kindness, but the round of activities tired him. He gave up an intended trip to Asheville. On arriving in New York, Wolfe was visited by Perkins, still in a conciliatory mood. Wolfe finally agreed to pay $1,425 as his share of the compromise settlement of the Dorman libel suit, plus legal fees of $1,320.05. As a result, his royalty account now showed a deficit. Quarrels with Perkins continued even after the formal break with Scribner's, and, according to an impartial observer, once resulted in a fistfight between Wolfe and Perkins.[22]

In April, 1937, Wolfe made the postponed trip to Asheville. Visiting relatives of his mother nearby, he got from an old veteran the facts he later developed into the story "Chickamauga." Wolfe tried for a time living in an isolated cabin in order to escape old family conflicts that broke out again with the return of his brother Frank. But Wolfe was unable to keep a servant for long, and he was totally unable to look after himself. In September he returned to New York, having completed "The Party at Jack's," published as a short novel in *Scribner's* after his death and later incorporated in *You Can't Go Home Again.* Before he returned to New York, however, Wolfe put in long-distance calls to various publishers, asking them point-blank if they would publish him. Wolfe's drunken voice was unconvincing to several, but Alfred Harcourt, of Harcourt, Brace, took the matter seriously and informed his friend Charles Scribner. The break, pending for months, was now public knowledge. In the autumn, Wolfe negotiated seriously with Houghton-Mifflin, but when the publisher's representative was unwilling to accept

full responsbiility for storing Wolfe's huge accumulation of
manuscript, the author withdrew. Harper's then offered ten
thousand dollars for Wolfe's next book, unconditionally. Wolfe
accepted, and, on December 31, he signed a contract.

After the long, tangled difficulties of 1936 and 1937, the spring
of 1938 was relatively quiet, and became a productive period
for Wolfe. He worked hard on a novel then called *The Vision
of Paul Spangler.* He won a minor law suit, in which Perkins
appeared as a witness in Wolfe's behalf. In May he was invited to
speak at Purdue University, which he did with great pleasure and
satisfaction. From Purdue he went on to Chicago, Denver, and
Portland, Oregon. With two Portland friends he went on a thir-
teen-day automobile trip of over four thousand miles, visiting
Crater Lake, Yosemite, Sequoia, the Grand Canyon, Zion and
Bryce National Parks in Utah, and Yellowstone. On July 2 this
trip, which Wolfe had enjoyed exuberantly despite long, hard,
hot days of travel, ended in Seattle.

After returning from a short boat trip to British Columbia,
Wolfe was ill. A week later, July 11, he was taken to the hospital with pneumonia. After the crisis was safely passed, and the
fever reduced, it became apparent that there was some further
and obscure difficulty. Severe headaches continued. On August
19 his sister Mabel arrived, joining his brother Fred, who had
already been with Wolfe for a month. Early in September,
Wolfe's mind became confused. Finally doctors advised that he
be taken to Johns Hopkins Hospital in Baltimore. Mrs. Wolfe
joined the party in Chicago. Edward Aswell, Harper's editor,
came down to Baltimore, and later Perkins. An operation on
September 12 disclosed miliary tuberculosis of the brain, so far
advanced that nothing could be done. On September 15,
Thomas Wolfe died; had he lived on until October 3 he would
have reached his thirty-eighth birthday.

Wolfe's body was taken to Asheville for burial. Despite the
long illness, Wolfe's family was distraught at the suddenness of
death. Prior to the funeral in the Presbyterian Church, the coffin
lay open in the old family residence, the scene of Ben's death
twenty years before, the "Dixieland" of *Look Homeward, Angel.*
Perkins has left a poignant account of the highly charged emotions of family and friends, so alien to Perkins' own instinctive
New England reticence. Across the country, and abroad, Wolfe's
death was startling news. By 1938 he was accepted as one of the

leading American writers. His vitality, his warm response to the rich variety of American life, and his denunciation of Nazism in 1937 had made him something of a national spokesman. In the year of Munich, this was important. It seemed incredible that Thomas Wolfe was dead. With the sense of loss there was mingled a conviction that he represented something important, something that must not be allowed to die. Through the paper-back reprints distributed during World War II, many a service-man discovered in his works the personal resonance of American life which gave meaning to the formal statements of patriotism.

Today, the visitor to Riverside Cemetery in Asheville finds on a beautifully shaded slope a large tombstone with this inscription:

T O M

SON OF

W. O. AND JULIA E.

WOLFE

A BELOVED AMERICAN AUTHOR

OCT. 3, 1900 — SEPT. 15, 1938

. . .

"THE LAST VOYAGE, THE LONGEST, THE BEST."

LOOK HOMEWARD ANGEL

. . .

"DEATH BENT TO TOUCH HIS CHOSEN SON WITH MERCY, LOVE AND PITY, AND PUT THE SEAL OF HONOR ON HIM WHEN HE DIED."   THE WEB AND THE ROCK

CHAPTER 5

The Webber Novels

A PECULIARITY of Wolfe's will was that, despite the break with Scribner's, Maxwell Perkins was made executor of the estate and administrator of all Wolfe's literary affairs. Thus, though the two Webber novels and a book of short fiction were brought out by Harper's after Wolfe's death, these books were published under the general supervision of Perkins, who remained senior editor at Scribner's. The cooperative spirit in which these publications were developed from the mass of manuscript left by Wolfe reflects great credit on Perkins and on Edward A. Aswell, the Harper's editor; and it testifies to the high respect both men had for Wolfe as a man and as a writer. In a long letter to Aswell, February 14, 1938, Wolfe stated his general plan for the story of George Webber:

> . . . the whole book might almost be called "You Can't Go Home Again"—which means back home to one's family, back home to one's childhood, back home to the father one has lost, back home to romantic love, to a young man's dreams of glory and of fame, back home to exile, to escape to "Europe" and some foreign land, back home to lyricism, singing just for singing's sake, back home to aestheticism, to one's youthful ideas of the "artist," and the all-sufficiency of "art and beauty and love," back home to the ivory tower, back home to places in the country, the cottage in Bermuda away from all the strife and conflict of the world, back home to the father one is looking for—to someone who can help one, save one, ease the burden for one, back home to the old forms and systems of things that once seemed everlasting, but that are changing all the time—back home to the escapes of Time and Memory. Each of these discoveries, sad and hard as they are to make and accept, are described in the book almost in the order in which they are named here. But the conclusion is not sad:

this is a hopeful book—the conclusion is that although you can't go home again, the home of every one of us is in the future: there is no other way.[1]

Though Wolfe goes on to say that this new book will be autobiographical, it will be so in a new way: ". . . this book marks not only a turning away from the books I have written in the past, but a genuine spiritual and artistic change. In other words, I feel that I am done with lyrical and identifiable personal autobiography; I am also seeking, and hope now to obtain, through free creation, a release of my inventive power which the more shackling limitations of identifiable autobiography do not permit" (714).

In other words, the value of the Eugene Gant type of character is his personal and romantic uniqueness, causing conflict with the world around him: in this sense, Eugene becomes a kind of romantic self-justification, and his greatest weakness lies in this fact. Wolfe further explained his intentions in the new novel:

> Therefore, it is first of all vitally important to the success of this book that there be no trace of Eugene Gant-i-ness in the character of the protagonist; and since there is no longer a trace of Eugene Gant-i-ness in the mind and spirit of the creator, the problem should be a technical one rather than a spiritual or emotional one. In other words, this is a book about discovery, and not about self-justification; it hopes to describe the pattern that the life of Everyman must, in general, take in its process of discovery . . . (714).

A seemingly trivial but probably psychologically important way in which Wolfe sought to objectify his protagonist was by making him a man of normal height, but so misproportioned that "Monk" was an inevitable nickname. Gradually, "Monk" discovers that his physical uniqueness is of no great importance. This wisdom represents his eventual identification with mankind.

Study of Wolfe's manuscripts in the light of his general aim enabled Aswell to edit the Webber story into two novels: *The Web and the Rock* (1939) and *You Can't Go Home Again* (1940). Aswell comments: ". . . the wonderful thing about the manuscript—the really incredible thing—was that once the extraneous matter was removed, once the unfinished fragments and great chunks of stuff that did not belong in the books were taken out, the parts that remained fell into place and fitted together like the pieces of a jigsaw puzzle." [2] There were a few gaps. These Aswell filled in with italicized passages based on Wolfe's own words as far as possible. In the more than fourteen hundred pages of the two novels, only eighteen pages are thus set off from the main text. Because the Webber story was published without Wolfe's personal supervision, and because the narrative is consecutive, it will be convenient to review it as a unit, recognizing that each volume has some degree of unity.

I The Web and the Rock

The Web and the Rock, like *Of Time and the River,* employs subtitles drawn from myth to suggest a symbolic conception not entirely consistent: "The Web and the Root," "The Child Calaban," "Olympus in Catawba," "Götterdämmerung." Such imaginative subtitles clash awkwardly with literal captions such as "The Theatre" and "Esther's Farewell." In the main title "Web" means growth, the creative principle associated with George Webber. "Rock" is the static quality which opposes growth: the city in some aspects, and later Foxhall Edwards, Webber's editor. [3]

The Web and the Rock is developed in two unequal parts. The first, made up of three books (about a third of the volume), narrates Webber's boyhood in Libya Hill, his years at Pine Rock College, and his bachelor life with other young Southerners in New York. The second part begins with Chapter 17, when George, returning from a trip to Europe, meets Mrs. Esther Jack. The remainder of the novel is devoted to their love affair, their mutual jealousies and their quarrels, the rejection of George's novel, his trip abroad in a fruitless attempt to break with Esther, and his return to New York and to Esther.

In outline, then, *The Web and the Rock* appears to be a retelling of the story of Eugene Gant, with an extension into Eugene's affairs with Esther Jack, who is mentioned in the last chapter of *Of Time and the River.* There are many differences, however, some superficial and some important. Libya Hill is Altamont, just as Altamont is Asheville. Pine Rock College is Pulpit Hill, just as Pulpit Hill is Chapel Hill and the University of North Carolina. What happens in these places in the new novel, is different in kind; and George Webber's passage to New

York is direct instead of by way of Harvard, as with Eugene and Wolfe himself. The effect is to compress George Webber's development into a single volume that covers a greater time span than *Look Homeward, Angel* and *Of Time and the River* combined.

Like Eugene, George Webber is isolated in boyhood, but in a different fashion. George's father had deserted his mother for the wife of another man, though he continued to live in Libya Hill. This scandal separated George from his father when the boy was only eight, and not long after, the mother died. The boy was then brought up in the family of an uncle, a Joyner, as George's mother had been. The Joyners were rigid people, with no tolerance for the scandalous behavior of George's father. Though George sees his father every day, he is not allowed to associate with him. With Mark Joyner and Mag lives Aunt Maw, an elderly sister of George's mother. Aunt Maw has some of the accents and qualities of Eliza Gant, but there is no other parallel to the Gant household.

George's boyhood is suggested through a series of episodes. The big boy of his neighborhood, Nebraska Crane, defends him against three bullies. Aunt Maw tells the boy stories of the early Joyners and of the Civil War. There is the thrill of the circus, with its suggestion of distant cities. There are accidents, like the one in which a neighbor boy is killed by an automobile. There is a chapter about the coarse-mouthed butcher who brings up his children with an ugly force. Most sensational of all is the frenzied mob killing of Dick, the kindly Negro, loved by all the boys for his knowledge of sports and respected by all adults for his good manners and piety. Insulted by a white man, Dick goes berserk, killing several persons before he is himself shot down. Finally, there are the bitter reminiscences of Uncle Mark, who hated his own father—Major Joyner—for his poverty, his military pretensions, and his fancied literary talent. Despite such rough and disillusioning glimpses of life, young George Webber dreams of achieving happiness, somehow, somewhere.

On the death of the boy's father in 1916, there was a small inheritance, enough to send George to Pine Rock College. His college life is briefly touched on in three chapters. Jim Randolph, the star football player, befriends George, who is thus identified with the glory of Jim's great victory over the University of Virginia and later with Jim's military career. A second friend is Jerry Alsop, a jolly, sentimental fancier of literature. Eventually George quarrels with Jerry over Dostoevski who, Jerry believes, cannot possibly be as great a writer as Dickens—and Jerry reads Sidney Carton's farewell speech to prove it.

In New York, with vaguely defined aspirations in journalism, George Webber settles in a cheap apartment with four college friends, one of them the former football star, Jim Randolph, who is now a sports reporter. Not far away is Jerry Alsop, eagerly acquiring a sophistication foreign to his college tastes. George quarrels again with Jerry, and not long afterwards moves out of the Randolph apartment in revolt against Jim's dominance. Living alone, George is alternately repelled by the coarse and empty street talk ("Dat guy. Nah—not *him!* Duh otheh guy!"), and is victimized by fantasies of love and wealth.

The objectivity Wolfe aimed at is reasonably well achieved in this first third of *The Web and the Rock.* The story of Negro Dick, separately published as "The Child by Tiger," a title keyed to Blake's poem, is full of sharp detail so managed that an overwhelming horror is evoked. The football game in which Jim Randolph stars, and the Dempsey-Firpo fight, which the young Southerners attend, are imaginative, interpretive journalism in which Webber's self-centered nature is uncondescendingly released into an identification with the crowd. Nebraska Crane, Aunt Maw, and Jerry Alsop have individual accents which the reader listens for and recognizes.

II *Rhetoric*

Yet, as in *Of Time and the River,* Wolfe turns easily aside into rhetorical elaboration. The rhetoric is often good. The four-page vision of the city, prompted by the coming of the circus, catches something of the dreamlike quality of adolescence: "That vision of the city was gathered from a thousand isolated sources, from the pages of books, the words of a traveler, a picture of Brooklyn Bridge with its great, winglike sweep, the song and music of its cables, even the little figures of the men with derby hats as they advanced across it. These and a thousand other things all built the picture of the city in his mind, until now it possessed him and had got somehow, powerfully, exultantly, ineradicably, into everything he did or thought or felt" (93).

A brief passage does not fully convey the rhythm and the

development of the whole, nor the curious way in which phrases—"brown-gold like morning" and "the chemistry and rhythm of his blood"—excessive in an ordinary context, are sustained by total effect, as harsh colors sometimes fit agreeably in the composition of a picture. Uncle Mark's condemnation of the Joyners has something of the vigorous hyperbole of old Gant (160-69). The invidious assertion of the superiority of North Carolinians over South Carolinians (13-16) is a shrewd satiric touch, and the essay on Southerners in New York (239-48) is discerning: "there is no one on earth who is more patriotically devoted—verbally, at least—to the region from which he came than the American from the Southern portion of the United States." Along with the satire is an insistence on the positive values of the Southern temperament: "They brought to all the multiplex and feverish life of all your ancient swarming peoples some of the warmth, the depth, the richness of the secret and unfathomed South."

Rhetoric even at its best, as someone has said, is will doing the work of the imagination. It seeks to persuade the reader by rhythmical repetition and elaboration. It has too obvious, "too palpable" a design upon him. Its language is general. It seldom permits the privilege of discovery and revelation that results from more imaginative methods. It is therefore disturbing to find Wolfe still relying so heavily on rhetoric and generalized exposition. Of the first ninety-four pages of the novel, which cover George's boyhood in Libya Hill, about twenty can be called rhetorical, and some thirty more are exposition and non-dramatic narrative. Only twenty-five show dialogue, and some of the speeches are merely typical comments of Aunt Maw, rather than dramatic utterances. In the later section on the city (218-93), nondramatic passages are even more obtrusive. The large proportion of nondramatic material in this novel explains why it is more likely to be skimmed than is *Look Homeward, Angel.*

III   *Esther Jack*

The second and longer part of *The Web and the Rock* narrates George Webber's love affair with Esther Jack, the rejection of his first novel, his trip to Europe to escape from Esther. Twelve chapters develop "The Magic Year," the meeting with

Esther on shipboard and the first year of their idyllic life together. Returning from Europe, George becomes acquainted with a man who knows two ladies traveling first class. The four have dinner together, and in one evening George is captivated with Mrs. Jack. From New York, George immediately goes south to Libya Hill for a two-week visit, but he thinks constantly of Mrs. Jack. Returning to New York, he writes a long, pretentious letter hoping to continue the acquaintance but at the same time awkwardly asserting his independence. Mrs. Jack telephones him the next day, and invites him to see a show for which she has designed the sets. Some time later, when they meet to celebrate George's twenty-fifth birthday at lunch, George drinks too much and quarrels outrageously with Esther. She overlooks this and telephones him the next day. He calls upon her and is impressed with the grandeur and the fine taste of her home.

At length she finds a large, cheap apartment which she and George can share. "This thing is ours," she announces. She sends around a drawing board so that she can do some of her work there. Daily she comes, cooks favorite dishes for George, listens to his despairs, and gives him encouragement about his writing. "The woman had become a world for him," especially as she could introduce him to the fascinating inner details of the city, society, and the theatre. Two chapters put together episodes from her childhood: her actor-father introducing her to the man who designed Brooklyn Bridge; her meeting with Richard Brandell, the great Shakespearean actor; and the success of her sister Edith as a dress designer. The passionate affection which develops between George and Esther has one ominous aspect: "Nothing was his own any more, not even the faintest, farthest memories of his childhood. She inhabited his life relentlessly to its remotest sources, haunting his memory like a witness to every proud and secret thing that had been his own" (451).

After this first magic year, another year passes, and George is writing his novel "with the full intensity of creative fury." Jealousies appear. Esther sees him looking at an attractive woman in a market, and she suspects him of bringing other women to "our place." When he replies that he is "free":

> "You're not free!" she said. "You belong to me and I belong to you forever."

"You have never belonged to me," he said. "You have a husband and a daughter. Your duty is to your family, Sister Jack," he said, in an oily tone. "Try to rectify the mistakes of your past life before it is too late. There is yet time if you will only repent sincerely" (458).

But George, despite his taunts, and his own jealousies, continues to admire the brilliant competence of Esther's genius. Her capacities are effectively organized; his are incorrigibly disorganized. His admiration only intensifies his jealousy. He loathes the theatrical crowd, he loathes her participation in society, he loathes in particular the lion-hunting admirers of literature he meets at her parties. He eats her cooking with great relish, but increasingly he resents her control of his life. She tries to help market his novel, and introduces him to a famous critic, a Mr. Malone, whose condescension infuriates George. Consequently a hundred pages of *The Web and the Rock* are devoted to a series of bitter quarrels, accusations, taunts, partings, and frustrated reunions; and the repetition is tedious. In a story of 1890, Howells has a character say that people in love become so completely interested in each other that they cease to be interesting to other people: their mutual absorption dissipates the sense of character. Despite the skillful dialogue—a resource seemingly always available to Wolfe—this long sequence of quarrels makes painful reading. At the end of the school year, George decides to end the affair by going to Europe. He receives Esther's affectionate farewell letter on shipboard and tears it up.

George's lonely wanderings lead him to the English Lakes, to Paris, to Munich. He longs to hear from Esther but is enraged by her letters. In Paris he is annoyed with American tourists who say, "Never again! The good old U.S.A. is good enough for me!" In Germany, however, the good food and the genial people are agreeable. He visits art galleries and struggles to improve his command of German. In October he visits the festival with a friend, and wakes up in a hospital, his head injured, his nose broken. The fight itself is not specifically explained. The last two chapters show Esther, lonely and disconsolate in New York, and George, ruefully surveying his face in a mirror and conducting a whimsical debate with the Body. As he thinks over his youth, the Body warns: "But—you can't go home again."

The second part of *The Web and the Rock* is more unified

than the account of George's youth given in the first three books. The rise and fall of the affair with Esther is the obvious explanation. The attachment is treated with a convincing blend of feeling and intelligence. There is every reason for George to be attracted to Esther, and a good deal of reason in her attraction to him. The failure to treat her husband is a conspicuous gap, but there is an implication that George has qualities he lacks. The decline of the love affair into bitter quarrels is almost wholly emotional. In theory there are reasons here as well— mutual jealousies, George's resistance to her possessiveness, his intense concentration on his writing, her own self-assurance—but these intelligible factors are so immersed in the tide of invective that the literary quality of this long sequence is impaired.

Aside from the affair with Esther, the latter part of the novel is made up of digressive and minor episodes. So little is said of George's novel—*Home to Our Mountains*—that the satiric picture of the publishers Rawng and Wright seems extraneous. Even the visits to the theatre, the parties, the episode of Mr. Malone's literary advice, important as they are in showing the basis of later quarrels, seem digressive because George tries so hard not to become involved in any positive way. George's visit to the theatre in Chapter 20, for example, becomes a satiric essay at the expense of theatre people in general. George is disgusted when he hears someone say, "The play is nothing, of course. But you really ought to see the sets." The birthday party becomes the occasion to describe at length a New York speakeasy of the time and to give a history of the proprietor. The visit to Esther's apartment includes a three-page essay on the difference between people "who have the quality of richness and joy" and those who do not. As Esther introduces George to "A New World," she does it by panoramic typical reports of her activities and acquaintances, rather than by episodes that have direct relevance. Chapters 26 and 27, the excursion into Esther's childhood, are a dreamlike expedition into a past which, for all its charm, is not made to focus sharply on the developing story of George and Esther. After the separation, George's wanderings in Europe are aimless, and seem so. It would matter little if the sequence of his itinerary were altered.

The Web and the Rock was naturally open to the charge that Wolfe was "merely" retelling the story of Eugene Gant. Only in the most general sense is this true. The differences in the

Webber novel are many and important. Home life and school life are almost ignored in the later novel. George's companions, Nebraska Crane and Negro Dick, suggest a wider horizon and a more solid external world than Eugene Gant encountered. There is no counterpart to the boyish fancies prompted by Eugene's early reading of romantic stories and his visits to the movies. George is treated more seriously, and there is less of the comic in his surroundings. This change is carried over into George's college years. George is not exposed to campus ridicule as a naïve and friendless boy. He immediately attracts the friendship of Jim Randolph, the football star, and he is an accepted member of Jerry Alsop's literary salon until an interest in Dostoevski leads him to defy Jerry. Instead of going to Harvard and trying to become a playwright, as Eugene did, George goes to New York and settles down to writing his novel. Though he becomes a college instructor, there is no mention of his students or colleagues. George's life in New York with four other Southern boys has no parallel in Eugene's experience. On the other hand, the first trip abroad, which filled the last third of *Of Time and the River*, is barely mentioned in *The Web and the Rock*. Hence the latter half of the later novel can be used to develop the love affair with Esther Jack.

Many of these differences were necessitated by the simple fact that Wolfe wanted to minimize the repetition of material already treated. Nevertheless, it is important that he did resourcefully confront his problem and that he did achieve a "different" book—a different emphasis on the basic story of the young man who aspires to become a writer. The person who has read the Gant books has certainly not thereby read *The Web and the Rock*. A broad difference is that, for all his self-centered isolation, George is a much more thoughtful observer of the social scene. His comments about the South are shrewd, though the satire is essentially good-natured—leaving aside the perhaps malicious ridicule of Jerry Alsop. The pathos of Jim Randolph's aimless maturity as an anticlimax to his athletic and military glory shows insight unspoiled by sentiment. George's revulsion at the hypocrisy of theatrical and artistic society reflects Wolfe's own jealous disappointment in not selling his plays in the middle 1920's, but there is something more than sour grapes. By the middle 1930's, when he was formulating *The Web and the Rock*, the naïve boy who had gone to Harvard in 1920 had come a long way. He had a larger stock of worldly wisdom through which to view the experience he looked back upon as fictional material. There is, perhaps, some doubt at the end of *The Web and the Rock* whether George really does look "calmly and sanely forth upon the earth," but the mood induced by his injury is more convincing than the paean to love at the end of *Of Time and the River*, when Eugene first catches sight of Esther.

IV You Can't Go Home Again

"You can't go home again" is part of the wisdom attained by George at the end of *The Web and the Rock*. The phrase itself, used by Wolfe in 1934, was given some special emphasis in conversation with Ella Winter, the widow of Lincoln Steffens, in 1937. He asked her if he could have it for a title, and in the letter of February 14, 1938, he suggested to Aswell that it might serve as a title for the whole Webber story. Appropriately, it did become the title of the second Webber novel. Again, mythical captions reach toward symbolic patterns—"The Quest of the Fair Medusa" (fame), "The Dark Messiah," "Young Icarus"— but they remain incidental allusions rather than structural elements. *You Can't Go Home Again* begins with George back in New York, feeling a new sense of direction in his life. "What had he learned? . . . He had learned that in spite of his strange body, so much off scale that it had often made him think himself a creature set apart, he was still the son and brother of all men living. He had learned that he could not devour the earth, that he must know and accept his limitations" (6).

In this spirit he had again taken up his life with Esther. The new place was now his, not theirs; they were to share love, but to lead independent lives. A letter comes from the James Rodney publishing company, and after an interview with the editor, George unbelievingly holds in his hands a five-hundred-dollar advance check and a firm acceptance of *Home to Our Mountains*. The novel is about George's home town in Old Catawba, but no details are given, as would be natural in an actual negotiation with an editor. Instead, the editor, Foxhall Edwards, and his phlegmatic assistant, Otto Hauser, are introduced with good-natured caricature.

As George is revising his novel, a telegram arrives, informing him of the death of Aunt Maw. George's trip to Libya Hill for the funeral is used to make him aware of the frantic real-estate boom in Libya Hill; to create a chance reunion with George's boyhood friend Nebraska Crane, now a professional baseball player; and to characterize Judge Rumford Bland, a blind old lawyer who has built up a fortune by lending money to Negroes at ruinous rates. Arrived at Libya Hill, George is greeted by his old friend Randy Shepperton and his sister, who best represent the town as he remembers it. Old memories are stirred as he goes to the funeral and sees his mother's grave. Later George is startled at the intensity of the real-estate boom. He is interviewed for the local paper, and his statements are distorted in accordance with the expansive optimism of the town. Nothing he sees in Libya Hill leads him to want to gratify Aunt Maw's often-expressed wish that he come back home to stay.

Back in New York again, exhilarated by the approaching publication of *Home to Our Mountains,* George agrees to attend a big party Mrs. Jack is giving. Mr. Jack and then Esther herself are described as they wake up and make ready for the day, self-assured, self-sufficient, and merely politely interested in each other's activities. An essay on Mr. Jack's business reduces the broker's complex functions to ruthless gambling. This glimpse of high finance is followed by a scene at the service entrance of the Jackses' apartment, where an argument develops about whether packages should be delivered at the front door or at the service entrance. Upstairs, Esther Jack surveys the tables, beautifully laid out for a buffet supper. Piggy Logan, the popular entertainer of the year, arrives with his paraphernalia. Esther's daughter arrives, and finally the guests. To George, Esther can give only incidental attention, and he wanders about in jealous frustration, resenting the elegance and display of wealth and hollow society. Piggy Logan's circus—a childish sequence of maneuvers with wired dolls—is duly applauded by some of the younger set, but it is greeted with amazed disgust by George, Mr. and Mrs. Jack, and many of the other guests. At what should have been the climax of the evening, smoke fills the air. Everyone in the great apartment house goes out in the street as rapidly as possible, though, as it turns out, the fire is in the basement and is soon put out. For the residents and for the guests at the party, the fire is thus an unexpected but hilarious lark, and soon all go back inside, oblivious of the fact that two elevator operators have died, overcome by smoke when the elevators were accidentally stopped. Back in the apartment with George, Esther is happy, and she tells him: "In the whole world there's nothing more. Love is enough." But George has doubts.

Publication of George's novel in November, 1929, created great excitement and resentment in Libya Hill. In New York it made George sufficiently famous to give him contacts with a variety of self-seeking admirers: "And yet, he would not have it thought that he was bitter." Shortly, the financial crash in Wall Street is reflected in bank failure at Libya Hill, the collapse of the real-estate boom, and the mysterious death of the mayor, apparently by suicide. Fuller knowledge of what has happened in Libya Hill comes from Randy Shepperton, who loses his job and comes to New York for a short visit with George. Finding the author irritable at his critics, Randy tells him: "George, of all the people I have ever known, you are the least qualified to play the wounded faun" (383).

After the party, Esther disappears from the novel. George moves to Brooklyn to work in solitude. His chief associate is now Foxhall Edwards, the editor who helped him to success with his first novel. Living with his wife and daughters, Fox is represented as frustrated by women. Yet he daily tips a hat-check girl a dollar because "she is the *nicest* person." As he reads his newspaper, Fox encounters the ills of the world with shrewd insight, but he has no remedy to offer. Nor has he an adequate remedy for the difficulties in George's new book. At last George goes to London to complete it. There he is startled one day to receive a telephone call from Lloyd McHarg, the successful American novelist. When he goes to see McHarg, they set out in a rented Rolls Royce for a visit in the country with one of McHarg's English friends. The saga of their wild adventures, lost on the roads east of London on a stormy night, fills a hundred pages. George then goes to Germany for the Olympic games and a round of parties with German admirers. Before he leaves Germany, George hears the political views of a skeptical friend who dislikes both the Nazis and the Jews. George considers this man's fears exaggerated, but on the train he sees a quiet little Jew arrested as he tries to escape from Germany. This event, like the party at the Jackses, convinces George that "There was no road back."

It is in this spirit that George composes the long letter of farewell to Foxhall Edwards which concludes the novel. The break with his editor signifies a new direction to his personal life and his career as a writer. There is first an expression of gratitude for the friendly help extended nine years earlier. Then George reminisces about Pine Rock College and his youthful interest in philosophy. This leads him to recall a college prank which resulted in the death of a fellow student. Serious as this incident was, George thinks it had no bearing on what Fox calls his "radicalism." He denies that he is a member of the "lost generation" to which their mutual friend Hunt Conroy belongs. George recalls that he came to New York to look for a news-paper job, but, failing that, accepted an instructorship in "one of the great educational factories of the city," living meanwhile with a group of young men who seemed to him very sophisti-cated. At this time George wanted the two things he had always wanted: love and fame.

Having achieved both, he discovered that neither was enough. Sharing Fox's own admiration for Ecclesiastes, George cannot rest in this conception of the world: "Man was born to live, to suffer, and to die, and what befalls him is a tragic lot. There is no denying this in the final end. *But we must, dear Fox, deny it all along the way.*" In such denial is the only hope of the future: "I believe that we are lost here in America, but I believe we shall be found. . . . I think the true discovery of America is before us. I think the true fulfillment of our spirit, of our people, of our mighty and immortal land, is yet to come. I think the true discovery of our own democracy is still before us. And I think that all these things are certain as the morning, as inevitable as noon" (737, 741).

The Webber novels, even more than the Gant story, are a departure from autobiography in any strict sense. Though George Webber, like Wolfe (and Eugene Gant), grew up in a Southern town, attended a state university, and lived in New York City, he has few of the experiences prominent in Wolfe's youth: a large family, a drunken father, a possessive mother, a summer love affair, the editing of college publications, the death of a beloved brother, three years at Harvard, a career as a dramatist, and a long, intimate association with New York Uni-versity. In George Webber's childhood the Negro Dick's going berserk is an authentic Asheville incident, but Wolfe's development of it is a normal kind of literary projection. Nebraska Crane, long thought to be a wholly invented character, seems by Wolfe's own comment (*Letters*, 722), to have had some factual basis. This may be true for the college episodes involving Jim Randolph and Jerry Alsop. Webber's life in New York with four young Southern friends was not part of Wolfe's experience. Webber's affair with Esther Jack is a radically simplified version of Wolfe's relationship with Mrs. Bernstein. Even when the full text of surviving correspondence is published, however, much of its living context will be beyond our reach. We can never be sure how specifically autobiographical the fiction is. The same is true regarding Foxhall Edwards, a fictional portrait of Maxwell Perkins. Malcolm Cowley has recorded Perkins' comment to Aswell when he first saw the manuscript: " 'That man he calls the Fox—I don't think Tom got him quite right.' Then, a few days later, he added, 'That man Tom calls the Fox—I took the passage home to show my wife and daughters, and they think he did get him right.' " [4]

But of course all the detailed associations of the two actual men are omitted in favor of the long, generalized satiric sketch, and the eloquent concluding letter. As to the "Gant-i-ness"—the egocentric rhapsodizing—which Wolfe came to see as a defect of the two earlier novels, there is some of it in the Webber story, but not much. It is most apparent in the story of George's affair with Esther, originally written as an extension of the Gant story. Composed perhaps as early as 1930, it has the element of self-justification which Wolfe later wished to eliminate.

You Can't Go Home Again, next to *Look Homeward, Angel*, is Wolfe's most admired book. There is in it much to commend. The satirical picture of the party at Jackses' is sustained with versatility and power for nearly two hundred pages. The wild ride with Lloyd McHarg has a blend of demonic and comic fantasy hard to match. The capture of the little Jew by Nazi police is convincing to the reader as well as to George, and it captures perfectly the mood of the late 1930's, when such stories were new. Beyond doubt Wolfe's eloquence reaches its peak in the long letter to Foxhall Edwards, addressed to a particular time, but still applicable.

Aside from these major passages, the novel is filled out with a large number of episodes which, though interesting in themselves, scatter instead of focus the attention. Mr. Katamoto, for instance, George's amusing neighbor, appears only in Chapter 3. Nebraska Crane, the boyhood chum now a professional baseball player, and Rumford Bland, the blind loan shark, appear only in Chapter 6. "The Lion Hunters," (Chapter 23) is a series of unrelated encounters with disagreeable people, as a result of George's fame as a novelist; apparently there were no agreeable encounters. The long episode of the suicide of C. Green, which Fox reads about in the *Times*, distracts attention from Fox rather than furthering the process of revealing his temperament through his responses to the news. Daisy Purvis, the British housekeeper, is surely an amusing minor figure, but Chapter 32 remains a sketch instead of a functional part of the novel's development.

It is fair to say that *You Can't Go Home Again* is the most objective of his novels and that the ideas in it show great potential unity. In its present state, the novel is episodic to a degree that prevents effective concentration. The climax intended in the letter to Fox, for all its eloquence, is a climax of rhetoric rather than a climax of character and incident. If one looks back across George's journey through the two novels, there is some doubt as to the depth of his new-found faith. The gesture of the break with Fox is nobly phrased, but it remains a gesture.

It must always be remembered, however, that Wolfe did not live to put the Webber novels in final form. To be sure, he did not put *Of Time and the River* in final form, for Perkins sent the manuscript to the printer without the author's consent. With Wolfe, more than with most authors, the reader must tolerate some rough roads and some detours if he is to enjoy the best scenery. The views in the Webber novels are surely different from those in the Gant novels, and their publication added stature to Wolfe's reputation as a writer.

CHAPTER 6

Wolfe's Shorter Fiction

F ROM 1929 until his death in 1938, Wolfe published about forty pieces of fiction in various magazines, including *The American Mercury, Cosmopolitan, Esquire, Harper's Bazaar, Modern Monthly, The New Republic, The New Yorker, The North American Review, Redbook, The Saturday Evening Post, Scribner's, Vanity Fair,* and *The Virginia Quarterly Review.* The variety of publications illustrates the wide appeal Wolfe had at this period. Most of the stories and sketches were revised for inclusion in the Gant novels or collected in the volume *From Death to Morning* (1935). After Wolfe's death, about twenty additional pieces appeared in magazines, most of them published later in slightly different form in the Webber novels, or in the posthumous collection *The Hills Beyond* (1941).[1]

The detailed study of these shorter pieces, their precise relation to the novels, and to such manuscripts as survive, has not been carried very far. Two more general questions will occur to many readers. What does Wolfe's shorter fiction add to the Gant-Webber saga? What light does this fiction throw upon the ways in which Wolfe might have developed had he lived another twenty years? Approximate answers to these questions may be given by examining the two volumes of short fiction as a single body of work and relating the themes of the stories in roughly chronological order to the four novels.

I *Gants, Pentlands, Joyners*

First, there is a considerable body of material on the North Carolina of Wolfe's ancestors and his parents, the North Carolina he pieced together from his reading and from the family

stories he heard over and over. "The Men of Old Catawba"—
Catawba is derived from an Indian tribe and is Wolfe's frequent
synonym for Carolina—is a whimsical historical sketch of early
times. "The earth is a woman, but Old Catawba is a man." This
is documented by a story of pillage by the Spaniards, who in
their search for gold anticipated the materialism of modern
times. Then follows a long dialogue on a hypothetical dispute
over a mule, in which "mawral rights" are pleaded to protect
greed. But the real history of Old Catawba, Wolfe concludes,
"is a history of solitude, of the wilderness, and of the eternal
earth. . . ."[2]

In "The Hills Beyond" (the title piece for the posthumous
volume) we see Catawba in the pre-Civil War period. The
Joyner family are the maternal ancestors of George Webber,
and are parallel to, perhaps identical with, the Pentlands of the
Gant story. In the 1850's Zachariah Joyner came to typify the
spirit of the West in its struggles against the wealth and pretensions of the East. The fabulous William Joyner, Zack's father,
had once bitten the nose off a bear in a fight, had broken a
blacksmith's ribs with a single blow, and at the judicial age of
forty had learned to read and write. Eventually William moved
out to Libya Hill and established a store in which, for a time,
Zack was a helper. Later his father said: "Well, I don't know
what to do with him unless I make a lawyer of him. He won't
work—that's certain. . . . But he won't starve, neither. Not Zack."[3]
Zack and a younger brother went off to law school, and by
1840 the Joyners were well established in Libya Hill as the first
lawyers to come from local stock. Zack's success as a trial lawyer
naturally led him into politics.

Ted Joyner, a younger brother, failed at the bar, and eventually set up Joyner Heights Academy. His boys volunteered for
service in the army, and Theodore built up for himself a legend
of military prowess. After the war "he grew into his role, until
at last . . . he looked a perfect specimen of the grizzled warrior."
He was respected by everyone except his brother Zack: "My
brother Theodore . . . is the only officer of my acquaintance who
performed the remarkable feat of getting completely lost in an
open field, and ordering an attack upon his own position."[4]
Theodore married Emily Drumgoole, who never let anyone forget she came from Virginia. Of their three children, Drumgoole,
the elder son, failed at West Point, attended the University of

Virginia, and returned to be a "Major" in his father's academy; Virginia attended a finishing school and returned home too good for the rest of the town; Dolph attended the University of Virginia, studied law, lived abroad at Heidelberg, and then migrated to the Oklahoma Territory. Mrs. Theodore Joyner continued to dominate Libya Hill Society, so that the wife of the Northern multi-millionaire was forced to call and—by implication—beg for recognition.

In 1881, on a stage bound for Libya Hill, Judge Robert Joyner and Senator Zack Joyner met John Webber, a Northern man coming to settle at Libya Hill. When Zack was pitched out of the stage, it was Webber who had the presence of mind to pour mange cure down the throat of the apparently lifeless man. "Great God!" roared Zack. "You've burnt me up!" It was Webber, a little later, who quickly found a way to get a circus wagon moving when it mired down and blocked the road. A little later still, when Judge Joyner planned an office, it was Webber who convinced him it should be built of brick instead of pine. "I don't like wooden houses. I come from Pennsylvania . . . where they know how to build." [5]

Judge Joyner's son Edward grew up in the period just after the Civil War, when his father, a veteran, was often visited by other veterans. Edward remembered one conversation, concluded when his father said in exasperation: "We could have *had* it! . . . The whole truth is we didn't really *want* it! . . . We didn't really *want* to win!" Young Edward could neither understand nor believe this remark. He dwelt on the glories of the war, daydreaming exploits in which he would like to have figured. He even wrote a romantic war story, which to their mutual anguish his father discovered. "Great God!" the father exclaimed. "Whoever read such Goddamned stuff as this since time began?"

Later when the boy wants to go to West Point, Judge Joyner gives his low opinion of war and of the military profession. "It's not the war that ruined us. Most of us . . . were ruined long before the war! . . . For every fake we had before the war we have ten new ones nowadays, and each of them is ten times as bad! . . . You find people like Old Looky Thar—who calls himself a 'Major' now, and never even rose up to a corporal's chevrons. Yes! and tells you of all the land and property he owned, and all the niggers that he lost!" Looky Thar was a veteran who made a career out of his record, his wooden leg, and an ugly hole in his mouth left by a wound, which he ceaselessly demonstrated, saying "Looky Thar!" Instead of military men like Looky Thar and Edward's Uncle Theodore—who had, after the war, resumed being a fool—Judge Joyner points to John Webber as a model of ambition and energy.

As Edward follows his father to the courthouse, he cannot share the contempt for Looky Thar. After all, he points out, "the man *has* got a wooden leg." He is unprepared for his father's rejoinder: "Just remember what I tell you. . . . *A wooden leg is no excuse for anything.*" A few months later, when reading a book about the war, young Edward comes across a passage: ". . . among others, I saw Joyner among his gallant mountaineers firing and loading until he was himself shot down and borne away by his own men, his right leg so shattered by a minie ball that amputation was imperative. . . ."

Startled, the boy shows the book to his mother: "'. . . does that mean that father ——'"

> And suddenly he saw that she was crying; she put her arms around his shoulders, as she answered:
> "My dear child, your father is so proud, and in some ways a child himself. He wouldn't tell you. He could not bear to have his son think that his father was a cripple."
> And all at once the boy remembered what his father had once said to him; and knew what he had meant.[6]

Some have seen in Wolfe's novelette "The Hills Beyond" the promise of a new and greater Wolfe, had he lived. This is a natural response to the very considerable interest of this forty-thousand word chronicle. There is in the anecdotes told about William Joyner a relish for the old life of mountain people. Wolfe did not know that life directly, but Julia Westall had come from the mountains and her son had an instinctive appreciation for mountain people and an insight into their narrowness. If he had been able to combine the pathos of his early play *The Mountains* with the rollicking good humor of "The Hills Beyond," he might have given this material the treatment it merits.

Yet as they stand, the early chapters of "The Hills Beyond" are hurried and loosely episodic. The treatment does not add greatly to the inherent interest of Joyner's fight with the blacksmith, for example. The later chapters, dealing with the effects of the Civil War, go much deeper. There is a recognition that the war did not mean the same thing to all parts of the South, and that North Carolina people felt defeat less than some other regions for the simple reason that they had so much less to lose. There is also a sharp awareness, shown earlier in the play *Mannerhouse*, of how romantic illusion entered into the war itself and into the postwar period. Looky Thar is a pitiless revelation, but not a malicious one. Edward's sudden insight into his father's whole view of the war is dramatic in the best sense. In these chapters Wolfe seems to have an understanding of the South between 1860 and 1900 that has been little employed in fiction. The subject was big enough to enlist his respect, remote enough to challenge his sense of historical perspective, and varied enough to have given an objective focus to Wolfe's best imaginative powers. Perhaps he might have become the needed chronicler of Reconstruction and post-Reconstruction.

Another use of Civil War material is "Chickamauga," the story which resulted from Wolfe's visit in 1937 to a great-uncle, John Westall, a veteran of ninety-five years who had fought in the great battle. Wolfe wrote to a friend: "He told about it all so wonderfully and in such pungent and poetic language, such as so many of the old country people around here use, that I couldn't wait to get back to New York to begin on it." [7] In a rambling style, the veteran is allowed to tell his own story. He and his friend Jim Weaver joined the Twenty-ninth North Carolina in August, 1861, on his nineteenth birthday. While they were in camp at Clingman, Jim met Martha Patton, and immediately decided he would marry her. His engagement to Martha made Jim hate the war that separated them. Jim and John (the narrator) are sent west with their regiment. They just missed the battle at Fort Donelson, but "we was thar on time at Shiloh. Oh Lord, I reckon that we was! Perhaps we had been country boys before, perhaps some of us still made a joke of hit before—but after Shiloh we wasn't country boys no longer." Jim was wounded and sent home on a two-month furlough, vowing he would not return to the war. But he did, "the grimmest, bitterest-lookin' man you ever seed." Not long after came Chickamauga, with days of bloody fighting back and forth in a cedar thicket. When the battle was seemingly won, the Union General

Thomas, "The Rock of Chickamauga," remained in position, and Longstreet tried to dislodge him by a series of charges up Missionary Ridge:

> The last charge happened jest at dark. We came along and stripped the ammunition off the dead—we took hit from the wounded—we had nothin' left ourselves. Then we hit the first line—and we drove them back. We hit the second and swept over them. We were goin' up to take the third and last—they waited till they saw the color of our eyes before they let us have hit. Hit was like a river of red-hot lead had poured down on us: the line melted thar like snow. Jim stumbled and spun round as if somethin' had whupped him like a top. He fell right toward me, with his eyes wide open and the blood a-pourin' from his mouth. I took one look at him and then stepped over him like he was a log. Thar was no more to see or think of now—no more to reach—except that line. We reached hit and they let us have hit—and we stumbled back.

Later the narrator goes back to find Jim's body: "I turned Jim over and got his watch, his pocket-knife, and what few papers and belongin's that he had, and some letters that he'd had from Martha Patton. And I put them in my pocket. . . . And I would go all through the war and go back home and marry Martha later on, and fellers like poor Jim was layin' thar at Chickamauga Creek." [8]

Not long before he wrote this story, Wolfe had sold "Child by Tiger," the story of the berserk Negro which later appeared in *The Web and the Rock,* to *The Saturday Evening Post,* and he was certain the same magazine would buy "Chickamauga." To his surprise, the editors rejected the story because it had too little "story element." Later it was published in *The Yale Review,* which paid a hundred dollars for it. The story has been variously evaluated. Some insist, with Wolfe, that it is one of his finest stories. Others object that it is too long—it is only thirty pages—and that it is something of a tour de force through being entirely the reminiscence of the old soldier. Nevertheless, there is in the battle scenes an objective intensity almost unique in Wolfe's writing. This story suggests that he might have assimilated the experience of the Civil War and developed the distinguished and imaginative treatment it has seldom received thus far.

"The Web of Earth," the concluding and longest story in *From Death to Morning,* is a ninety-page monologue by Eliza Gant, full of remembered anecdote and rambling comment. Written in 1932, after Mrs. Wolfe had visited her son in New York, the story presents Eliza, talking to Eugene and hearing from time to time the boats in the harbor. She starts out to explain the "voices" that years before, "the year the locusts came," had said to her "Two . . . Two," and "Twenty . . . Twenty." Random digressions intervene. She remembers childhood fears, the Sherman troopers, the strange death of her father "as the clock was striking the last stroke of six," the homecoming of the Southern soldiers: "Lord God! do I remember! I reckon that I do!" The son's reminding query about the mysterious "two and twenty" only sets Eliza off on further stories. She repeats the conversation her husband Will Gant had with Mel Porter, the lawyer who was dejected at the thought of the imminent hanging of three murderers he had unsuccessfully defended. Then she tells the story of how Will Gant, in a drunken fit, began to talk about his earlier wife Lydia as if she were still living.

This memory leads to an explanation that Lydia was not really his first wife; the first wife was Maggie Efird, a fact Eliza discovered when she saw the divorce papers in Gant's dresser drawer. Then there was an affair between Gant and Lydia's sister-in-law, Eller Beals: "This Eller Beals was a little dark black-and-white sort of a woman: she had this white skin, and hair as black as a raven's and coal-black eyes. She had this easy sugary sleepy way of talkin', all soft and drawly—like she'd just waked up out of a good long sleep. I could a-told him the first time I laid eyes on her that she was no good: she was a bad egg if ever I saw one, a charmer out to get the men and lead them on, you know, and bleed them out of everything they owned."

Lydia died, knowing of this affair, and accusing Gant, whose guilty conscience conjured up fears of her ghost come back to haunt him. Gant also had a strange drunken superstition about Chinamen. When the Boxer Rebellion broke out, Gant wanted to enlist. Eliza talked him out of this idea, but the wanderlust was in him. As an old neighbor said: "They're all alike! I never saw a man yet that could stay where he was five minutes." Then there was Gant's illness, his trickery in obtaining liquor at the hotel while awaiting admittance to the Johns Hopkins Hospital, and his loss of the laundry ticket identifying his shirts at a Chinese laundry.

Next, Eliza brings up the trial of Dock Hensley, the policeman, for murder. During the trial, three murderers escaped from prison. Once again the initial mystery of the "two . . . twenty" phrase is mentioned. "I know exactly when it was—I'm goin' to tell you now," says Eliza. One of the escaped murderers, Ed Mears, finds Eliza alone. She gives him shoes for his bare feet, and talks him into leaving his pistol with her. On Gant's return, Eliza dissuades him from giving the alarm. "Maybe it's the best way, after all," he says. "But that's the strangest thing I ever heard about. By God it is!" Then one day, Eliza felt birth pains, and when Doctor Nelson came he said, "It's *your* time, sure enough."

> And sure enough, it was. Why! that was it, of course!—that's what I've been telling you, boy!—that explained it all.
> "Two . . . two," the first voice said, and "Twenty . . . Twenty" said the other:—
> *Twenty* days later from that evening Ed Mears came there to our house, to the minute, at twenty minutes to ten o'clock on the seventeenth day of October, *twins* were born—Ben and Grover were both born that night. . . .
> "What do you think of that?" I said to Mr. Gant. "You see, don't you?"
> His face was a study. "It's pretty strange when you come to think of it," he said. "By God, it is!" [9]

No synopsis can suggest the vitality of Eliza as she ranges freely over the long years, every incident connected with every other by some thread of association invisible to the reader, but sufficient for Eliza's ceaseless recollection. Maxwell Perkins and Elizabeth Nowell agreed with Wolfe himself that "The Web of Earth" was one of his best achievements. To a friend, Wolfe wrote: "I really believe, although this is a terribly boastful thing to say, that I knew this old woman better than Joyce knew that woman at the end of 'Ulysses' and furthermore that my old woman is a grander, richer and more tremendous figure than his was." [10]

There may be readers who find ninety unrelieved pages of Eliza tedious, but the unity of tone is undeniable. Eliza sums it up in a little sermon near the end to the dejected Miller Wright, who had "lost everything": " 'No,' I said, 'not everything. There's something left.' 'What is it?' he said. 'We've got the earth,' I said. 'We've always got the earth. We'll stand upon it and it will save us. It's never gone back on nobody yet.' " [11]

Only one other slight sketch adds to the story of Will Gant. "The Four Lost Men" describes him (identifiable not by name but by speech) as reminiscing about former presidents Garfield, Arthur, Harrison, and Hayes: " '. . . all of them are dead. . . . I'm the only one that's left,' he said illogically, 'and soon I'll be gone, too.' And for a moment he was silent. 'It's pretty strange when you come to think of it,' he muttered. 'By God it is!' " [12]

The narrator then speculates: "And for me they were the lost Americans: their gravely vacant and bewhiskered faces mixed, melted, swam together in the sea-depths of a past intangible, immeasurable, and unknowable as the buried city of Persepolis." Such a sketch is not very important in itself, but it illustrates Wolfe's habit of projecting himself back into the world his parents knew before he himself was born. Gant's rumination on four of the least memorable presidents is made to suggest, too, that something of the past is irrecoverable.

Several sketches are variations on characters or situations associated with Eugene Gant. "No Cure for It" tells of Doctor McGuire's examination of seven-year-old Eugene when his growth seems dangerously disproportionate. McGuire delivers a boisterous but cheerful verdict: " 'I've seen them when they shot up like weeds, and I've seen them when you couldn't make them grow at all,' he said, 'but I never saw one before who grew like a weed in one place while he was standing still in another! . . . Look at those arms and legs!' he cried." On hearing this Gant complains to Eliza in familiar accents: " 'you have given birth to a monster who will not rest until he has ruined us all, eaten us out of house and home, and sent me to the poorhouse to perish in a pauper's grave!' " But upon being reassured by McGuire, Gant shifts to a tender tone seldom allowed him in the Gant novels: " 'Well, son,' he said kindly, putting his great hand gently upon the boy's head, 'I'm glad to know that it's all right. I guess it was the same with me. Now don't you worry. You'll grow up to be a big man some day.' " [13]

When the boy is a little older, "Circus at Dawn" describes how he and his stuttering brother (neither boy is named) hurry through their paper routes to go down to watch the tent being put up and the circus people "eating their tremendous break-fasts with an earnest concentration, seldom speaking to one another, and then gravely, seriously and briefly."[14]

"Gentlemen of the Press," dramatic in form, is a wartime scene in the newspaper office where Ben works. Ben is inciden-tal to the sketch, which contrasts the tough-talking newspaper world with the evident sentiment of the city editor when a dispatch carries the news of a local boy's death in the Lafayette *Escadrille*. Aswell says this is one of a series of sketches for a book of nighttime episodes planned in 1930 or 1931. Another wartime sketch, "The Face of the War," gives a fuller descrip-tion of Eugene's observations at Norfolk while doing war work in 1918.[15] A Southern white gang boss brutally beats a frightened Negro. An officious military guard abuses three youngsters who are trespassing out of innocent curiosity. A young boy meets a prostitute whom he remembers as a girl from his home town. A white lieutenant is driven frantic by the imperviousness to discipline of the black troops under his command. These two pieces typify Wolfe's effort to develop objectivity and unity of effect through multiple action.

In "The Lost Boy" Wolfe expanded the treatment given to the death of Grover in *Look Homeward, Angel* (51-59). Divided into four sections, "The Lost Boy" is really a novelette, about half the length of "Web of Earth." The first section presents Grover as an eleven-year-old, paying for candy in stamps which he is unjustly accused of stealing. When he tells his father about it, Gant takes him back to the candy store and denounces the storekeeper: " 'You were never a father. . . . You never knew the feelings of a father, or understood the feelings of a child; and that is why you acted as you did. But a judgment is upon you. God has cursed you. He has afflicted you. He has made you lame and childless as you are—and lame and childless, mis-erable as you are, you will go to your grave and be forgotten!' "

Section II shows the Gant children and their mother on the train in Indiana, headed for the St. Louis Fair of 1904. Eliza recounts the story, years later, to Eugene. What a trader Grover was! How reliable! On the train Grover fell into conversation with a man and asked so many questions that Eliza rebuked him. But the man said: "Now you leave that boy alone. He's all right . . . he doesn't bother me a bit. . . ." In Section III, Eugene's sister reminisces. She remembers how Grover took her to a restaurant for a treat, and became sick. When they got home, Grover's fatal illness had set in. The concluding section describes Eugene's visit, years later, to the house in which the family lived when Grover died. When he explains to the woman who now lives there why he has come, she invites him in, and he recognizes all the familiar places. But "the lost boy was gone forever, and would not return." It is interesting that Wolfe told the story of Grover's death twice; it is even more interesting that the second telling is more tender than the first.[16]

"The Return of the Prodigal" presents in two parts an imagined and an actual return to Altamont when Eugene is a famous author. In the imagined return, the unrecognized Eugene takes a room in his mother's boarding house. In the middle of the night he wakes to hear his brother's voice saying: "Brother! Brother! . . . what did you come home for? . . . You know now that you can't go home again!" Written in 1934, this concluding remark anticipates the title of the posthumous novel. In the second part of the story Eugene stops off in Zebulon, where his mother's people welcome him heartily, and where by chance he is witness to a fatal gunfight. Back in Altamont, everyone is cordial to Eugene. No one is angry any more about Eugene's book: "The only ones who are mad today are those you left out!" At home it takes Eliza six pages just to explain about all the telephone calls that have come for Eugene.[17] In a briefer story, Wolfe gives a sequel to the Uncle Bascom sequence in *Of Time and the River.* "A Kinsman of His Blood" tells how Bascom's son Arnold breaks with him and disappears. When Eugene meets him one night, Arnold denies his identity.

The Gant material in these shorter pieces shows that, like Faulkner, Wolfe had in his mind a locale and a set of characters capable of indefinite expansion. The tenderness of Gant, hardly hinted at in *Look Homeward, Angel,* is shown in "No Cure for It." Eliza, the grasping and unlovely boardinghouse keeper, is in "The Web of Earth" endowed with a rich and convincing love of life. "The Hills Beyond" illustrates a sense of family traits rooted in a traceable past comparable to that revealed in Faulkner's Sartorises. Wolfe looks backward with a historical imagination free from sentimentality and pedantry. It is our loss that the epic of the Gants and Pentlands was interrupted, in part by the shift to the Webber cycle, in part by the business troubles of 1935 to 1938, and most of all by Wolfe's death.

II *The City*

Besides the Gant material, the short stories are less a proof of accomplishment than of resourceful experiment. It is sometimes maintained that Wolfe's long residence in New York (1924 to 1938) was a mistake. His best material was in the South, the argument runs, and therefore he should have "gone home again" before it was too late. This argument is plausible, for there is more enjoyment when one reads in Wolfe's pages about the Altamont of old days than when one reads about New York and Europe. Yet part of one's enjoyment is simple nostalgia for a past whose charm increases as it recedes.

It is a simplification of Wolfe's nature and of the world in which he grew up to argue that he could or should have remained in the South. The city angered him, but it fascinated him too. His love affair with Aline Bernstein, who was New York and Europe to her fingertips, prevented him from leaving New York in his late twenties; but even had this affair never occurred, it is hard to believe that Wolfe could have fulfilled himself by returning permanently to the South. He sensed that New York, good or bad, was an essential part of American experience; and he intended to have that experience—all of it. Faulkner made another choice; and his best, most characteristic achievements are a recapture and transfiguration of the past. Wolfe, dealing much with the past, could not rest content in it. As a result, there is in Wolfe's work as a whole a directly contemporary quality which Faulkner does not try to achieve.

Four sketches make satirical use of street dialect in the manner found in *Of Time and the River* and in *The Web and the Rock*. Of the four, the most ambitious is "Death the Proud Brother." Wolfe was greatly impressed by seeing four deaths on the streets of New York, all in circumstances emphasizing the callousness of the surrounding "manswarm." In the story an Italian street vendor is killed in a traffic accident, a beggar dies from a fall on an icy sidewalk, a steel worker is hit and over-balanced by a flaming rivet. It is the fourth death, however, the least violent, which is climactic. As a man sits quietly on a bench in a subway station, his heart stops beating. The self-importance of the bystander grates on the ear:

"Sure! Sure!" he cried. "Dat's what I'm tellin' yuh. I seen him when he passed out. I was standin' not ten feet away from 'im! Sure! I watched 'im when he stahted gaspin' t' get his bret'. I was standin' dere. Dat's what I'm sayin'. I tu'ns to duh cop an' says, 'Yuh'd betteh look afteh dat guy,' I says. 'Deh's somet'ing wrong wit' 'im,' I says. Sure! Dat's when it happened. Dat's what I'm tellin' yuh. I was standin' dere," he cried.

"Death the Proud Brother" has much solid detail and convincing dialogue, but the linking of the four deaths seems schematic and artificial. The rhetoric is often strained, and never more so than in the concluding apostrophe: "Proud Death, wherever we have seen your face, you came with mercy, love, and pity, Death, and brought to all of us your compassionate sentences of pardon and release." Of satirical intention in this conclusion there is no trace.[18]

Much more successful are the less pretentious "No Door" and "Only the Dead Know Brooklyn." The first is really an essay on rich friends who think it "wonderful" to live in picturesque Brooklyn. For his own satisfaction, the narrator sets down a conversation which reveals the sterility of life in his neighborhood:

. . . you remember how two windows were thrown up, and you heard two voices—a woman's and a man's—begin to speak in that soft tragic light. And the memory of their words came back to you, like the haunting refrain of some old song—as it was heard and lost in Brooklyn.

"Yuh musta been away," said one, in that sad light.

"Yeah, I been away. I just got back," the other said.

"Yeah? Dat's just what I was t'inkin'," said the other. "I'd been t'inkin' dat yuh musta been away."

"Yeah, I been away on my vacation. I just got back."

"Oh, yeah? Dat's what I t'ought meself. I was t'inkin' just duh oddeh day dat I hadn't seen yuh f'r some time, 'I guess she's gone away,' I says." [19]

"Only the Dead Know Brooklyn" is a nameless Brooklynite's account of his meeting with a man asking directions for Bensonhurst, "because he liked duh name." The stranger's desire to "know" Brooklyn and his bright confidence that a map will solve most of his problems vaguely exasperate the Brooklynite: " 'Map or no map,' I says, 'yuh ain't gonna get to know Brooklyn wit' no map,' I says. . . . What a nut *he* was! I wondeh what eveh happened to 'im, anyway!' "[20]

Thinking about these pieces we can gauge their quality by asking what Sinclair Lewis would have made of the same material. The satire would be there, in dialogue and description. The perspective would be different. Lewis was usually content to treat a subject from the outside, with uncompromising resentment and malicious exaggeration. Wolfe, though guilty of malice on some occasions, does not betray it here. He resents the callousness of feeling, so perfectly expressed in the ugly idiom and monotonous rhythm of the dialect. He grasps the humor of these caricatures of human nature. But also with the insight of a poet he broods upon what the city has made of men. Pathos is indirectly implied by a tragic sense of waste. Such emphasis is possible for Wolfe because he also had an awareness of the city's magic. "In the Park" is similar to the reminiscences of Esther in chapters 26 and 27 of *The Web and the Rock*. An unnamed woman tells of happy days when she and her actor-father dined often at Mock's with Father Doland and Father O'Rourke. One day all four of them took their first ride in an automobile. So excited were they that they rode around the park all night long: "and the sun came up, and it was like the first day of the world. . . ." [21] As Wolfe writes about it, the city is an experience, not merely a subject for satire and denunciation.

A few sketches suggest the way Wolfe might have developed his projected novel about the James Rodney Publishing Company, part of which was used in the portrait of Foxhall Edwards in *You Can't Go Home Again*. "The Lion at Morning," based on an anecdote about Charles Scribner II, is a rather artificial story about a wealthy man who discovers that the minister of his own church is involved in scandal. A chuckle of good humor follows the old man's rage: "By God! I didn't know he had it in him!" [22] An uncollected piece, "Old Man Rivers," is a satirical portrait of Robert Bridges, retired editor of *Scribner's Magazine;* he is represented, under the name of Rivers, as being enormously proud of himself as he reads proof on his own *Who's Who* biography, hardly aware that he is now out of touch with current activity and the younger men.[23] A related but unpublished story, "No More Rivers," is mentioned by Elizabeth Nowell; at Wolfe's request she submitted it to Perkins, who was much annoyed and embarrassed by the manuscript since he himself had given Wolfe much of the information used.[24] "The

Portrait of a Literary Critic," possibly an offshoot of the novel about publishers, ridicules a "sane" critic who always wants to stay safely with the crowd. Another uncollected piece, published posthumously as a small book, *A Note on Experts*, is an attack on journalism: "You know that if the worst is not bad enough, the whore of print will make it so."[25] These brief pieces seem inconsequential beside Wolfe's larger themes, the Gants, and the city. Despite singularly good fortune and kind treatment, Wolfe's attitude toward publishers in his last years had too much spleen to call out his best powers.

III *Short Novels and Episodes*

For Wolfe, the writing of short fiction was incidental to "the Book," and was dictated by his need of money and by his desire to keep his name before the public. Nevertheless, he became interested in his stories, analyzed the problems he was trying to solve, and considered certain stories among his best achievements. The importance of his short fiction, long overshadowed by the novels, has been vigorously asserted by Professor C. Hugh Holman's recent edition of *The Short Novels of Thomas Wolfe*. From the two volumes of short stories reviewed in this chapter, Holman reprints only "The Web of Earth." The other novels in this new collection are: "The Portrait of Bascom Hawke," later rearranged and fragmented when included in *Of Time and the River;* "The Party at Jack's," expanded to double its original length in *You Can't Go Home Again;* "I Have a Thing to Tell You," also included in *You Can't Go Home Again;* and "No Door," of which only the first section was published under this title.

Bascom Hawke (Pentland in the novel) is a truly Dickensian character, with a strictly American accent. To read of him in "The Portrait of Bascom Hawke" without the distractions of Eugene Gant's other Cambridge activities underlines the high quality of Wolfe's achievement. "The Party at Jack's" in its expanded form in the novel is, as has been said, resourcefully developed, and many readers would not willingly part with such additions as Stephen Hook, the art critic; old Jake Abramson, who has been everywhere and seen everything; Hirsch, the lawyer interested in the Sacco-Vanzetti case; and Miss Heilprinn of the art theatre. Yet, as Professor Holman says, the long version is less sharply focused. The last two short chapters of the magazine story (little more than a page) round off the story with a formal completeness which Wolfe could manage more often than his critics have recognized.

"I Have a Thing to Tell You," the story of the Jew arrested by Nazi soldiers at the border, Professor Holman thinks close to Hemingway in directness and simplicity. He reminds us that, as originally published, this story ended with the two paragraphs now used to conclude Webber's long letter to Foxhall Edwards. Though they are effective as the last paragraphs of the novel, they are more pertinent at the end of "I Have a Thing to Tell You," and the familiar version of the episode in the novel is thus impoverished. The paragraphs read as follows:

> I have a thing to tell you:
> Something has spoken to me in the night, burning the tapers of the waning year; something has spoken in the night; and told me I shall die, I know not where. Losing the earth we know for greater knowing, losing the life we have for greater life, and leaving friends we loved for greater loving, men find a land more kind than home, more large than earth.
> Whereon the pillars of this earth are founded, toward which the spirits of the nations draw, toward which the conscience of the world is tending—a wind is rising, and the rivers flow.[26]

Thomas Wolfe's break with Germany was an altogether larger enterprise than George Webber's break with Foxhall Edwards. It cost him royalties, good friends, and another "home" to which he could not return. Wolfe's awareness of economic problems was somewhat doctrinaire; his insight into Hitler's Germany was real. The rising wind of 1936, when the story was written, was prophetic.

"No Door" has a complex history. The story of this title included by Wolfe in *From Death to Morning* (1935), already described, is only the first of four sections designed to be published as a small book in 1934. With this first section, contrasting a wealthy couple's "picturesque" conception of Brooklyn with the sterile reality, Wolfe planned to combine three other episodes emphasizing the general theme of loneliness. Several passages, later used in various parts of *Of Time and the River*, describe Eugene's frantic reading, his return to his home with thoughts of his dead father and brother, and the voice of his mother echoing in his mind. Another episode, also included in *Of Time and the River,* is Eugene's encounter with the Coulsons at "Hill-top Farm" near Oxford; they are part of the impenetrable English world, and touched with some mysterious disgrace in local reputation. The fourth section, eventually part of *You Can't Go Home Again,* centers on a man who sits silent across the street, seeming to be "the face of darkness and of time," imperturbable above the hubbub of the street and the passion of Webber's love affair with Esther. These four episodes were introduced by a prologue essentially the same as that finally used for *Of Time and the River:* "Where shall the weary rest? Where shall the lonely heart come home?" In a sense, then, "No Door" in its original form constituted a stage toward the conception of the novel. Whether or not these episodes do achieve so great a unity of effect as Holman asserts, it is apparent that Wolfe set himself a difficult artistic problem in shaping the materials of memory and observation.

Professor Holman's *Thomas Wolfe Reader* further emphasizes Wolfe's command of form in his short stories and in unified passages from the novels. Besides a half-dozen stories, most of which have been discussed in this chapter, twenty-seven passages from the novels are presented as capable of standing alone. Usually a consecutive passage is given, without excision, as in "The Death of Ben Gant," or, from *Of Time and the River,* "Flight Before Fury," part of Eugene's northward journey. Four selections from the second novel and one from *The Web and the Rock* bring together related passages which Wolfe separated in order to bring in other themes of the novel. Certainly "Professor Hatcher's Celebrated Course" gains much emphasis by concentration of four passages scattered over two hundred pages of the novel. The same is true of "A Portrait of Abe Jones," the exasperating student, and of "Oktoberfest" in *The Web and the Rock.*

If it is true that Wolfe could conceive and execute powerful, unified episodes, often of considerable length, why did he not become a master of the short story and the *novella?* One of the sources of his power was his intuitive sense of relationship. Like Coleridge, he was convinced that everything *was* related to everything else. To treat material in small, disparate segments was, Wolfe felt, somehow to violate it. *Look Homeward, Angel,* it is true, was "finished." It told a phase of his experience which could be thought of as a whole. When, however, he tried to reach forward to the experience of the 1920's and 1930's, backward into the history of the Pentlands, outward toward the whole span of European culture, he could find no satisfying form. Driven by necessity to publish short works, he yet continued to talk about "the Book" as if the published stories and even *Of Time and the River* were fragments escaped into print against his will. Yet what he attempted, strengthened importantly what he achieved. If one finds his stories and episodes more satisfying than his work as a whole, this is because time and convention set limits that he rebelled against. If one insists on fine-cut gems, one ought to recognize that they exist at all only by virtue of enormous pressures. In its imperfection, Wolfe's total work allows readers to feel those pressures more fully than they do in the work of more finished craftsmen.

IV *Wolfe's Plans*

Besides the novels and stories, we have a good deal of information as to Wolfe's further intentions. As early as May, 1923, he wrote his mother of his ambition to explore everything, to write everything. "I know this now," he says: "I am inevitable." After enumerating for more than a page some of his sharpest memories, he explains: "This is why I think I'm going to be an artist. The things that really mattered sunk in and left their mark. Sometimes only a word—sometimes a peculiar smile— sometimes death—sometimes the smell of dandelions in Spring— once Love. Most people have little more mind than brutes: they live from day to day. I will go everywhere and see everything. I will meet all the people I can. I will think all the thoughts, feel all the emotions I am able, and I will write, write, write." [27]

Since *Look Homeward, Angel* dealt only with his youth, it was but prologue. In *The Story of a Novel* Wolfe describes his "whole gigantic plan," gradually realized during the writing of *The October Fair*, part of which became *Of Time and the River:* "It was not until more than a year had passed, when I realized finally that what I had to deal with was material which covered almost 150 years in history, demanded the action of more than 2000 characters, and would in its final design include almost every racial type and social class of American life, that I realized that even the pages of a book of 200,000 words were wholly inadequate for the purpose." [28]

So tangible was this intention that the first edition of *Of Time and the River* carried this publisher's note:

> This novel is the second in a series of six of which the first four have now been written and the first two published. The title of the whole work, when complete, will be the same as that of the present book, "Of Time and the River." The titles of the six books, in the order of their appearance, together with the time-plan which each follows, are:

> *Look Homeward, Angel* (1884-1920)
> *Of Time and the River* (1920-1925)
> *The October Fair* (1925-1928)
> *The Hills Beyond Pentland* (1838-1926)
> *The Death of the Enemy* (1928-1933)
> *Pacific End* (1791-1884)

This seemingly fixed plan constantly underwent changes of title, of names of characters, of amplifying episodes, and of digressions. *Look Homeward, Angel,* for example, was first called *The Building of a Wall,* to signify Eugene Gant's isolation; later it was called *Alone, Alone,* an echo of "The Ancient Mariner"; when submitted to publishers it was called *O Lost;* not until 1929 did Wolfe supply the final title. The Gants and the Pentlands of the first novel became the Webbers and the Joyners of the posthumous novels. In two separately published short stories—"The Portrait of Bascom Hawke" and "The Web of Earth"—the name Hawke was substituted for Pentland. In 1932, publication of *K 19,* Wolfe's series of travel episodes, was announced, but later canceled. Another title for this material was *Fast Express,* and some use of the conception was made in the first part of *Of Time and the River.* At various times, Wolfe planned *The Good Child's River,* based on Mrs. Bernstein's childhood in New York; a modern Robinson Crusoe tale "in the desert island of this world"; *The Man on the Wheel,* an expansion of the Robert Weaver episodes in *Of Time and the River;* a book about a writer writing a book; one about the James Rodney Publishing Company; a "Book of the Night"; and another about an itinerant filling station attendant.

Wolfe's letters of 1930 and 1931 show active planning for *The October Fair.* His application for a Guggenheim Fellowship speaks of this work as ready for publication in the spring or autumn of 1931. Its dominant theme will be related to that of his first novel: ". . . it tries to find out why Americans are a nomad race (as this writer believes) . . . why thousands of the young men, like this writer, have prowled over Europe, looking for a door, a happy land, a home, seeking for something they have lost, perhaps racial and forgotten; and why they return here; or if they do not, carry on them the mark of exile and obscure longing." [29]

In a letter the following June, Wolfe announces to Wheelock that he has completed "the first section of the first part—it is called *Antaeus,* and it is as if I had become a voice for the experience of a race." He then enumerates a long series of scenes representing the variety of movement in America and the desire for "love, the earth, a home, fixity," now identified as the female principle of life. "Through it all," says Wolfe, "is poetry—the enormous rivers of the nation drinking the earth away at night. . . ." A week later he writes with more restraint to Perkins that his book will have four parts: (1) "Antaeus"; (2) "The Fast Express"; (3) "Faust and Helen"; (4) "The October Fair." It is, he assures Perkins, "full of rich detail, sounds and talk."

Two weeks later he writes Perkins that he thinks of calling the whole work *Immortal Earth.* He enlarges upon the male principle of wandering, which he says is "not only a masculine thing, but that in some way it represents the quest of a man for his father." The hero of the work will be named David Monkey Hawke, "a mixture of the ape and the angel," of normal height and not identifiable with Wolfe himself. The fables and legends in which the book will be formulated will also prevent autobiographical interpretation. By December, 1930, he thinks of *The October Fair* with this subtitle: *Time and The River: A Vision.* Following the subtitle he would put this list of captions: "The Son, The Lover, and The Wanderer; The Child, The Mistress, and The Woman; The Sea, The City, and The Earth." Then would come the verse from Ecclesiastes: "One generation passeth away, and another generation cometh; but the earth abideth forever." It is evident, despite the variations, that in Wolfe's mind the book which we know as *Of Time and the River* was only the first part of a unified conception. Wolfe's failure to complete the sequel in proportionate scale resulted in the "formlessness" most readers feel.[30]

Originally planned in 1936 as a separate work, "The Vision of Spangler's Paul" (later "The Ordeal of Bondsman Doaks") was grafted onto the plan of *The October Fair*. Wolfe explained the idea in a letter to a German friend: ". . . it is the story of a good man abroad in the world—shall we say the naturally innocent man, the man who sets out in life with his own vision of what life is going to be like, what men and women are going to be like, what he is going to find, and then the story of what he really finds." [31] Wolfe added that this is similar to the idea behind many great books: *Don Quixote, Pickwick, Candide, Gulliver, Faust,* and *Wilhelm Meister.*

Later in 1936 Wolfe wrote Perkins that this work would be his own *Ulysses,* and that he would develop it with all the independence Joyce had employed. Miss Nowell points out that some of the material in *The Vision of Spangler's Paul* found its way into the Webber novels. It is this *Vision* about which Wolfe wrote in elaborate detail to Edward C. Aswell, the Harper's editor, in the long letter dated February 14, 1938. Though the letter was never sent to Aswell, we may assume that most of the ideas in it came to Aswell in the long conversations he had with Wolfe. The book, Wolfe says, is a book of apprenticeship. It will have satire in it, for this story is about an innocent man journeying through life. Wolfe gives a long description of the protagonist, not yet so named, but recognizable as George Webber.[32]

The Hills Beyond Pentland was announced as dealing with the period 1838 to 1926. In 1930 Wolfe wrote appreciatively to James Boyd about a bear hunt in Boyd's novel. This episode reminded Wolfe of the wonderful pioneer material he wanted to get into his own book. Two years later he completed "The Web of Earth," and though the narrator is Delia Hawke, her experience is part of the Pentland story from 1860 on. To a friend Wolfe wrote: "I wish to God Max Perkins would let me write a whole long book about her"; fascinated as he was with this material, "The Web of Earth" was at that time a digression from *The October Fair*. In August, 1933, Wolfe wrote Perkins that he was "completing" the book titled *The Hills Beyond Pentland*. In 1935, a few weeks after *Of Time and the River* appeared, the book he was "living for" was that about the Pentlands. Later in 1935 he was outlining it, and planning to include in it a section on nighttime in America.[33]

Wolfe's shorter fiction, including separately published episodes from his novels, is a substantial body of work. Subjects of great range and variety are resourcefully handled. There is formal excellence that quite contradicts the legendary flow of undirected energy. There is meaning without propaganda, the meaning of insight into character. The plans, which seem so grandiose and chaotic when detached from the context of Wolfe's actual accomplishment, illuminate his success. What he planned had relevance to what he accomplished. What he accomplished was never isolated from the vitalizing stimulus of a vast undertaking. This remains true even when one concedes—as one must—that grave defects of Wolfe's temperament limited his career.

CHAPTER 7

The Man

MANY PHOTOGRAPHS SURVIVE to help us visualize Wolfe and his family as they were. That of the family group, taken a few months before Tom was born, shows the old house on Woodfin Street, now torn down. In the foreground are Effie and Frank, with their bicycles. Behind the low fence stand Mr. and Mrs. Wolfe, with Mabel, Fred, Grover, and Ben between them. Fred and Ben, though nearly eight, still wore curls. Mr. Wolfe is tall, slender, thin-faced, and wore a drooping mustache. Mrs. Wolfe, less clearly shown, is a pleasant-faced woman, wearing the long-sleeved shirt waist and skirt typical of the period. Later pictures of Mr. Wolfe show little change in his appearance. Those of Mrs. Wolfe present a round-faced woman of average height with a rather quizzical expression in the eyes.

In a picture of Tom when he was seven, he wears a dark sailor suit and dark curls that come to his shoulders, a family fashion, to judge from the group picture just described. Tom's face at seven is rounded and a little serious; most people would think from the large dark eyes and the full lips that he was "a sensitive child." As Tom grew older, there are many stories of his unkempt appearance and of his thin, gangling awkwardness. On at least one occasion in college, however, he appears neatly dressed, tall and slender, and quite eligible for dating, a side of college life he seems to have neglected. At Harvard in 1921, he is already heavier of face and figure, and almost grimly serious. In 1929 he posed for a portrait which emphasizes his wavy hair and a moody, almost tormented expression in the eyes. Six years later he stands by one of his famous crates of manuscript, his hair ruffled, his head small in proportion to his tall body. Two years after this, in a family group, he is heavy-jowled and massive. Pictures from the 1938 trip through the National Parks show him overweight, but happy and relaxed.[1]

How big was Wolfe, particularly how tall? Six feet six inches seems to be the accurate figure,[2] and in later years he weighed up to two hundred and fifty pounds. His unusual size, his frequently ill-fitting clothes, his long, unruly hair, and his violent movements combined to create in those he met an unforgettable impression. His impetuous monologues, delivered in a slightly hoarse voice, captivated and sometimes exhausted his auditors, although at other times he was overawed by strange surroundings and became awkwardly silent. In keeping with his huge size, Wolfe had an enormous appetite, which continued to astonish his friends. When he had money, he ordered great rare steaks. Entertained in San Francisco in 1935, he astonished the Chinese cook by breakfasting on a dozen eggs, a loaf of bread, and two quarts of milk. Despite his physical energy, there was about him what one of his students called an "otherworldliness." It was this quality which made Maxwell Perkins think of Shelley the first time he ever saw Wolfe.[3]

In the fourteen years that centered in New York, Wolfe's way of living was chaotic. He liked to work at night, and often to prowl the city alone. Since he traveled much, he had no settled home but lived in a sequence of hotels and apartments, near Washington Square, in Brooklyn, and back in Manhattan again. Where he lived and how did not greatly matter to him. He was content to camp out in disorder. He did not care whether the chest of drawers had handles or not. He did not care if his heaps of manuscript looked untidy so long as he could find what he was hunting for. He wanted space, so that he could pace up and down as he worked over difficult passages. He wanted solitude, except for his typists, who came in to transcribe his long-hand penciled manuscript.

What social life he had was elsewhere. For years he got his mail at the Harvard Club. In the early 1930's he was almost an inhabitant of Scribner's office. And to Wolfe, a bar was always a friendly place. He cashed most of his checks at a liquor store because he could never remember to get to the bank during banking hours. On many occasions he drank excessively, getting himself into petty quarrels that embarrassed him and often his friends. The binge in Montreux has been alluded to. The months of 1936 and 1937, when the quarrel with Scribner's was in progress, were marked by midnight telephone calls in which his drunken voice would announce to a friend at Scribner's, "You betrayed me!" or to his literary agent, "I've done it now!"— meaning that at last he had broken with Scribner's, when actually he was still thinking about it. Even before the years of his fame, women threw themselves at him, and some of his promiscuous affairs may have been provoked by his extreme jealousy of Mrs. Bernstein. After he broke with her, there was no stable relationship with any woman.

Wolfe's complex temperament has best been summarized by Elizabeth Nowell, once a Scribner's employee, later Wolfe's literary agent, and, after his death, the editor of his letters and author of the fullest biography:

He had his mother's penny-pinching frugality, but his father's lavish love of spending. He could never bring himself to throw things away, but he lost things—hats, coats, manuscripts, and uncashed checks—continually. He had a gourmet's passion for good food, but he starved himself day after day, with only cigarettes and strong black coffee to sustain him. He had a tendency toward alcoholism, but he put in more long, sober, grueling hours than any one on earth. He loved women and was somewhat over-sexed, but he resented any trickery or possessiveness from them and preferred the good companionship of men.

He was completely ignorant of how to shape a piece of writing and make it publishable, but he had a deep instinctive feeling for his work which rarely played him false. He was fascinated by the concept of time in all its aspects, but he always was an hour or more late to his appointments. He loved to ride on boats and trains, but he had the greatest difficulty in catching them. He loved baseball and read all the dope about it in the New York papers, but he seldom found the time to watch a game. He had what he called "a mountaineer's suspicion of people from outside," which sometimes made him accuse even his best friends of "betraying" him, but he was the most naïve and trusting man on earth and wanted everyone to be his friend. He had "black moods" so deep that he sometimes was afraid of going crazy, but he also had periods of the greatest hope and joy. He had a humorless self-pity, but a sense of humor that was superb. He had the greatest difficulty in making decisions, but when he made one, he did it utterly, irrevocably, and with a bang. He had a ruthlessness in breaking free from too smothering relationships, but he had depths of loyalty which never changed. He was driven wild with exasperation at his family, but he worried endlessly about them and gave them hundreds of his own much-needed dollars during hard times. He was in many ways an adolescent boy, but he had the philosophy, the hope, the resignation of a great man. Even his physical appearance varied greatly: when he saw a nice thick sirloin steak, a bottle of good wine, or a pretty woman, he would crow and ogle like a suckling babe, and when he told his comic stories and tall tales, he would roll his eyes and grin like Wordsworth's idiot boy; but in repose of meditation, his face had the grandeur and the genius of the Höfel Beethoven, and his eyes were always dark and sad with a knowledge of the strangeness and the tragedy of life.[4]

With such contradictory and inconsistent elements in his makeup, it was inevitable that Wolfe would have no easy passage through life. Some examination of his difficulties is desirable at this point, for they had a great bearing on his accomplishments and his failures. If the accomplishments are to be understood and rightly valued, the praise and blame heaped upon Wolfe as a man deserve analysis. Furthermore, we must consider some questions in regard to his family, his teachers, Mrs. Bernstein, and his publishers.

To begin with, it is worth pointing out that Wolfe was one of the most fortunate writers of recent times. Despite his frequent complaints against his family, they aided him financially, and they stood by him in what neighbors regarded as an unjustified assault upon the family and the town of Asheville in *Look Homeward, Angel.* As Wolfe points out, there had never been a writer on either side of the family. If his family did not understand his strange ambition, at least they did not greatly interfere with it. There was no rigid expectation or insistence on what his vocation should be. His father, to be sure, would have been better pleased if Tom had gone into law; but he made no great protest when Tom rejected this profession. Despite the fact that the family had neither intellectual interests nor imposing social position, there was a freedom and competitiveness that Tom reflects in his own vigorous independence. At the age of twelve Tom was sent to private school, an advantage enjoyed by none of the other Wolfe children. The school may have been weak in some respects, but the friendly interest of Margaret Roberts was a major asset to Tom for years to come.

At the University of North Carolina, Wolfe had the admiring comradeship and recognition of his fellow students. He made a good record and was never in any academic or disciplinary trouble. He had as close personal friends three able faculty men—Horace Williams, Edwin Greenlaw, and Frederick Koch—whose impact was so different that no one of them could dominate him too much. At Harvard, Wolfe liked the course work, did well in it, and recognized the intellectual stimulus he received. In particular, he took work with Lowes at the very time when *The Road to Xanadu* was in the making, one of the most literate and usable books for a writer to come from any American campus in this century. At the 47 Workshop Wolfe was associated with people older, more experienced, less provincial than himself. From the beginning and for three full years, Wolfe was close to Baker, then the only academic man in the country to be much respected in the professional theatre. As a student of Baker, Wolfe had immediate contacts with the Theatre Guild and with other art theatres then developing. It has already been shown in Chapter II that Wolfe's "failure" was relative and by no means justified abysmal depression in a young man of twenty-three.

If Wolfe was to teach at all, his experience at New York University was, for an aspiring writer, probably the most fortunate he could have had. He was in New York, the theatrical and publishing center, with a number of young colleagues who also had literary aspirations. The teaching was onerous, but he learned something from it, and there is good evidence that he enjoyed it. He taught only parts of six years, for, with economy and assistance from his family and from Mrs. Bernstein, he enjoyed long periods abroad. In most ways Wolfe's relationship with Mrs. Bernstein was extraordinarily good luck. She was intelligent, witty, shrewd, but optimistic by nature. Her life included nearly everything Wolfe had missed, and she eagerly shared her intimate knowledge of the theatre and other arts, her feeling for city life, her acquaintance with famous people. She was immediately certain of Wolfe's talent, and with infinite patience she gave him the encouragement without which it is doubtful whether *Look Homeward, Angel* could ever have been completed.

In finding a publisher for his huge manuscript, Wolfe had some initial discouragement, yet nine months after it was completed it had been accepted by a major publisher. Perkins' interest and his warm encouragement, his intelligent grasp of

Wolfe's problem, his deferential manner, and his patience astonished the young author. The success of the book was rapid and
substantial. It was a critical success and a lucrative one. On the
strength of it, Scribner's was eager for him to get on with the
next book, and the Guggenheim Foundation granted him a
year's fellowship. At twenty-nine, few authors have done so
well. Nine years later, Wolfe was dead. In the interval he had
published one major novel, a volume of short stories, and a
number of scattered pieces; and he had accumulated a vast body
of manuscript. During these nine years—the years of fame—
Wolfe was unhappy. He enjoyed himself hugely on many occasions, to be sure: in Europe, and on the Western trips of 1935
and 1938. Yet his life was so disorganized, his struggles with
his writing so full of frustration, that unhappiness was a common mood.

Since, on the surface at least, the external circumstances of
Wolfe's life were so fortunate, one will have to look elsewhere
for an explanation of his deep discontent. The large body of
published letters helps one to look within Wolfe's nature and to
answer some of the questions raised by his fiction. For instance,
why in *Look Homeward, Angel* does Wolfe present so unfavor-
ably a recognizable picture of his family, his private school, and
of the University of North Carolina? In 1923 Wolfe wrote to a
friend, "I wonder if, in some respects, I'll ever cease being a
child."

In some respects he never did. Psychologists could make much
of the fact that he was not weaned until he was past three,
that he slept with his mother "until he was a great big boy,"
that he was the youngest of a large family, and that he was the
one to accompany his mother on her numerous trips.[5] Yet as a
boy he felt neglected, and wandered between the Woodfin
house and the boardinghouse. After graduation from Chapel
Hill, Wolfe was dependent on his mother for continuing his
education at Harvard, and his letters show an uncomfortable
alternation between affection and distrust, between dependence
and independence. "I shall not call upon you for more help,"
he writes his mother with injured pride in September, 1920; yet
he was to call upon her again and again for years. In 1924 he
says aggrievedly: "You never write. You never think of me. If
I should die here you'd forget me in two months."

The later letters are full of reassurances that he is working hard and all is going well. On the other hand, he occasionally comments censoriously, as he did in 1926: "Money in our family has been a deadly poison—for it you have lost comfort, peace, and in the end, money itself. . . ."[6] In 1925 he could say of Mabel; "The simple and terrific fact is that with all her fuming, fretting, weeping, her love of adulation, I have never seen her do a selfish thing." Yet in 1938 he wrote Mabel a long letter of recriminations about the old quarrel over their father's estate.[7] Such allusions to his family—and many more could be cited—suggest that Wolfe never grew up. Since he did not marry and have children of his own, he did not have the experience of his own family as a check and balance upon his continuing relations with the family he had grown up with. He continued to justify himself or to feel aggrieved in the way a child does.

With Mrs. Roberts, and with the University of North Carolina, the pattern of relationship was much the same. He could express affection and a deep sense of obligation. Yet Harvard and New York had conferred a more sophisticated outlook than that of school and college. For him this development was not an easy, natural development, but a rapid shift that disturbed deep loyalties. He was growing, and he had to wrench himself free from his origins. Yet he needed those origins, too, for they were his creative material. The satire in his fiction was his gesture of freedom. The lyric passages were his hymns of praise. Both were "sincere." But was there malice in the satire? Did he, consciously or unconsciously, use the novel as a means to score off the petty tyrants of his youth?

No doubt he did, and while this must have given him great satisfaction as he saw the words on the manuscript, the public reaction to cold type created in him a sense of guilt from which he never fully recovered. Trying to explain his psychological difficulties in the early 1930's, he wrote to Mabel: "I think that I got afraid after the first book."[8] A similar explanation applies to his treatment of Professor Baker and his New York University experience in *Of Time and the River*. These satiric episodes were his means of freeing himself from loyalties that he felt interfered with his growth. He was illustrating the old cynical proverb: "We rise by a series of disgusts." The disgusts were real enough, and they were an important part of the truth of his observation. He knew, however, that they were not the whole truth. The gap bothered him; it accounts for his great efforts at self-justification in his letters and in *The Story of a Novel.*

I   *Aline Bernstein*

Wolfe's meeting with Mrs. Bernstein took place on board ship just before the "Berengaria" docked in New York in August, 1925, as Wolfe was returning from his first trip abroad. The manuscript of *Mannerhouse* had been stolen in Paris. He had had a disappointing love affair with a friend of Kenneth Raisbeck and had quarreled with Raisbeck himself. He had had money troubles. And he had accomplished very little writing, except for a new draft of the stolen play. Mrs. Bernstein was at this time a woman of forty-two, rich, talented, competent.[9] More important, she had beauty, charm, gaiety. Her children were now grown, and she had just begun in 1924 a very successful career as stage and costume designer. Through her association with The Neighborhood Playhouse she had actually read the manuscript of Wolfe's *Welcome to Our City,* and was thus familiar with his name. Apparently the attraction was mutual and immediate.

In the summer of 1926 he went abroad again, joining Mrs. Bernstein in England. While they were together at Ilkley, in the Lake District, Wolfe began to think of writing a novel, having decided that further effort to become a playwright was useless. When Mrs. Bernstein returned to New York in August, Wolfe remained to work on the novel now known as *Look Homeward, Angel.* On December 29, when he landed in New York, Mrs. Bernstein met him at the dock. She had already secured an apartment for him, and in January, 1927, Wolfe was settled at 13 W. Eighth Street. Mrs. Bernstein persuaded him to give his whole time to the novel, and that spring he did not teach, as he had expected to do. In July, Wolfe made his third trip abroad, spending part of the time with Mrs. Bernstein. In September he was teaching again, but by March, 1928, the novel was finished.

By this time there had been sufficient quarreling between Wolfe and Mrs. Bernstein that they did not see each other while they were both abroad that summer. It was in October, 1928, that Wolfe went to Munich and was hospitalized by injuries received in a fight. He wrote Mrs. Bernstein of this, and by correspondence a reconciliation was brought about. Shortly thereafter she cabled him that Scribner's was interested in his novel. Returning home late in December, Wolfe signed a contract and was soon engaged in revising his manuscript while teaching half-time at New York University. The association with Mrs. Bernstein was renewed, and in the summer she was with him in Maine, where he was reading proof. On October 18 the book was published, carrying a dedication "To A.B.," followed by a verse from Donne. Two weeks before, Wolfe had given her his carbon copy of the manuscript with an inscription which said, in part: "To Aline Bernstein. On my twenty-ninth birthday, I present her with this, the first copy of my first book. This book was written because of her, and is dedicated to her. At a time when my life seemed desolate, and when I had little faith in myself, I met her. She brought me friendship, material and spiritual relief, and love such as I had never had before." [10]

Wolfe resigned from New York University in January, 1930, and on May 10 he sailed for Europe with the help of a Guggenheim Fellowship. Before he did so, he made a will, naming Mrs. Bernstein and his mother as co-beneficiaries. The dedication of the novel and the terms of the will seem to indicate a continued close relationship, but this is not entirely true. Mrs. Bernstein's opposition to his plan of going abroad resulted in a serious quarrel. The provision of his will was chiefly an acknowledgment of a financial obligation.

As Mrs. Bernstein suspected, the trip abroad in 1930 was in part an effort to break with her. She made repeated attempts to communicate with him, and Wolfe thought she tried to have friends spy on him. Mrs. Bernstein's sister talked with Wolfe on one occasion. When he did return to New York in February, 1931, there was no reconciliation. In April, when Mrs. Bernstein attempted suicide, Wolfe sent an affectionate telegram and visited her in the hospital. Apparently not long afterward, Mrs. Bernstein had a stormy meeting with Wolfe's mother, who visited him in New York about this time. When *Of Time and the River* was published in 1935, Wolfe sent a copy to Mrs. Bernstein, with the words "My dear" written in the margin of the concluding passage in which Eugene first sees Esther.[11]

On his return from Europe in July he found a letter from her, which he answered most affectionately. A few days later,

Wolfe, who was with Perkins, encountered Mrs. Bernstein at a bar near Scribner's. Wolfe was unnerved, and the three adjourned to the Scribner's office. There she appeared to be making another attempt at suicide, but was prevented by Wolfe. After this dramatic episode, their association was renewed, and in October it was Mrs. Bernstein who decorated Wolfe's new apartment on First Avenue. During the last three years of Wolfe's life, however, there was little or no contact. When Wolfe was ill in the Johns Hopkins hospital, Mrs. Bernstein wanted to visit him, but she was dissuaded by Perkins.

After Wolfe's death she seems to have raised no objections to publication of the Webber novels, with their story of Esther Jack. Miss Nowell acknowledged Mrs. Bernstein's cooperation in preparing the edition of the *Letters* (1956) and the biography (1960). Mrs. Bernstein permitted publication of several letters to her, but her death in 1955 prevented her from editing herself a more complete selection of the correspondence.

Before the Esther Jack episodes in Wolfe's posthumous volumes were published in 1939 and 1940, Mrs. Bernstein had made her own fictional use of the affair. In 1933 appeared *Three Blue Suits,* a slender volume of seventy-five pages in an edition of six hundred copies. The first blue suit is that put on in the morning by Mr. Froelich, the well-to-do and self-sufficient husband of a gay and attractive woman. The second blue suit is that of Herbert Wilson, an extravagance on the part of a newly widowed man, which fails to soothe his abject loneliness now that he can "do as he likes." The third blue suit is that of Eugene. The lady who tells the story comes into Eugene's apartment and finds him asleep. She has groceries for lunch, but finds Eugene has an appointment with his publisher. So the food is to be saved for dinner, and Eugene promises to be back at three. When he finally returns at seven, he tells her that he has accepted a Guggenheim Fellowship, and will soon be going abroad. Enraged, she accuses him of selling her out: "You promised you would never leave me, darling."

Wolfe's first knowledge of the published book was a notice of it in the *Times.* He immediately bought a copy, read it, and wrote Mrs. Bernstein a letter of some four thousand words. The tone is friendly but distant. He is sorry she did not let him know about the book herself. Of the three sketches, he is most moved by the middle one. He knows of no counterpart in life for Mr. Wilson, "but I cannot tell you how moved I was by that story and how proud I am to know you could have done it." As for the other two stories, Wolfe alludes to the fact that she had sent them in manuscript "over a year ago," and on comparison he finds them little changed. He accepts them as portrayals of himself and her husband (Mrs. Bernstein later denied that "Mr. Froelich" was so intended). Wolfe objects— seemingly on Asheville principles!—that "you have sometimes been uncharitable and unjust, and that you could have shown them as better people than you make them without injuring the truth or the quality of your writing." He objects to her story of Eugene as an oversimplified and therefore distorted picture of their love affair. The Guggenheim Fellowship was not the cause of their break, he reminds her; it was an incidental decision against a background of long disagreement between a woman past fifty and a man not yet thirty. He adds: "In all your stories you show the remarkably sharp, accurate and cynical observation of your race—a quality which I must confess I never knew you had to such a degree, but which may be a most characteristic thing about you." This long letter is one of the most fascinating in the Wolfe correspondence, and I do not know a parallel to its detailed examination of a fictional portrait by the subject portrayed. Wolfe tries to draw a distinction between his own fictional method and that of Mrs. Bernstein. It is hard to follow his reasoning. And there is a morally superior tone that is as offensive as it is false.[12]

In the spring of 1938 appeared Mrs. Bernstein's *The Journey Down*, a short novel based on the affair. In the novel, the couple (never named) meet at a shipboard party. He berates her for being part of the theatrical world, and she tells him she has read his play. The second chapter shows the couple wonderfully happy in England, except that he is slightly jealous when her fashionable friends call unexpectedly. A sequence of scenes, all lightly touched, mingle their days together: their quarrels, their fondness for food, her childhood memories of the stage, of London, of Mr. Wilkie Collins, her rehearsals, her visit to a fortune teller, and her accidental meeting with the former lover who is now merely a friend. The book closes with her recovery in the hospital from an attempted suicide. At the theatre one day she had diagnosed the cause of their estrangement:

The strange thing was that while I was so horrid I watched myself perform. . . . The double life went on, I was completely conscious of them both. Nagging, tearful, self-centered woman above, and my love sang below, murmured, pulsed, beat out its lovely music on my soul, struggled, gasped for fear of death. All I had of goodness, all I knew from life, I should have used them for our salvation and happiness. . . . My life with him had been complete reality, and it was more than I could manage, it was a greater measure than I could hold (158-59).

The tone of the book is sadly sweet, with intelligence and wit enough to keep it from being sentimental. There is no bitterness. In 1941 Mrs. Bernstein published *An Actor's Daughter,* the story of her childhood. Since it ends with the death of her father, it has no direct connection with Wolfe. It does, however, fill out the reminiscences given in *The Journey Down* and paralleled in *The Web and the Rock* (chapters 26 and 27). It is evident that "In the Park," a story in Wolfe's *The Hills Beyond,* closely resembles Chapter 14 of *An Actor's Daughter.* In all three of Mrs. Bernstein's books there is a charm that goes far to explain Wolfe's interest in her, and a sympathy for the creative temperament which is both warm and deep. Yet it remains true that her books have been forgotten except for the relevance they have to Wolfe's story.

Wolfe's own fictional treatment of the love affair simplifies actual events as they are known. Omitted are the summer trips abroad in 1926 and 1927, when progress on the novel was central to the love affair. Omitted also are details of the reconciliation in Europe after the Munich fight and before the return to New York. Permanent separation from Esther is implied after "The Party at Jack's," and she is not mentioned again. Since the stock-market crash follows the party by only a few days, the final separation is dated in 1929. We have seen that, with some interruptions, Wolfe's association with Mrs. Bernstein continued until 1935. Thus like the Gant story, there was more to be told about Esther Jack.

About the affair itself, and Wolfe's conduct in it, there is not much to be said in judgment. The reasons for the attachment are self-evident, but they are precisely the same reasons that eventually led to estrangement. Wolfe in 1929 was a very different man from what he was when Mrs. Bernstein met him in

1925. Mrs. Bernstein herself remained much the same. In a sense, Wolfe received far more than he gave; and he looks shabbily ungenerous. In another sense, it was not "fair" for Mrs. Bernstein to try to possess him as completely as she did, and it was not "unfair" in Wolfe to escape if he could. It was not his nature to withdraw in easy, friendly fashion from an association so intimate and so intense. Mrs. Bernstein must have realized this even as she strove to keep his love and close companionship. Her own books are evidence that, in the end, she bore no grudge.

II Maxwell Perkins

Wolfe's relationship to Maxwell Perkins, Scribner's editor, was from the beginning both personal and professional. Aline Bernstein had seen Wolfe through the composition of *Look Homeward, Angel,* but when Wolfe returned from Europe at the end of 1928, they were already somewhat estranged. The kind of help Perkins could give was what Wolfe needed, and he received it gratefully. Until the publication of *Of Time and the River* in 1935, both men worked together with only the kind of disagreements that could be resolved after a drink or a good night's sleep. Like Mrs. Bernstein, Perkins was extremely competent, capable of working long and rapidly without losing a calm, clear-headed deliberateness. Unlike Mrs. Bernstein, he was incapable of jealousy or emotional extremes. In the eight years of association with Wolfe, the closest Perkins came to losing his temper was in his own house early in 1937, when Wolfe insisted on reiterating his grievances against Scribner's. Perkins is reported to have said: "All right then, if you *must* leave Scribner's, go ahead and *leave,* but for heaven's sakes, *don't talk about it any more!*" [13]

When Perkins looked up to greet the tall young man in the doorway of his office in January, 1929, he had been with Scribner's nearly nineteen years. Born of a distinguished New England family—his grandfather had been a United States Senator—Perkins had graduated from Harvard in 1907, had a brief experience as reporter on the New York *Times,* and in 1910 had joined Scribner's as advertising manager. Four years later he became assistant to W. C. Brownell, the senior editor. In a quiet way, Perkins persuaded the conservative firm to publish a remarkable number of new, important authors. By 1929 the list included Fitzgerald, Hemingway, Ring Lardner, James Boyd, and a number of lesser but popular writers like Willard Huntington Wright, whose Philo Vance detective stories were extremely successful.

Perkins inspired unusual respect and affection in his temperamental authors by genuinely valuing their talent. What he wanted to do was to help them see their own aims more clearly. In 1921 he began a letter to Fitzgerald: "Don't ever *defer* to my judgment. You won't on any vital point, I know, and I should be ashamed, if it were possible to have made you; for a writer of any account must speak solely for himself." He then went on to distinguish between Fitzgerald's intention in a scene of *The Beautiful and Damned* and the probable antagonism of readers to a detail unnecessary to the intention. In another letter to Fitzgerald, after raising some questions about characterization in *The Great Gatsby,* he adds: "The general brilliant quality of the book makes me ashamed to make even these criticisms."

Perkins' published letters to Wolfe are all written in the same spirit. He respected Wolfe's talent, he understood many of his difficulties, and he showed unfailing courtesy even under severe strain. In the middle of the arguments with Scribner's, Perkins wrote Wolfe: "Ever since 'Look Homeward, Angel' your work has been the foremost interest in my life, and I have never doubted for your future on any grounds except, at times, on those of your being able to control the vast mass of material you have accumulated and have to form into books. You seem to think I have tried to control you. I only did that when you asked my help and then I did the best I could." [14]

Wolfe's appreciation was eloquent. On December 24, 1929, he wrote Perkins a Christmas note, saying that what had happened in the past year was "a miracle": "You are now mixed with my book in such a way that I can never separate the two of you. I can no longer think clearly of the time I wrote it, but rather of the time when you first talked to me about it, and when you worked upon it . . . you are chiefly 'Scribners' to me: you have done what I had ceased to believe one person could do for another—you have created liberty and hope for me." [15]

The word "liberty" is worth noting. By August 29, 1931, Wolfe was "in doubt" about his progress. He was, he said, "not sure about anything." The success of "The Portrait of Bascom

Hawke" the following spring raised his spirits, but in December, 1933, he was desperate. At this point Perkins informed him that he thought the novel was completed. The incredulous Wolfe was instructed to assemble his manuscript in the best order he could and bring it in. This he did, asking Perkins to estimate "its value or lack of value." Wolfe thought the manuscript included some of the best writing he had done, but he added, "I must shamefacedly confess that I need your help now more than I ever did." Perkins saw the manuscript as two books, one of which ultimately became *Of Time and the River*, and one, called *The October Fair*, which eventually became *The Web and the Rock*. He advised Wolfe to concentrate on the first book, cutting where possible and adding transitions where necessary.

Early in 1934 Perkins and Wolfe settled down to a nightly process of detailed revision, the strictly literary aspect of which will be discussed in the next chapter. In July, 1934, without Wolfe's permission, Perkins sent the manuscript to the printer. At the time, Wolfe resented this, but Perkins had watched Wolfe since 1929 with mounting concern about the nervous strain under which he worked. Even before December, 1933, Perkins felt Wolfe "could not go on like this," and he therefore called for the manuscript. Similarly in July, 1934, he felt that the manuscript must either undergo interminable revision or be taken from the author and sent to the printer. These are the circumstances under which Perkins, as Wolfe later said, "took the book away" from him. It is Miss Nowell's opinion that this unusual editorial decision was virtually forced on Perkins by Wolfe's fatigue and tension.[16]

Despite some resentment, which showed itself in Wolfe's failure to read proofs, he submitted to Perkins a three-page preface, praising Perkins' great assistance in editing *Of Time and the River*. Perkins expressed his pleasure at this gesture, but with unusual insight, even for him, advised against including the preface: ". . . you cannot, and should not, try to change your conviction that I have deformed your book, or at least prevented it from coming to perfection. It is therefore impossible for you sincerely to dedicate it to me, and it ought not to be done."[17] Wolfe withdrew the intended preface—later to be expanded into *The Story of a Novel*—but, without Perkins' knowledge, he inserted the following dedication:

To
MAXWELL EVARTS PERKINS

A great editor and a brave and honest man, who stuck to the
writer of this book through times of bitter hopelessness and
doubt and would not let him give in to his own despair, a work
to be known as "Of Time and the River" is dedicated with the
hope that all of it may be in some way worthy of the loyal
devotion and the patient care which a dauntless and unshaken
friend has given to each part of it, and without which none of it
could have been written.

With good grace Perkins acknowledged this as "a most generous and noble utterance. Certainly for one who could say that of
me I ought to have done all that it says I did do." This was on
February 8, 1935. On December 31, 1937, Wolfe signed a formal contract with Harper's, somewhat melodramatically quoting
Martin Luther as he did so: "*Ich kann nicht anders.* I can't do
otherwise: I have no other choice." [18]

The external circumstances leading to the break with Scribner's do not adequately explain Wolfe's action, but they must
first be summarized. Disregarding Perkins' warning, Wolfe
expanded his intended preface into a long lecture delivered in
July, 1935, at Boulder, Colorado; published it serially in *The
Saturday Review of Literature* the following spring; and finally
published it as a small book entitled *The Story of a Novel.* This
essay emphasized his struggles with his materials and his great
debt to his editor, not named, but well-known. Publication of
this work not only triggered Bernard De Voto's famous attack,
"Genius is Not Enough"; it also revived the charge that his
fiction was "merely" autobiography, exactly as Perkins had pre-
dicted it might.

At first Wolfe was not unduly concerned about this criticism.
More immediately in his mind was a petty dispute over the
price of the small book, which had been increased from a tentative $1.25 to $1.50 without his knowledge, and over a cut in
his royalty from 15 per cent to 10 per cent in view of the small
size of the book. To these complaints Wolfe added his indignation at a bill for $1,100 for excessive author's corrections in the
proofs of *Of Time and the River.* Some of these corrections had
been made by Scribner's staff, it is true, but this was because
Wolfe himself did not read most of the proofs. Wolfe felt that
Scribner's was indulging in sharp business practice at his

expense. He felt that Perkins, as his friend, should protect him from such mistreatment. Perkins restored the 15 per cent royalty on the book and reminded Wolfe that he had not been charged for author's corrections in *Look Homeward, Angel*, even though about seven hundred dollars was chargeable according to contract. Perkins' defense of Scribner's policies was vigorous, though courteous throughout. Wolfe wrote a letter of apology, but at the end of it reiterated the charge of sharp business practice.

Wolfe's doubts about Scribner's were increased by a series of financial difficulties and lawsuits which led him to feel that fame had made him a target for extortion. Even at Harvard he had been sued by a typist, apparently for the simple reason that he had not asked for an estimate in advance of her bill for typing his play. In 1930 he was incensed at what he considered an overcharge for dental work, and turned to Perkins for advice. In May, 1935, while in Germany, Wolfe received news that his literary agent, Mrs. Madeleine Boyd, who had brought *Look Homeward, Angel* to Perkins, was suing him for commissions on *Of Time and the River*. There had been no contract covering the second book, but there had also been no formal release; the case was finally settled out of court in May, 1936, at a cost of nearly a thousand dollars.[19] At this same time, progress with *The October Fair* was held up by Mrs. Bernstein's threat of a libel suit if the novel were published. In November, 1936, suit was brought against Wolfe and Scribner's for alleged libel in his story "No Door," by a Brooklyn family named Dorman. Because Wolfe's conduct as a witness in court was hard to predict, lawyers for Scribner's advised settlement out of court. Though Scribner's paid half the cost of settlement and of the lawyer's fees, Wolfe's share of $2,745.05 was a heavy loss in the spring of 1937. He continued to feel that the suit should have been fought in court, and could have been won. In 1936, Wolfe himself was forced to take legal action against a young man to whom he had entrusted some of his manuscript for sale. The case, finally tried in February, 1938, was decided in Wolfe's favor, with Perkins as a chief witness.

All of these difficulties were serious distractions for Wolfe. Yet it is difficult to believe that even the most serious and costly—the Dorman libel suit—would have been sufficient to cause Wolfe to change publishers, or to do it in the protracted, highly emotional way he did. Behind the charges of disloyalty he leveled at Scribner's and Perkins was an instinctive feeling that he must move on in order to be himself, to grow. Later, Perkins himself considered the break inevitable.[20] Wolfe was, however, so deeply indebted to Perkins that he could not leave without what in "The Men of Catawba" are satirically called "mawrul grounds." Leaving Scribner's could not be a simple matter of business. It had to be a stand on principle against the power and wealth of a great publishing house. The long delay in definitely going with Harper's suggests that he hoped against hope that Perkins would somehow find a way that would permit him to stay on with Scribner's. At the same time, the querulous tone of the long sequence of long letters was a defense against just such an outcome.

One of the strange things about the whole relationship is the continued friendship between Wolfe and Perkins, even after the close association stopped. It was in the midst of the controversy, on April 17, 1937, that Wolfe's new will named Perkins as administrator of his estate. In August, while Wolfe was in the South, Perkins thoughtfully paid the rent on Wolfe's apartment. In February, 1938, as has been mentioned, Perkins served as a witness in Wolfe's behalf, and after the decision, he, Wolfe, and Mrs. Jelliffe (a mutual friend) celebrated in the old happy way. It was the last time Perkins saw Wolfe alive. Wolfe's letter from the Seattle hospital the following August—the last letter he wrote—has been quoted many times:

> DEAR MAX:
>
> I'm sneaking this against orders, but "I've got a hunch"— and I wanted to write these words to you.
>
> I've made a long voyage and been to a strange country, and I've seen the dark man very close; and I don't think I was too much afraid of him, but so much of mortality still clings to me— I wanted most desperately to live and still do, and I thought about you all a thousand times, and wanted to see you all again, and there was the impossible anguish and regret of all the work I had not done, of all the work I had to do—and I know now I'm just a grain of dust, and I feel as if a great window has been opened on life I did not know about before—and if I come through this, I hope to God I am a better man, and in some strange way I can't explain, I know I am a deeper and a wiser one. If I get on my feet and out of here, it will be months before I head back, but if I get on my feet, I'll come back.

Whatever happens—I had this "hunch" and wanted to write you and tell you, no matter what happens or has happened, I shall always think of you and feel about you the way it was that Fourth of July day three years ago when you met me at the boat, and we went out on the café on the river and had a drink and later went on top of the tall building, and all the strangeness and the glory and the power of life and of the city was below.

Yours always,
Tom[21]

By the terms of Wolfe's will, as has been mentioned, Perkins was the administrator of Wolfe's estate, and in this capacity could have prevented publication of the Webber novels. Even with regard to the satirical treatment of Foxhall Edwards, recognizably modeled after Perkins, he wanted no changes made. He considered the final letter of Webber to Fox "magnificent." [22] On personal grounds, Perkins' relation to Wolfe is beyond criticism. At every point, Perkins did in friendship what he felt had to be done. Those who feel that Perkins "dominated" Wolfe should consider the alternatives open to Perkins. If Perkins had set Wolfe adrift as simply unmanageable—and most editors would have done so before 1933—he would most certainly have been blamed by Wolfe's friends. In 1934, had Wolfe suffered some kind of nervous breakdown, as Perkins feared, he would also have been blamed. Having seen Wolfe through *Look Homeward, Angel*, Perkins—at great cost to himself—took risks far beyond the call of editorial duty. If it is maintained that Wolfe "ought" to have stood up to Perkins, or that he ought not to have permitted Perkins to dominate him as much as he did, the fact remains that Wolfe asked for help. Perkins should hardly be blamed in any personal way for giving it. Some of his decisions and suggestions may be open to question, but nobody else—Wolfe included—was at the time capable of getting *Of Time and the River* in print.

After the book was in print, Wolfe was bound to blame the book's imperfections on Perkins, rather than on his own weaknesses. Even though he paid high tribute to Perkins, there was a deep feeling that he must still prove himself as an independent creative writer. He must be free of Perkins. The conflict between his loyalty to a friend and his need for independence parallels Wolfe's relation to his family, to Mrs. Roberts, to the University of North Carolina, to Harvard, to New York Univer-

sity, and to Mrs. Bernstein. The lawsuits and business disagreements of 1935 to 1938 made it possible for Wolfe finally to
create a distinction between Scribner's and Perkins. Scribner's
was the enemy, against whom all his moral indignation was
concentrated. Perkins, as a friend, should have protected him;
but perhaps he could not. At least he did not. Give Max time,
though, and perhaps he could work things out. When Max did
not provide the magic formula, Wolfe, like Luther, could not
do otherwise than break with Scribner's. But he could and did
preserve something of his friendship with Perkins.

A narrow view of Wolfe would condemn him for "betraying"
Perkins and a long list of earlier friends. The notable fact
is that—despite specific acts charged with malice, rudeness,
thoughtlessness—Tom Wolfe seldom lost a friend. Men of high
talent are rare, and much is pardoned them. Pained and embarrassed as Wolfe's friends and family often were, and justified as
their complaints might be, they found in this unique man much
to remember gratefully: his laughter, his passionate response to
beauty, his dedication to literature. This loyal appreciation is
notable in Wolfe's family, in his college friends, and in many
of his colleagues at New York University. Most of all, it is
notable in Aline Bernstein and Maxwell Perkins.

III *Social Views*

Wolfe's personal relationships were so intense and so subjec-
tive that he is likely to be thought of as completely egocentric.
Though this side of his nature is most conspicuous, and probably most important, he had more concern with society and its
problems than has generally been thought. It is particularly
important to recall that in college Wolfe was a joiner and a
leader. He took philosophy seriously, and the Worth Prize essay
is a high-minded insistence that the whole nature of man will
not be served by regarding labor as merely a marketable commodity. As has been seen, Wolfe's plays dealt with important
social themes: the struggle of the young idealist against such
outworn ways as the feud; romantic illusion as an obstacle to
clear thought about the present, particularly in the South; mate-
rialistic greed, as represented in the real-estate boom; and,
incidentally, the race problem. Having failed to develop such
substantial social ideas into a saleable play, Wolfe retreated

into the egocentric autobiography of *Look Homeward, Angel* and of *Of Time and the River*. Since these novels bring Eugene Gant's story only to 1925, they do not reveal much of Wolfe's social awareness in the important years from 1925 to 1935.

Wolfe's letters in the 1920's reflect a good deal of the debunking spirit then so prevalent. After a visit to Asheville in 1922, he complained to Mrs. Roberts of the townspeople: "The disgusting spectacle of thousands of industrious and accomplished liars, engaged in the mutual and systematic pursuit of their profession, salting their editorials and sermons and advertisements with the religious and philosophic platitudes of Dr. Frank Crane, Edgar A. Guest, and *The American Magazine*. The standards of national greatness are Henry Ford, who made automobiles cheap enough for us all, and money, money, money!! And Thomas A. Edison, who gave us body-ease and comfort." [23]

The following year he darkly told his mother that in his plays:

> I will step on toes, I will not hesitate to say what I think of those people who shout "Progress, Progress, Progress"—when what they mean is more Ford automobiles, more Rotary Clubs, more Baptist Ladies Social Unions. . . . What I shall try to get into their dusty little pint-measure minds is that a full belly, a good automobile, paved streets, and so on, do not make them one whit better or finer,—that there is beauty in this world,—beauty even in this wilderness of ugliness and provincialism that is at present our country, beauty and spirit which will make us men instead of cheap Board of Trade Boosters, and blatant pamphleteers.[24]

In 1927 he wrote to Mabel an amusing but condescending description of a sales convention he had visited with her husband. In another letter to Mabel he ridiculed women's clubs: "Apparently the women are getting all the 'culture'—What do the men do?" When *Look Homeward, Angel* came out he announced to Mabel: ". . . my book is not a book that every realtor, attorney, druggist, or grocer should read. They should stick to *Collier's* and *The American*, and the S.E.P. [*Saturday Evening Post*]." [25]

Despite this condescension toward the middle-class businessman, then so fashionable, Wolfe was even more bitter toward so-called artists, whom he usually thought of as impostors. "I have a horror of becoming like those wretched little rats at Harvard who are at the mercy of their pangs and quivers, who

whine about their 'art,' who whine that the world has not given
them a living." Wolfe told of attending a "terrible studio party"
in New York. After meeting Carl Van Vechten, Elinor Wylie,
and Will Benét, he said, "I hated them so that I managed to
insult them all before the evening was over." The publication
of his first book intensified this distrust of "artistic" people. "I
have found that although there are millions of people who
swear they are willing to live and die for what is good and
beautiful, I have never known a half dozen who were willing
to be out of fashion. And this is more true of the critics, the
reviewers, the writers, than anyone else—most of them have the
spirits of rats: they are humanists now, romantics next season,
something else again." [26]

The urge to be independent in all circumstances, so evident
in his personal relationships, is equally evident in the subjects
which Henry Volkening lists as habitual targets for Wolfe's
invective: aesthetes who loaf around waiting for inspiration;
propagandists; lawyers; gossip columnists, and their readers;
café society; dentists and doctors; "the whole damned theatre
crowd"; most modern painters; opera singers; mystics; women,
"for their inherent incapability of detached and impersonal
thought"; the women's club favorites; sophisticated writers
(except Aldous Huxley); book reviewers; and most Southerners.[27] Such half-serious and comically exaggerated prejudices
perhaps do not merit consideration under the heading of social
views, but if there is a common denominator in this list it is
a hatred of pretentiousness.

Wolfe's political views are not stated at length in his letters,
but a few allusions suggest a pattern of development. Wolfe's
father was a Northern man and a Republican. His mother was
Southern and a Democrat. The early letters do not refer to the
campaigns of 1920 or 1924, or to any issues. In 1928, Wolfe was
disappointed by the election of Hoover and the defeat of Smith.
"Why is it," he wrote Aline Bernstein from Budapest, "that the
good people, the right people are so often the underdogs?" The
following spring he commented to Mabel that prosperity was a
very uneven thing: "I think if I had any politics, I'd be a
socialist—it's the only sensible thing to be (if you're not a capi-
talist, and I'm *not*). But you think that's 'wild talk,' don't
you?" [28] In 1931 he speculated in a letter to his mother: "The
system of overproduction will not improve, will get worse,

unless something is done to control it—I think we are at the end of a period: it may be that the whole Capitalistic system is finished—if so, I think we should welcome some other one that is not so stupid and wasteful." [29]

In the published letters there is no reference to the 1932 campaign, but by 1936 his recent trips to Europe had begun to make him conscious of international issues. To a friend, he described indignantly the extreme attacks on Roosevelt as "a vile Communist," "a sinister Fascist," and "a scheming and contriving Socialist." [30] Wolfe had talked with Ambassador William E. Dodd in Berlin, and accepted his favorable view of Roosevelt. Nevertheless, Wolfe refers to "the disquieting expenditure of money," and to unspecified "grievous errors" of the administration, though he thinks the election of a reactionary government would be "the worst calamity that could happen." Therefore, he tells his friend: "I want to take the stump. I want to write letters to the newspapers." There is no record that he did so.

Perkins says that as early as 1934 Wolfe wanted to inject Marxian ideas into *Of Time and the River,* but he was finally dissuaded by Perkins' argument that such sentiments did not fit the period of Eugene Gant's life covered in the novel. Wolfe, said Perkins, "wanted at that time to be a Communist, the last thing he truly was, as his last book shows." There is no evidence that Wolfe ever made any careful study of communism, or of any economic theory. Such comments as have been quoted in this paragraph merely reflect the widespread dissatisfaction with "the system" which had allowed the Depression to occur. "The Party at Jack's," published after Wolfe's death and later included in *You Can't Go Home Again,* is an exposure of ostentatious wealth and callous unawareness of social interdependence. Wolfe himself insisted it was "not at all Marxian." [31] It is in no way prescriptive of a remedy. The call to social conscience is a generalized one, not propaganda for a program. It is more an appeal to democratic tradition than to revolution.

An intuitive grasp of liberal tradition, rather than elaborate analysis of special information, likewise led Wolfe to his denunciation of the Nazi regime in 1936-37, certainly his most immediately useful stand on any social or political matter. By this time he had a considerable personal acquaintance with Europe, though no profound knowledge of it. He had made trips of varying length in 1924, 1926, 1927, 1928, 1930, from which he discovered nothing more startling than "the fundamental honesty of the English," the passion of the French for glory, and the importance of the belly in Germany. The letters written on his travels are extremely readable. He can make one see "a Cockney at mortal sword-play with an English aristocrat," or "a sort of German—young gentlemen with dueling scars on their face, and older ones with shaven bullet heads, small porky eyes, and three ridges of neck over the back of their collars." [32] Essentially, however, his letters are tourist's letters.

Despite his injuries at the Munich Oktoberfest in 1928, and his frequent uncomplimentary remarks, Germany was Wolfe's favorite European country. When he returned there in 1935, gratified by the current success of *Of Time and the River,* he was so lavishly entertained that he naturally discounted the stories he heard about Nazi atrocities. Martha Dodd, daughter of the American ambassador, has described the great enthusiasm for Wolfe, even among some Nazis.[33] When he left the country after his short stay in 1935, Germany was still, for him, the country of Goethe. In 1936, however, particularly through Heinz Ledig-Rowohlt, his publisher's son, he made the discoveries narrated in "I Have a Thing to Tell You." The publication of this story in 1937 made it impossible for him to go back to Germany. Though the Nazi tyranny seems obvious enough now, plain speech about it was not yet popular. The following year *The Nation* published a symposium under the heading "How to Keep Out of War." Wolfe's short letter was forthright and dead serious in tone, one of the best utterances he ever made:

> Aside from the question whether even peace can be worth any price that we can pay or that can be demanded of us—a view which was seriously maintained by many people until a year or two ago—I do not think that peace can ever be won and kept in such a way. I further think that "isolation" is a rhetorical concept, useful to politicians for the purpose of strengthening the majorities at home and of reassuring their constituencies, and perhaps useful to other people who project the metaphysical idea that it is possible for a nation of one hundred and thirty million people to live sealed up hermetically in peace in a world that is ravaged by war. . . . It becomes increasingly apparent that the only effective way to meet armed aggression may be armed resistance: the wheels of a great war machine, such as

THOMAS WOLFE

that which Germany has today, are not going to be stopped,
once they have begun to roll, by a handful of reproving phrases,
or by a batch of diplomatic protests. Just as the foundations of
Fascism are rooted in the hopelessness and despair of a bankrupt
and defeated people who, having nothing more to lose, submit
to any promises of gain—this would have been apparent to
anyone who visited Germany as I did in 1928 and 1930—so does
the success and growth of Fascism depend upon submission, and
flourish upon compromise and vacillation. . . . The failure of the
major democratic powers thus far effectively to oppose the
aggressions of Germany, Italy and Japan has not weakened my
belief in the possibility of collective action and has not destroyed
my faith in the power of the major democratic powers to act
effectively. Sooner or later, it seems to me, they will have to.
They will have to when they decide that democracy is valuable
enough to be saved, and is worth fighting for, if need be, by
those who believe in it. In the end, I think we may all have to
make that decision. For Fascism is a creature that thrives [on]
but is not appeased by compromise.[34]

This was published April 2, 1938. It will be remembered that
on the day of Pearl Harbor, December 7, 1941, the America
First group was still active.

Regarding the menace of fascism in Spain, Wolfe had less to
say, no doubt because he had never visited that country. Early
in 1937 he spoke of sympathy for Loyalist Spaniards as a sentimental gesture. "The miseries of home, I suppose, are not
romantic enough, not noble enough, and, above all, oh dear yes,
not ideological enough." [35] In 1938, however, Wolfe contributed
to *The Nation* a letter satirically directed at the atrocities of
Franco's forces.

Wolfe's views on race are nowhere elaborately developed.
Toward the Negro he began with the typical Southern feeling.
Writing his mother from Boston in 1923, he states a belief that
he sees challenged:

For one thing our constitution has perpetrated the most damna-
ble political theory ever conceived—namely that men are created
equal. Now, I appeal to your judgment, to your good hard
sense—did you ever see two people who were equal in any
respect? In intelligence, in physical strength, in imagination, in
courage, in judgment, in any of the things that help us through
this tempestuous world? Furthermore, we Southerners, more
than anyone else, recognize the falsity of the doctrine in practice

at any rate, while defending it hypocritically in practice. Do we admit the equality of the negro? Do we give him the vote? Yet no one is better at whooping up equality than one of our quack Congressmen on the stump.[36]

Here, of course, Wolfe ignores the classic eighteenth-century concept of equality before the law, resting on equality in the sight of God; it is evident that he thinks the Negro has his place and should stay in it. Yet the only work in which the Negro figures importantly is his play *Welcome to Our City*. In this, as has been seen, Negro characters are presented realistically; they are shown as exploited, and it is left an open question whether enough of them have the courage to assert themselves as men. Perhaps a stronger pro-Negro treatment would have made the play more appealing to the Theatre Guild, but the text cannot fairly be called anti-Negro. After 1920, Wolfe lived most of his life in Northern cities. At New York University there is a story of an altercation with a Negro elevator operator, but it is a single incident. By leaving the South, Wolfe escaped the problem of the Negro.

Prejudice against the Jews is present in Wolfe's life and in his work, but it is incidental in both. He knew few Jewish people in Asheville; and, to judge from *Look Homeward, Angel*, the anti-Semitism he participated in was an occasional cat-call. Nevertheless, when Wolfe went to New York University in 1924, he specifically acknowledged prejudice in a letter to a friend. According to Oscar Cargill, Wolfe consulted two colleagues about how to deal with his prejudice. The fictional treatment of college classes suggests that his anti-Semitism was strong. Two students are on record, however, that they never saw any evidence of it in classes they attended.[37] In 1936 it was the seizure of a Jew which crystallized Wolfe's awareness of Nazi tyranny. The glaring and inescapable presence of anti-Semitism is in the posthumous novels which treat Esther Jack. Though direct references to Esther's race are only occasional—"A damned, crafty Jezebel of a Jew!"[38]—the intensity of the protracted quarrel seems to embody the irrational hatred in anti-Semitism. Wolfe's own diary references to Mrs. Bernstein as "the Jew"[39] reveal a habit of thought tinged with some racial feeling. As is so often true, Mrs. Bernstein's "race"—the term used by Wolfe—may have been merely a convenient peg on which to hang resentments generated in other ways.

Pertinent to Wolfe's social views is an essay published in the *American Mercury* in 1941 as "The Anatomy of Loneliness," and included in *The Hills Beyond* as "God's Lonely Man." In this essay, Wolfe gives this reason for rejecting Christianity: ". . . though the way and meaning of Christ's life is a far, far better way and meaning than my own, yet I can never make it mine. . . . For I have found the constant, everlasting weather of man's life to be, not love, but loneliness." [40] Aswell says the essay was written as early as 1930, but that it belongs to Wolfe's whole life. It is at variance, however, with the growing concern in his last years for man's relation with society. In May, 1938, he wrote of what he planned to say to the students at Purdue: "I do want to show them if I can that the writer is not a strange and mysterious creature, but very definitely a citizen of mankind, a living, breathing, acting member of the human race, with work to do, a place to fill, a function to perform like everyone." [41] This is very much in the mood of Webber's letter to Foxhall Edwards. Had the mood continued, Wolfe might have added a sequel to "God's Lonely Man."

It is not entirely idle to project the probable course of Wolfe's life had he lived on to 1950 or later. "My longing for America amounts to a constant ache," he wrote from London in 1930.[42] The expansive pleasure he felt as he traveled west in 1935 and again in 1938, together with his hatred of the Nazis, suggests that the war would have focused his energies as nothing in the confused 1920's and 1930's ever did. The exasperation with America's defects would not have disappeared. It would simply have been minimized in favor of more immediate and more serious business. World War II would for Wolfe have been very much the crusade that the Great War of his college days had been. One may imagine him as a wartime journalist, or as a special assistant in government service, trying to keep abreast of global strategy and changes on the home front. With his natural optimism, he would probably have had high hopes for cooperation with the Russians and for the practical success of the United Nations. Almost certainly his racial attitudes would have been modified. Concern with all these things would have removed whatever "Gant-i-ness" remained in 1938. The best of his later work shows a man strong within, but looking outward. In a sense, he was Everyman at thirty-eight, when he died.

CHAPTER 8

The Writer

WOLFE'S PRINCIPAL UTTERANCE on his view of himself as a writer is in *The Story of a Novel.*[1] He begins modestly, mentioning his editor's help and saying that he himself does not yet know how to write a story or a novel. From childhood he thought of writers as a race apart. His father's interest in poetry and his own experience in playwriting at the University of North Carolina and at Harvard are mentioned as influences in making him a writer. Beginning his first book in London, he recalled with special power his youth in America. He tells of the acceptance of his first novel, briefly mentions the pain of revision, and notes with satisfaction that its success gave him a position as writer. His real problem came with the second novel, particularly in the light of vigorous attacks in his home town. He insists that, basically, all creative work is autobiographical, but he concedes that his use of his materials may have been "too naked and direct for the purpose of a work of art."[2]

He then tells of the Guggenheim award and his trip to Europe in 1930. Being already familiar with Europe through his previous trips, he discovered that Europe was not really necessary as a place to work, and that its chief value was to evoke memories of America. Thus he saw his materials in so new a way that the difficulty of organizing them was intensified. He wrote not in terms of narrative structure, but in terms of realizing the vast and varied materials of his experience. The central idea or purpose remained the same: ". . . the deepest search in life, it seemed to me, the thing that in one way or another was central to all living was man's search to find a father, not merely the father of his flesh, not merely the lost father of his youth, but the image of a strength and wisdom external to his need and superior to his hunger, to which the belief and power of his own life could be united."[3]

In his ledgers he explored his experience for some two years and a half, putting down quantities of information about rooms and houses he had lived in and cities and countries he had visited. Returning from Europe to New York in 1931, Wolfe tells of his struggle to organize his second novel. One of the baffling difficulties was his sense of time:

> The first and most obvious was an element of actual present time, an element which carried the narrative forward, which represented characters and events as living in the present and moving forward into an immediate future. The second time element was of past time, one which represented these same characters as acting and as being acted upon by all the accumulated impact of man's experience so that each moment of their lives was conditioned not only by what they experienced in that moment, but by all that they had experienced up to that moment. In addition to these two time elements, there was a third which I conceived as being time immutable, the time of rivers, mountains, oceans, and the earth; a kind of eternal and unchanging universe of time against which would be projected the transience of man's life, the bitter briefness of his day.[4]

Despite the obstacles presented by this concept of time and by the vastness of his material, he persisted for some time in thinking of his work as a single book, to be entitled *The October Fair*. In his struggle to bring it to completion, he was sustained by his editor and by the evidence, furnished by the Depression days, of man's capacity to survive. Eventually, in the middle of December, 1933, the editor "calmly informed me that my book was finished." When Wolfe protested that the book would never be done, the editor insisted that he assemble the material he had in proper order. Since the manuscript described "two complete cycles" of events, it was divided into two parts. When the editor was satisfied that the cutting had been done and that the various parts were properly linked together, he sent the manuscript to the printer. Though at the time Wolfe protested, he came to see the editor's decision as one of "complete justice."[5] In the whole laborious process by which *Of Time and the River* was produced Wolfe saw the great difficulty and complexity of the modern American artist's task.

I *The Debt to Perkins*

In the light of *The Story of a Novel*, of Wolfe's dedication of his second novel to Perkins, and of the published correspondence, any estimate of Wolfe as a writer must take into account the editorial help given by Perkins. Yet this can be done only in a general and tentative way, for the documents that survive—even the manuscripts and proofsheets—are but fragmentary suggestions of the hundreds of hours in which the two men worked toward the printed book. Revision of *Look Homeward, Angel* seems to have been relatively simple. Wolfe was so delighted at the acceptance of his manuscript that he was at first willing to agree to almost any change. As previously noted, Perkins has told how he cut some ninety pages at the beginning because they dealt with the boyhood of W. O. Gant, and thus postponed too long the introduction of Eugene, the central character. Another change was to separate two Joycean passages, one dealing with Gant's return to Altamont, the other describing Eugene's return home from school. Three letters from Wolfe to Wheelock (assistant to Perkins) refer to various cuts, but the points raised by the author are all for clarification. The fact that proofs were coming through by midsummer suggests that the revision was not very much greater than would normally occur in a long first novel.[6]

In an article written not long after Wolfe's death, Perkins recalled his impression of the manuscript of *Of Time and the River:* "The book was far from finished. It was in great fragments, and they were not in order. Large parts were missing. It was all disproportioned. Tom, who knew all this, would come in at eight or so, and I would point these things out, part by part. But I could tell Tom nothing, if it were right, that he did not easily see, and perhaps had already seen."[7]

The opening scene of the novel, the sequence with the family as they wait for the train that is to take Eugene north, Perkins cut from thirty thousand words to ten thousand words. Editor and author agreed that the deleted passages were well written but that the episode was disproportionately long.[8] The death of Gant, previously deleted from *Look Homeward, Angel,* was not only introduced in the second novel, but, Perkins thought, unreasonably expanded by the emphasis upon Eugene's sister.

When Wolfe had finished the episode, nearly a hundred pages, Perkins admitted that he had been wrong.[9] He considered the death of Gant one of the great episodes of the book. Wolfe himself speaks of deleting an episode of eighty thousand words devoted to four people talking. He also tells of reducing many chapters from fifty thousand words to ten thousand words, and once or twice of cutting more than the editor was willing to allow.[10]

An important idea for which Perkins seems to have been responsible is the ending of the book with Eugene's meeting with Esther. Perkins says: "What seemed to me the very hardest part was that about his association with Esther. This never seemed right, and I dreaded the struggle we would have over it. But then it occurred to me that we might end the book with the first meeting with Esther, in France." [11] When *Of Time and the River* was finally sent to the printer, Wolfe felt that at least a dozen chapters should still be added. It seems likely that these chapters would have extended the association with Esther. Perkins persuaded him to let the book stand as it was. The affair with Esther was thus postponed to the posthumous books.

The process by which these and other unrecorded revisions were worked out was long and painful. In February, 1934, the two men were having daily sessions after business hours, first in the late afternoon and then in the evening. In June, Perkins wrote to Hemingway: ". . . Tom does actual writing at times, and does it well, where pieces have to be joined up. We are organizing the book. That is the best part of the work we are doing. It will be pretty well integrated in the end, and vastly more effectively arranged. The fact is, Tom could do the work, but his impulse is all away from the hard detailed revision. He is mighty ingenious at times, when it comes to the organization of material. The scheme is pretty clear in his own head, but he shrinks from the sacrifices, which are really cruel often." [12]

Perkins speaks of these daily conferences with Wolfe as "the most difficult work" he ever engaged in, and once at least Wolfe put their relationship most unfairly. Regarding a particular cut, he asked, "Well, then, will you take the responsibility?" Perkins replied, "I have simply got to take the responsibility. And what's more, I will be blamed, either way." [13] But there were lighter moments. Once Wolfe looked over at the coat rack, where a rattlesnake skin hung, the recent gift of Marjorie Kinnan

Rawlings: "Aha," said Tom, "the portrait of an editor." [14] Wolfe writes of the "fascinating work" with scissors and paste and copies of *Scribner's Magazine* (perhaps containing the Bascom Hawke story) which he and Perkins are doing. And he cheerfully announces in a letter to a friend on July 8, 1934: "Perkins and I finished getting the manuscript ready for the printer last night." Only a few days later he mentions that Perkins "has already got together the material for a long book of stories." Though the errors in *Of Time and the River* made Wolfe write unhappily from England in March, 1935, that "we should have waited six months longer," in September he was ready to work on the same basis again. He asks Perkins, "What are we to work on next—'The October Fair,' the Pentland book, 'The Book of the Night,' short stories—or what?" [15]

On the evidence available, it is difficult not to accept Perkins' flat statement: "There never was any cutting that Tom did not agree to." [16] That Perkins was practical and resourceful in dealing with a difficult author is obvious. In the first two novels and in the short stories published during Wolfe's life there must be many details that should be credited to Perkins. Yet this would be true of many authors if the full story of the editing of their works were recorded. Wolfe's relation with Perkins is an extreme case of editorial assistance, injudiciously publicized by Wolfe himself, and naturally exaggerated in the subsequent bitter quarrel with Scribner's. In 1943 Perkins wrote to an unidentified correspondent, objecting to what he considered a libelous misrepresentation of his assistance to Wolfe. He concluded: "Editors aren't much, and can't be. They can only help a writer realize himself, and they can ruin him if he's pliable, as Tom was not." It is important to add that Wolfe quite evidently expected to work with Aswell as he had with Perkins. Despite his protest in a letter to Aswell that he does not "need" that kind of help, he also speaks of "the magnitude of the task before us." [17]

Wolfe's own capacity for revision has probably been underestimated. His initial written proposal for the revision of *Look Homeward, Angel* is businesslike.[18] His queries to Wheelock on the proofs of this first novel are sensible and responsible. So are his list of errors in *Of Time and the River* and his queries on the galley proofs of *From Death to Morning*.[19] A letter from Perkins to Frere (Wolfe's English publisher) implies that Wolfe's failure to read proofs for *Of Time and the River* was not typical. In Wolfe's absence, Perkins says he has corrected proofs on the short stories "so far as I dared." [20] The most important direct statement regarding Wolfe's own capacity to revise is in Aswell's account of his editing of Wolfe's manuscript:

> . . . Tom had become a tireless reviser and rewriter. Whether this was true of him in his younger days I cannot say, but it was certainly true of him later. Much as he had told me and shown me of what he had been doing in those last years, I was not quite prepared to discover, when I came to deal with the whole manuscript, how vitally essential rewriting had become to his whole method. Far more often than not I found that there would be at least two different versions of the same episode, and sometimes there were as many as four or five versions. There would be a first draft hastily sketched out, then later drafts that filled in the details, and it was fascinating to see how the thing had changed and grown under his hand. When he was dissatisfied with a scene or character he would not, as a rule, simply revise his draft and get it recopied: he would put it aside and rewrite it some different way from start to finish.[21]

II *Literary Influences*

Wolfe himself emphasizes the influence of James Joyce on his development as a writer. In *The Story of a Novel* he says that, like Joyce, he wrote about things he had known or experienced; unlike Joyce, he felt he had no great literary experience.[22] It should be remembered that Joyce was forty when he published *Ulysses* in 1922; Wolfe, only twenty-nine when he published *Look Homeward, Angel.* Twice Wolfe saw Joyce—in 1926 and 1928—but was too much in awe of him to approach him. In 1930 he wrote his English publisher that he had read Joyce's works "very assiduously and if some flavor of them has crept into my book I can not deny it. . . ." In 1932 he mentions Joyce as justification for his own so-called autobiographical way of writing. Joyce's "attempt to approach and penetrate reality" was so successful that he created "what is almost another dimension of reality."[23] Nevertheless, Wolfe says in *The Story of a Novel* that despite the influence of Joyce, *Look Homeward, Angel* was his own book: "the powerful energy and fire of my own youth played over and, I think, possessed it all."

How important was Joyce's influence on Wolfe? Various critics have alluded to Wolfe's Joycean use of multiple scenes—discontinuous comments from various points of view—but Nathan L. Rothman has made a careful study of the general question.[24] He points out many Joycean parallels to phrases and stream-of-consciousness passages in *Look Homeward, Angel,* particularly in the handling of Gant and Eugene. Burlesques such as Eugene's daydreams over cheap fiction, the trick of satiric comment through literary quotation, and the lyrical refrains are other examples of Joycean technique. The idea of the search for a father, and the poetic sense of time are concepts found in both authors. Yet Mr. Rothman is satisfied that Wolfe's use of Joyce was creative rather than parrot-like. Moreover, after Wolfe's first novel the Joycean influence is slight. Accepting Mr. Rothman's analysis as sound, one may still doubt whether Joyce's influence was of major importance. Wolfe's impulse to write came before he had read Joyce. In the other writers of his time there was much to emulate in his own individual fashion. Joyce, however, must certainly have increased Wolfe's conviction that autobiography was a powerful mode of writing, and one psychologically appealing to him—especially when he turned from the stage in 1926. Joyce also may have encouraged Wolfe to see the artist as pitted against a coarse, hostile environment. Wolfe's emphasis on lust in his first novel—it is much diminished in his later ones—may owe something to Irish example. Whatever the precise indebtedness, the relative clarity of Wolfe's novel is a testimony to his independence in controlling the influence of a writer who has contributed more than anyone else to making incoherence fashionable.

Other literary influences are indefinite. Wolfe read widely up through the Harvard period, and because of his retentive memory this early reading had lasting importance. Soon after he went to New York, his concentration on his own writing seems to have limited his reading, as he admitted at Purdue in 1938.[25] There are comparatively few literary references to new books in his letters, and he had not a scholar's taste for rereading, collecting, or keeping up with new material on old favorites. Wolfe's friend Volkening describes Wolfe's bookshelf in the late 1920's, when he was at work on *Look Homeward, Angel.*

"Look," he would say, pointing to a shelf of books above his
working table, "there in one small row is much of the best that
has ever been written, and half of those they've [his colleagues]
never really read." And there were Burton's *Anatomy of Melan-
choly,* Melville's *Moby Dick,* Dostoevski's *Brothers Karamazov,*
Heine, Shakespeare, Donne, Goethe, Homer, Plato, Euripides,
Walt Whitman, Joyce's *Ulysses* (freely marked-up), the Bible,
Swift, Boswell's *Johnson,* Voltaire's *Candide,* Milton, Coleridge
(including the essays), Herrick, De Quincey, Anderson's *Wines-
burg, Ohio,* DeFoe's *Moll Flanders,* Bennett's *Old Wives' Tale,*
Fielding's *Tom Jones,* and a few others which I have forgotten.[26]

In a letter in 1932 Wolfe repeated many of these writers and
titles as "books I like best," and added *War and Peace* and the
plays of Molière. For Lewis Gannett's syndicated column he
specified Wyatt, Blake, Wordsworth, Keats, and Robert Brown-
ing, along with previously mentioned favorites.[27] On the whole,
Wolfe's list of favorite authors and books is conventional, even
professorial.

Among older authors, Coleridge seems to have influenced
Wolfe most directly. Coleridge's infinite curiosity and his capacity to perceive analogies and relationships naturally evoked
Wolfe's admiration. Presented in terms of Lowes's approach,
Coleridge had relevance to the problems of a creative writer.
Wolfe's term paper in Lowes's course was a study of the supernatural in Coleridge and Irving. In a letter of 1932 Wolfe says
that "The Ancient Mariner" was not an escape from reality. He
mentions Lowes's study with great respect, and sees a similarity
between Coleridge's methods and his own use of diverse materials to shape *Look Homeward, Angel.*[28]

Of older American writers, Wolfe alludes to Emerson and
Henry Adams. Melville he says he never read until 1930, and
then in order to find out who it was reviewers were comparing
him to.[29] Whitman he likewise professed ignorance of before
publication of *Look Homeward, Angel.*[30] As early as 1922, however, Wolfe mentions reading Whitman, and at New York
University one of his classroom remarks was, "That has the
Whitman sweep and breadth." Much later he wrote Sherwood
Anderson that he thought of him with Whitman and Twain as
"men who had seen America with a poet's vision." Oddly, this
seems to be almost his only allusion to Twain.[31]

Wolfe's attitude toward writers of his own day was greatly

influenced by his fierce hatred of literary cliques: "The dear Moderns, you will find, are cut from the same cloth and pattern all over the world.—Unplatitudinously they utter platitudes, with complete unoriginality they are original. Whenever they say something new you wonder where you heard it before, you believe you have not heard it before, you are sure you have heard it forever, you are tired of it before it is uttered, the stink of a horrible weariness is on it, it is like the smell of the subway after rush hours. . . . they hate life, but they won't die." [32]

So anxious was Wolfe to avoid literary fashion that in 1922 he considered J. M. Barrie "the most significant dramatist in the English-speaking world today." Shaw, unfortunately, spent his great powers on the thesis play. Wolfe was apprehensive about Eugene O'Neill because he seemed to be "looking backward." In the letter giving these opinions, he mentioned that he had been reading in the same weekend—seemingly with equal enthusiasm—Wells's *The Undying Fire* (a retelling of the Job story), some of Emerson's essays, Leslie Stephen's life of Pope, and Swift's *Tale of a Tub*. "Oh for a Swift to flay the free versists," he exclaimed.[33] Later, he refers to "trash by Wilder," to *Gone With the Wind* as "that immortal piece of bilge," and to Robert Nathan with condescension.[34] His only comment on Hemingway is irritation in 1935 at Hemingway's facetious suggestion that suffering in Siberia might help Wolfe achieve greater control.[35] About the same period he agrees with Stark Young that what Faulkner writes "is not like the South, but that yet the South is *in* his books, and in the spirit that creates them." [36] T. S. Eliot he associates with "the futility boys and girls." [37] There are admiring references to Max Beerbohm, Ford Madox Ford, Aldous Huxley, Somerset Maugham, and Hugh Walpole. Wolfe was not particularly pleased by his first sampling of D. H. Lawrence in 1930.[38] Of European writers he read with some enthusiasm Thomas Mann, Wasserman, Anatole France, and Proust.

Strangely, Wolfe's closest association with a writer of his own generation was with Scott Fitzgerald. Both were Scribner's authors, and at the suggestion of Perkins, Fitzgerald looked Wolfe up in Paris in 1930. They liked each other but differed at once. Wolfe reported to Perkins: "I said we were a homesick people, and belonged to the earth and land we came from as much or more as any country I knew about—he said we were not, that we were not a country, that he had no feeling for the land he came from." [39]

Despite this difference, Fitzgerald telegraphed in August that he had read *Look Homeward, Angel* in twenty consecutive hours and was "enormously moved and grateful." Wolfe's pleasure in this praise was somewhat dampened a month later when Fitzgerald begged Wolfe for an introduction to a wealthy female acquaintance then in Paris. Writing to his friend Volkening, Wolfe is full of contempt for "this poet of the passions," "the great analyst of the soul," "this great philosopher," who assured him that every writer is a social climber.[40] In 1936 Fitzgerald was in Asheville, in very bad shape. Wolfe, writing to Hamilton Basso, another North Carolina writer, spoke sympathetically of Fitzgerald's plight, but he was uncertain how he could help him. Thinking about Fitzgerald's career, he said that *Tender is the Night* had never been done justice; "I admit the deficiencies and weaknesses in the book, but I still think that he went deeper in the book and did better writing in it than in any of his previous books." [41]

This is the background for the famous exchange of letters in 1937. Fitzgerald wrote to Wolfe from Hollywood expressing great admiration for Wolfe's talent, but urging him to follow the example of Flaubert rather than that of Zola by giving more attention to selection and form. Wolfe's reply fills nearly four large pages of print. He is good-humored, but he vigorously asserts his own view of writing:

> You say that "Madame Bovary" becomes eternal while Zola already rocks with age. Well this may be true—but if it is true isn't it true because "Madame Bovary" may be a great book and those that Zola wrote may not be great ones? Wouldn't it also be true to say that "Don Quixote," or "Pickwick" or "Tristram Shandy" "becomes eternal" while already Mr. Galsworthy "rocks with age"? . . . Now you have your way of doing something and I have mine; there are a lot of ways, but you are honestly mistaken in thinking that there is a "way."
>
> I suppose I would agree with you in what you say about "the novel of selected incidents" so far as it means anything. I say so far as it means anything because every novel, of course, is a novel of selected incidents. There are no novels of unselected incidents. You couldn't write about the inside of a telephone

booth without selecting. . . . You say that the great writer like Flaubert has consciously left out the stuff that Bill or Joe will come along presently and put in. Well, don't forget, Scott, that a great writer is not only a leaver-outer but also a putter-inner, and that Shakespeare and Cervantes and Dostoievsky were great putter-inners—greater putter-inners, in fact, than taker-outers—and will be remembered for what they put in—remembered, I venture to say, as long as Monsieur Flaubert will be remembered for what he left out.[42]

In literary taste as in personal associations, the key word for Wolfe was independence. He is not the kind of author to be very much explained in terms of his sources. He was widely read, even bookish, as a very young man. In maturity he was not bookish. He valued books for their capacity to energize his own vision of experience. Therefore he could use so great a writer as Joyce without slavishly imitating him. In Coleridge he caught the creative ideas but bypassed the pedantry. Though he and Fitzgerald were poles apart in temperament, he could see Fitzgerald's excellence. But Wolfe went his own way.

III *Poetry and Humor*

Wolfe's way was the way of a poet and a humorist. In theory, poetry and humor should go together, since both involve imagination. In practice, the two often seem opposites. So rigid is the conventional separation, that Wolfe's immediate reputation for writing "poetic" prose obscured his success as a humorist. When Burton Rascoe reviewed *Of Time and the River,* he objected that Wolfe "has no evident sense of humor; nor any true sense of comedy." Wolfe's comment to Perkins should be better known: "The Rascoes say he has no sense of humor—this, to the man who created old Gant, wrote the lunch room scenes in the *Angel,* Bascom Hawke in the *River, The Web of Earth,* Oswald Ten Eyck, the Countess, the Englishmen at the inn and all the others."[43]

To this brief catalogue we may add from the posthumous volumes: the Jerry Alsop scenes and the chapters on Esther's girlhood in *The Web and the Rock;* Mr. Katamoto, the satire of "The Party at Jack's," "The Universe of Daisy Purvis," Mr. Lloyd McHarg, and the portrait of Foxhall Edwards from *You*

Can't Go Home Again; and the early chapters about the Joyners in "The Hills Beyond." These humorous scenes—and those previously mentioned in the discussion of *Look Homeward, Angel*—stand up very well indeed. They have a fresh vitality because they come in a context of deeply felt experience. They are not stereotyped gags, such as the professional humorist is forced to resort to. They derive from a sense of character. What other American writer—including Twain himself—has given us so varied a gallery of humorous characters, so great a range of humorous tone?

Humor—sometimes boisterous, sometimes delicately restrained—is one evidence of Wolfe's strong natural feeling. The elaboration of serious emotion is another. Is this emotional elaboration, as De Voto insisted, placental material that should have been excised? Is it "mere" rhetoric, pounding in with insistent rhythm a generalized emotion? Or does Wolfe really achieve genuine poetry through imaginative insight? The answer to all three questions is yes, depending on the passage one picks. Chapter XCVII of *Of Time and the River* might well illustrate the placental material. It is a twelve-page interlude in Eugene's stay in Tours, which dilates upon the "incomparable substance of America" as Eugene thinks about it in a foreign land. Following a generalized contrast of the energy of America with the settled softness—"the wool-soft air"—of Europe, are the dialogues which point up the shallow cynicism of American expatriates in Paris and the uncomprehending superiority of the Oxonian's view of America. Then come three pages evoking America through names of battles, of states, of Indian tribes, of railroads, and of rivers. These are transcriptions from Wolfe's ledgers of Amount and Number. There is a certain interest in all this, but the whole chapter could be omitted without damage to the narrative or to one's understanding of Eugene, for the idea of the homeland is registered elsewhere. Such a chapter might be characterized as "placental," though the term is unnecessarily derogatory.

In this same chapter a paragraph may be cited as an example of rhetoric; it follows a long list of Indian tribes: "Of wandering forever, and the earth again: in red-oak thickets, at the break of day, long hunters lay for bear. The arrows rattle in the laurel leaves, and the elmroots thread the bones of buried lovers. There have been war-cries on the Western trails, and on the plains the gunstock rusts upon a handful of bleached bones. The barren earth? Was no love living in the wilderness?" [44] The words here are general and external. The writer attempts to subdue the reader by rattling consonants instead of winning him with information and insight.

The concluding paragraph of the chapter is another example of rhetoric, which tries to subdue the reader by the insistent beat of parallel phrases: "We are the sons of our father, whose face we have never seen, we are the sons of our father, whose voice we have never heard, we are the sons of our father, to whom we have cried for strength and comfort in our agony, we are the sons of our father, whose life like ours was lived in solitude and in the wilderness, we are the sons of our father, to whom only can we speak out the strange, dark burden of our heart and spirit, we are the sons of our father, and we shall follow the print of his foot forever." [45]

The claim that Wolfe rose above such rhetorical effects to achieve true poetry has been most vigorously made by John Hall Wheelock, Perkins' assistant at Scribner's, and himself a poet of reputation. The year following Wolfe's death, Wheelock published a volume called *The Face of a Nation* composed of poetical passages selected from the Gant novels, the stories in *From Death to Morning*, and from *The Story of a Novel*. Wheelock concludes his brief introduction: "It is not possible to read the selections here included without coming to a fresh realization of the genius of Thomas Wolfe. The essential Thomas Wolfe is here, and he is a poet. In these pages, Tom's wish to be a poet rather than anything else in the world is gloriously fulfilled." [46]

Of the sixty or more passages that support this claim, most readers will find a good many that bear frequent rereading, the best test of poetic quality. In the first reading of a poem, and even more in the first reading of a novel, one seeks a sense of the whole. If the poem—or novel—is worth rereading, it is through its capacity to enrich the reader's experience as he more fully assimilates the detail contributing to the total effect. Readers who know Wolfe well may find in Wheelock's volume that strange combination of novelty and familiarity when they come upon this detached paragraph of Eugene's observation:

"He caught and fixed the instant. A telegraph messenger wheeled vigorously in from the avenue with pumping feet, curved widely into the alley at his right, jerking his wheel up sharply as he took the curb, and coasted down to the delivery boy's entrance. And post o'er land and ocean without rest. Milton, thou should'st be living at this hour." [47] The precision of the words in this paragraph—"pumping," "curved widely," "jerking his wheel up sharply"—is an abstracting of pure form from a commonplace observation. At the end of the paragraph the quotations from Milton's sonnet on his blindness and from Wordsworth's tribute to Milton are a whimsical juxtaposition, seemingly satiric, but then in a sense appropriate. The imaginative insight of this passage goes far beyond rhetoric.

From *Of Time and the River* the description of October in Chapter XXXIX is as superfluous to the narrative as Chapter XCVII, discussed above. October, however, is evoked by sharply phrased detail, the kind of detail that creates inner realization. Eugene thinks of burning leaves:

> "There is a smell of burning in small towns in afternoon, and men with buckles on their arms are raking leaves in yards as boys come by with straps slung back across their shoulders. The oak leaves, big and brown, are bedded deep in yard and gutter: they make deep wadings to the knee for children in the streets. The fire will snap and crackle like a whip, sharp acrid smoke will sting the eyes, in mown fields the little vipers of the flame eat past the black coarse edges of burned stubble like a line of locusts. Fire drives a thorn of memory in the heart." [48]

In 1954, John S. Barnes edited a volume called *A Stone, A Leaf, A Door,* arranging prose passages on the page as free verse. In the "Foreword," Louis Untermeyer said: "In no prose and only in a small body of verse has there been expressed a greater sense of American life: its range and richness, its vast pride and intemperate gusto, its unhappy adolescent yearnings and insatiable appetite." [49]

Though this second collection includes fewer panoramic passages than the earlier collection, the device of arranging Wolfe's words as free verse does accentuate his gift for phrasing and underlines his cadences. From Chapter 28 of *The Web and the Rock,* part of George Webber's magic year with Esther, come these lines:

SPRING

Autumn was kind to them,
Winter was long to them—
But in April, late April,
All the gold sang.

Spring came that year like magic,
Like music, and like song.
One day its breath was in the air,
A haunting premonition of its spirit
Filled the hearts of men
With its transforming loveliness,
Working its sudden and incredible sorcery
Upon grey streets, grey pavements,
And on grey faceless tides of manswarm ciphers. . . .[50]

Unusual phrases, too, stand out on the page: the earth, "most weary unbright cinder," "the little ticking moments of strange time," the "bridge whose winglike sweep," "the bridgeless instancy of dreams," "the clean, hard rattle of raked gravel," "the timeless, yearless sea." [51] Such phrases are not frequent enough, but they do lighten the effect of rhetorical rhythms.

Writing in 1933 to a friend who asked for criticism of one of his own poems, Wolfe commented: "It is true I have read and known a great deal of poetry but to speak of it critically and academically to scan its lines has always been too much even for my own audacity. . . . I can never endure to hear a poem read . . . nor did I ever feel competent to express honest judgment of any poem, particularly of any poem that was any good after a first reading." [52] Wolfe's intuitive response to poetry suggests that his own writing was usually impetuous and unconsidered.

In contrast to this impression, Aswell quotes a passage from *You Can't Go Home Again* as more accurately describing Wolfe's own method:

> In his effort to explore his experience, to extract the whole, essential truth of it, and to find a way to write about it, he sought to recapture every particle of the life he knew down to its minutest details. He spent weeks and months trying to put down on paper the exactitudes of countless fragments—what he called, "the dry, caked colors of America"—how the entrance to a subway looked, the design and webbing of the elevated structure, the look and feel of an iron rail, the particular shade of rusty green with which so many things are painted in America.[53]

To the extent that Wolfe's writing is memorable—and these collections of poetic passages are evidence that it is memorable—Wolfe's sense of form was successful. Even passages that are faulty, Aswell insists, are not "formless":

> His inner eye was fixed upon the form of every line he wrote. If you wish to test this statement, try the experiment of cutting one of his sentences. Pick, if you like, some long-winded sentence that is repetitive and full of adjectives. Strike out everything you think redundant and superfluous, and then read aloud what you have left, which represents your improvement on Wolfe. If you have an ear for music, ten to one it will set your teeth on edge. By just a little injudicious tampering, those sonorous sentences which have the majestic swing and roll of mighty music can be reduced to limping dissonance.[54]

Thus, Aswell argues, much of Wolfe's verbosity can be accounted for by his effort to secure a rhythmical—a formal—effect.

IV Ideas

Grant that Wolfe had a talent for language, that he could powerfully evoke his own intense youthful experience, that he could suggest, like Whitman, the vast panorama of America. Did he achieve anything more memorable than fragments? Does his work add up to any substantial meaning? *Look Homeward, Angel*, it is generally agreed, is Wolfe's most satisfactory book. It does tell a reasonably unified story of how a sensitive and talented youth escapes from a well-meaning but coarse-grained family. There is youthful illusion, but there is humor and tragedy; and in Eugene's temperament there is the poetic response that makes the book transcend its own realistic elements.

It is interesting to contrast Wolfe's first novel with Sinclair Lewis' *Arrowsmith*, published in 1925 when Lewis, at forty, was at the height of his powers. In less than five hundred pages Martin Arrowsmith is taken through college, country practice as a doctor, public health service, and scientific research in a great medical center. The novel moves rapidly from Martin's youth to middle-aged disillusion, with many of Lewis' most memorable scenes and characters. Who can forget Gottlieb, the great research professor, or Pickerbaugh, the public health charlatan?

To Martin's boyhood and college years Lewis devotes little more than a hundred pages.

Look Homeward, Angel devotes all six hundred of its pages to Eugene's youth. Lewis compresses by never going within. Wolfe expands by doing exactly that. Lewis' account is the way a middle-aged man would remember it; Wolfe's, the way a boy lived it. Moreover, Martin Arrowsmith is deliberately made sensible and shrewd, while Eugene is visionary, still uncommitted at the end of college. For many readers, Eugene is a more interesting character than Martin Arrowsmith, and deserves the fuller treatment he gets. A journalistic treatment is suitable for Arrowsmith. It is the "poetry"—the poetic dimension—of *Look Homeward, Angel* that makes the difference.

Of Time and the River, as has been said, is all middle; but there is some movement toward Eugene's realization of himself and his realization of America from the perspective of Europe. The posthumous novels suggest how Eugene Gant might have developed in *The October Fair* to a convincing maturity. Perkins believed that ". . . it was a horrible crime that he should have departed from his inevitable scheme by trying to change his mother into an aunt, and himself, who had been Eugene, into George Webber. He should never have violated his own plan." [55]

Despite the distinctions Wolfe tried to establish between Eugene Gant and George Webber, most readers of the four novels will take the Webber novels as an extension of the Gant story under the Webber name. When this is done, a sense of wholeness does emerge. Eugene Gant–George Webber does slowly mature, as Philip does in *Of Human Bondage;* and, even more important, his view of himself is altered by the social pressures of his time. The economic problems rouse his social conscience, as in "The Party at Jack's"; and the German tyranny is exposed as an inescapable threat. The world is moving, and Eugene Gant–George Webber, realizing that fame and love are not enough, is ready to move with it.

What other American writer has told so much of the essential story of America from 1900 to 1938? Without allying himself with "the lost generation" and without becoming a propagandist, Wolfe wrote vigorous, shrewd satire; but he also expressed an abiding faith in his own country and a generous appreciation of Europe's best culture. Whatever one's personal preference may be as between Wolfe and his chief American contemporaries—

Anderson, Dos Passos, Dreiser, Faulkner, Fitzgerald, Hemingway, Lewis, O'Neill, Steinbeck—Wolfe's career and achievement
are unique and substantial.

Granting then, an approximate unity in the Gant–Webber
chronicle as it stands, does Wolfe achieve any inner meaning to
transcend the external events? Is a vital symbolism involved?
To these queries, the answer is less clear. In *Look Homeward,
Angel* he had begun with "a stone, a leaf, a door," which are
"the lost lane-end into heaven." Used as a refrain, these phrases
become symbols of Eugene's search.[56] In *Of Time and the River*,
as has been pointed out, the subtitles by which Wolfe strove to
unify his story with traditional myths are often ornamental
rather than structural, and are sometimes awkwardly applied.
That Wolfe gave much thought to the myths as analogues for
his own story is evident from the letters of 1930. From his
reflection on them he derived his concept of the male and female
principles, implicit in *Look Homeward, Angel* but now consciously used. Probably more important, the parallels between
the myths and his own experiences contributed something to
his concepts of time, already quoted from *The Story of a Novel*:
present time, past time (available through memory), and abso-
lute time as represented by "rivers, mountains, oceans, and the
earth." This multiple concept of time could readily be associated
with another concept, the search for a father: "not merely the
father of his flesh, not merely the lost father of his youth, but
the image of a strength and wisdom external to his need and
superior to his hunger. . . ."[57] Mastery of time, then, provides
the necessary wisdom.

It cannot be argued that these ideas were systematically
carried over into his books. Yet there is an inner consistency.
The search for a father (wisdom) begun in *Look Homeward,
Angel* is naturally carried forward in *Of Time and the River*,
and there it is deepened by the multiple sense of time and the
male principle of wandering. *The Web and the Rock* contrasts
growth with fixity, the artist and the city. In the love affair and
quarrel with Esther, the conflict of the male and female principles is represented. The burning memory of Esther, even while
Eugene tries to forget her, shows the conflict between present
and past. In *You Can't Go Home Again*, home is the past, and
the title is a kind of ultimate wisdom. Webber's final letter to
Fox concedes that fixity, like Ecclesiastes, has a basic truth.

But, says Webber, we must deny it! "The essence of Time is Flow, not Fix." [58] Stated in this way, there is a degree of relationship—and very little inconsistency—in the symbolic bearings of the four novels. In terms of time, wisdom is possible and faith is not a mirage.

A great deal has been said by various critics about Wolfe's "search for a father," and his "search for a mother." Mrs. Roberts and Mrs. Bernstein were "mother-substitutes"; Baker and Perkins were "father-substitutes." Vardis Fisher even says that Perkins was a "mother-substitute." [59] Wolfe, of course, encouraged this by passages in his fiction and in *The Story of a Novel*. Wolfe's addition of the phrase "the image of a strength and wisdom external to his need and superior to his hunger" is often overlooked. The phrase "search for the father" alone, or even more "father-substitute," has the effect of reducing a complex matter to a psychological stereotype. It blurs the uniqueness of the relationships that existed between Wolfe and Baker, and later Perkins. Wolfe nowhere uses the term "mother-substitute," but he does state the female principle this way: "They want love, the earth, a home, fixity." Mrs. Bernstein does not entirely fit this statement, nor is she adequately suggested in the term "mother-substitute." Such terms have their clinical uses, but in the hands of amateur psychologists they confuse more than they illuminate.

What, then, of Wolfe's promise? Aswell says:

> Of one thing we can be sure. If he had lived, his final books would have turned out to be somewhat different from what they are. Many sections of the manuscript which had to be altogether eliminated because they were left unfinished would have been completed and put in their proper place. The gaps would have been filled as he had meant to fill them. The love story would have been recast, along with the other material that had been written earlier. And in the end there might have grown out of the manuscript, not three books, but perhaps four, five, or even six. [60]

One could chiefly hope that "The Hills Beyond," little more than a hundred and fifty pages of the book of this title, would have been greatly expanded. Wolfe had achieved a perspective, and the atmosphere of the next ten years or so would have been favorable to an imaginative recovery of earlier generations of Pentlands and Joyners.

V *Conclusion*

In 1950 Faulkner was asked how he ranked himself in relation to other American writers. He listed five authors in this order: Thomas Wolfe, William Faulkner, John Dos Passos, Ernest Hemingway, and John Steinbeck. His comment on placing Wolfe first was: "He had much courage and wrote as if he didn't have long to live." [61] The high rank assigned to Wolfe has generally been regarded as Faulknerian perversity, and the reason given has seemed inadequate. Not long before this Mark Schorer had written: "The books of Thomas Wolfe were, of course, journals, and the primary role of his publisher in transforming these journals into the semblance of novels is notorious. For the crucial act of the artist, the unique act which is composition, a sympathetic editorial blue pencil and scissors were substituted. . . . his books are without interest as novels." [62] In this book such extremes of judgment have been rejected.

The recognition of Wolfe's courage, great as it was, will not cancel the defects in his work, nor bring the fragments of "the Book" into a completed whole. At the same time it is senseless to talk of Wolfe's novels and stories as "journals," when so many episodes are triumphs of form controlled by recognizable artistic intention; and there is no reasonable basis for saying that the role of Wolfe's publishers was "primary." Wolfe's success with shorter episodes, however, does not warrant the easy conclusion that he should have confined himself to stories of ten thousand words. The success he had was informed and energized by the great undertaking.

There is in his boundless ambition a youthfulness and an individualism sometimes egocentric and even frantic. Yet Wolfe shows greater awareness of society than has usually been thought. His view of the South, evident in the 47 Workshop plays as well as the fiction, is shrewdly satiric, but never shrill. Coming from the rural South into the urban North, Wolfe saw much that he hated; yet he saw the creative side of the city also, and did not, like the Agrarians, seek to turn the clock back. He relished the American past, but he was not victimized by nostalgia. His response to Europe was appreciative but independent, and his evaluation of the Nazi movement was unequivocal.

As a writer of fiction, Wolfe saw the limitations of the realistic tradition he had inherited. Through rhetoric and imagination he sought to give a larger utterance to man's whole nature. By his concept of search and his concept of multiple time he created a poetic approach to actuality. The Purdue lecture of 1938, much of it parallel to George Webber's letter to Foxhall Edwards in *You Can't Go Home Again,* is not the utterance of a man burned out by his own energy. The *Western Journal,* in hurried, vivid phrases, testifies to his continuing relish for new experience. Legend would have it that Wolfe died from excessive creative activity. The fact is that he died from tuberculosis of the brain.

The twenty-five years since Wolfe's death make his work now seem remote. Never once does his fiction describe an airplane. When he died, World War II and the Space Age were still to come. Most of the stereotypes by which Wolfe is still catalogued—the adolescent, the man demonically possessed, the uncontrolled torrent of words—are relics, too, of the literary wars of the now remote 1930's. Pamela Johnson has characterized recent low estimates of Wolfe as part of the inevitable "kicking season" which overtakes all literary reputations. [63] Perhaps the "kicking season" is about over. Perhaps new readers will see Wolfe with fresh eyes and find in him the durable stuff of literature.

An English critic has said: "I have yet to meet a person born into any kind of Establishment who understood Wolfe; I have yet to meet a provincial who has cracked open a big city who does not acknowledge that Wolfe expressed his own struggle for escape into larger experience." [64] The world is full of provincials. If they discover Wolfe, he will never lack an audience. If there is—or is to be—an American Establishment, it will need the understanding of youth and provincialism which Wolfe provides. In curious ways unanticipated by Establishments, provincialism often provides the key to universal insights.

Notes and References

Chapter One

1. *Look, Homeward, Angel* (New York, 1929), p. 557.
2. *Thomas Wolfe's Letters to His Mother Julia Elizabeth Wolfe,* ed. John Skally Terry (New York, 1943), pp. 41-42. Hereafter referred to as *Letters to Mother.*
3. *Letters to Mother,* pp. 46-47.
4. These facts are largely drawn from Hayden Norwood, *The Marble Man's Wife* (New York, 1947). See especially pp. 136, 165, 183.
5. Mabel Wolfe Wheaton with Legette Blythe, *Thomas Wolfe and His Family* (New York, 1961), p. 235.
6. *The Letters of Thomas Wolfe,* ed. Elizabeth Nowell (New York, 1956), p. 2. Hereafter referred to as *Letters.*
7. *Letters,* p. 123.
8. *Letters,* p. 193.
9. Robert Coleman Gibbs, "Thomas Wolfe's Four Years at Chapel Hill: A Study of Biographical Source Material," M.A. thesis, University of North Carolina, 1958, pp. 41, 49.
10. *Letters,* p. 66. Compare Elizabeth Nowell's *Thomas Wolfe: A Biography* (New York, 1960), pp. 35-36. Hereafter referred to as *Thomas Wolfe.*
11. *Letters to Mother,* p. 144.
12. *Letters,* p. 6.
13. These contributions to *The Carolina Magazine* appeared as follows: "A Field in Flanders," November, 1917, p. 77; "To France," December, 1917, p. 165; "The Challenge," March, 1918, pp. 223-24; "A Cullenden of Virginia," March, 1918, pp. 234-39; "To Rupert Brooke," May, 1918, pp. 314-15; "The Drammer," April, 1919, pp. 72-74; "An Appreciation," May, 1919, p. 79; "Russian Folk Song," June, 1919, p. 191.
14. Pp. 6, 13, of the pamphlet publication of the essay, Chapel Hill, 1919.
15. *Thomas Wolfe,* pp. 37-38.
16. Comment in Harvard Appointment Office dossier, quoted in full in Thomas Clark Pollock and Oscar Cargill, *Thomas Wolfe and Washington Square* (New York, 1945), pp. 15-17.
17. Quoted in Ann Preston Bridgers, "Thomas Wolfe, Legends of a Man's Hunger in his Youth," *The Saturday Review of Literature,* April, 6, 1935, p. 599.

18. Wisner Payne Kinne, *George Pierce Baker and the American Theatre* (Harvard University Press, 1954), p. 213.

19. *Letters,* p. 52n.

20. *The Correspondence of Thomas Wolfe and Homer Andrew Watt,* ed. Oscar Cargill and Thomas Clark Pollock (New York, 1954), pp. 3-8.

21. *Letters to Mother,* p. 122.

Chapter Two

1. Sam Selden and Mary Tom Sphangos, *Frederick Henry Koch: Pioneer Playmaker* (Chapel Hill, 1954).

2. "The Return of Buck Gavin," *Carolina Folk Plays,* Second Series, ed. F. H. Koch (New York, 1924), pp. 31-44. Reprinted in *Carolina Folk Plays,* ed. F. H. Koch (New York, 1941), pp. 113-23; and in *North Carolina Drama,* ed. Richard Walser (Richmond, Va., 1956), pp. 93-102.

"The Third Night," *Carolina Playbook* (September, 1938), pp. 70-75. Reprinted, *Carolina Folk Plays* (New York, 1941), pp. 125-43.

"Deferred Payment," *Carolina Magazine,* June, 1919, pp. 139-53.

"Concerning Honest Bob," *Carolina Magazine,* May, 1920, pp. 251-61.

3. *Letters,* p. 384.

4. See Kinne's biography of Baker, cited in Chapter I.

5. *Letters to Mother,* p. 13.

6. "Thomas Wolfe as a Dramatist," New York *Post,* September 21, 1938. Reprinted in Brown's volume, *Broadway in Review* (New York, 1940), p. 284. It is sad to report that this line does not appear in the Harvard Dramatic Club manuscript copy of this play.

7. *Letters to Mother.* p. 25.

8. Information in this paragraph is drawn largely from *The History of the Theatre Guild: The First Nineteen Years, 1919-1937,* a pamphlet issued by the Guild. Beginning with 1919-20, Burns Mantle's annual volumes of *Best Plays* give the number of performances.

9. *Mannerhouse* (New York, 1948), p. 182.

10. Information on the Yale production was furnished by Professor Norman Holmes Pearson and the Librarian of the Yale School of Drama. The play was produced May 5, 6, and 7, 1949. The *Yale Daily News* printed discussions of it on May 6 and 7. In 1941 production of *Mannerhouse* was considered at Kenyon; see *Editor to Author: the Letters of Maxwell E. Perkins,* ed. John Hall Wheelock (New York, 1950), p. 187. A German translation, *Herrenhaus,* was successfully performed at Hamburg and elsewhere in Germany in 1953; see Horst Frenz, "A German Home for 'Mannerhouse,'" *Theatre Arts,* XL (August, 1956), 62-63, 95.

11. "Welcome to Our City," *Esquire*, XLVIII (October, 1957), 58-83. This play has never been published in book form.

12. *Letters to Mother*, p. 48.

13. In the Wolfe MSS at the University of North Carolina.

14. *Our American Theatre* (New York, 1923), p. 128.

15. *Thomas Wolfe*, p. 102. For a somewhat less favorable view of Wolfe's dramatic experiments, see chapters 3, 5, 6, 8 of Richard S. Kennedy's *The Window of Memory* (Chapel Hill: University of North Carolina Press, 1962). Professor Kennedy says, p. 84, that Wolfe "served his apprenticeship but never got his papers as a journeyman."

Chapter Three

1. *Thomas Wolfe*, p. 127.

2. Jonathan Daniels, "Wolfe's First Is Novel of Revolt," *News and Observer*, October 20, 1929, Raleigh, N.C.

3. *Look Homeward, Angel* (New York, 1929), p. 27.

4. *Letters*, p. 198.

5. *The Marble Man's Wife*, pp. 20, 81, 113, 131, 133, 103, 109, 163, 62, 143.

6. *Ibid.*, pp. 16-19.

7. *Thomas Wolfe and His Family*, p. 117.

8. *Ibid.*, pp. 45, 84, 118, 64, 101, 111, 98, 70.

9. *Ibid.*, pp. 15, 57, 143-44, 111, 70, 164-65.

10. *Look Homeward, Angel*, pp. 123, 125, 225.

11. *Ibid.*, pp. 384, 425.

12. *Ibid.*, pp. 460, 143.

13. *Letters to Mother*, p. 5.

14. Legette Blythe, "The Thomas Wolfe I Knew," *The Saturday Review of Literature*, August 25, 1945, p. 19.

15. Quoted in Ann Preston Bridgers, "Thomas Wolfe, Legends of a Man's Hunger in His Youth," *The Saturday Review of Literature*, April 6, 1935, p. 599.

16. *Letters to Mother*, p. 12. Kennedy (*Windows of Memory*, p. 47) says an episode satirical of Koch survives in manuscript.

17. *The Autobiography of Mark Twain*, ed. Charles Neider (New York, 1961), p. 9.

Chapter Four

1. *Letters*, p. 264.

2. *Letters*, p. 347.

3. *Of Time and the River* (New York, 1935), p. 85.

4. *Letters to Mother,* p. 49.

5. Carlton was later one of Wolfe's colleagues at New York University. Robert Dow suggested to Wolfe that he apply at New York University. Olin Dows was a wealthy young man whose estate on the Hudson Wolfe later visited. George Wallace had been an advertising man; Wolfe also knew him later in New York.

6. To Edwin Greenlaw, *Letters,* p. 30.

7. *Thomas Wolfe at Washington Square,* p. 28.

8. *Of Time and the River,* p. 479. See *Thomas Wolfe at Washington Square,* p. 26.

9. *Letters,* p. 67. See also an earlier letter to Day, p. 61.

10. *The Enigma of Thomas Wolfe,* ed. Richard Walser (Cambridge, 1953), p. 35. Volkening's essay, "Penance No More," first appeared in *The Virginia Quarterly Review* (Spring, 1939).

11. *Thomas Wolfe at Washington Square,* pp. 23, 150, 30. A sample theme is reproduced, p. 96.

12. *Letters,* p. 59.

13. *Letters,* p. 61, *Thomas Wolfe at Washington Square,* p. 88.

14. *Letters,* pp. 69, 109, 117, 133.

15. *Of Time and the River,* p. 420; see *Thomas Wolfe at Washington Square,* p. 33.

16. *Letters,* pp. 133-34.

17. *Thomas Wolfe at Washington Square,* p. 65.

18. *Look Homeward, Angel,* pp. 269, 309-10, 508.

19. *Of Time and the River,* pp. 215, 256, 265, 273.

20. *Letters,* p. 460.

21. *The Enigma of Thomas Wolfe,* pp. 140-48. The essay first appeared April 25, 1936, in *The Saturday Review of Literature.*

22. *Thomas Wolfe,* p. 376n.

Chapter Five

1. *Letters,* pp. 711-14. This letter was not sent to Aswell but was found among Wolfe's papers. In *You Can't Go Home Again,* Aswell used the passage defining this phrase as part of an italicized transition, p. 706.

2. Edward C. Aswell, "A Note on Thomas Wolfe," *The Hills Beyond* (New York, 1941), p. 372. This "Note" is not the piece included in *The Enigma of Thomas Wolfe.*

3. This symbolism is stated in *You Can't Go Home Again,* pp. 740-41.

4. "Unshaken Friend," *The New Yorker,* April 1 and 8, 1944, p. 36 of second article.

Chapter Six

1. For the full list of stories included in these volumes, see the Selected Bibliography. A few minor sketches in these volumes are not discussed in this chapter. In *From Death to Morning*, "Gulliver" is a fantasy on the isolation of the very tall man. "The Bums at Sunset" concerns a young vagrant who joins two experienced tramps. "The Far and the Near" is an O. Henry-esque tale about a railway engineer. "One of the Girls of Our Party" satirizes an Ohio schoolteacher touring Europe. "Dark in the Forest, Strange as Time" sympathetically records the death of an old Jew in a German railway train. In *The Hills Beyond*, the piece entitled "On Leprechauns" is a discarded expository passage from the Webber narrative.

2. *From Death to Morning*, p. 204.

3. *The Hills Beyond*, p. 248.

4. *Ibid.*, p. 274.

5. *Ibid.*, pp. 300, 306, 308.

6. *Ibid.*, pp. 312, 319, 323, 326, 341, 345-46.

7. *Letters*, p. 625

8. *The Hills Beyond*, pp. 89, 91, 105-7.

9. *From Death to Morning*, pp. 242, 303-4.

10. *Letters*, p. 339.

11. *From Death to Morning*, p. 303.

12. *Ibid.*, p. 121.

13. *The Hills Beyond*, pp. 46-48.

14. *From Death to Morning*, p. 210.

15. With "The Face of the War," *From Death to Morning*, pp. 71-90, compare *Look Homeward, Angel*, pp. 523-25.

16. *The Hills Beyond*, pp. 13, 21, 42.

17. *Ibid.*, pp. 120, 132.

18. *From Death to Morning*, pp. 57-58, 67.

19. *Ibid.*, pp. 12-13.

20. *Ibid.*, pp. 95-97.

21. *Ibid.*, p. 184.

22. *The Hills Beyond*, p. 185.

23. "Old Man Rivers" has been published only in *The Atlantic Monthly*, CLXXX (December, 1947), 92-104.

24. *Thomas Wolfe*, pp. 321-22.

25. *A Note on Experts: Dexter Vespasian Joyner*, ed. Maxwell E. Perkins (New York, 1939), [p. 14].

26. *The Short Novels of Thomas Wolfe*, ed. C. Hugh Holman (New York, 1961), p. 278.

27. *Letters to Mother*, pp. 49, 53.

28. *The Story of a Novel* (New York, 1936), p. 53.

29. *Letters,* p. 212.
30. *Letters,* pp. 234, 235, 236, 238-40, 242-45, 278.
31. *Letters,* p. 526.
32. "Justice Is Blind," in *The Enigma of Thomas Wolfe,* pp. 91-100, is a brief episode from the Spangler story. It is satirical of "Old Sir Kenelm"—Christopher Morley published essays in *The Saturday Review of Literature* under this pseudonym—and of lawyers.
33. *Letters,* pp. 225, 339, 381, 462, 487. Delia Hawke was later re-named Eliza Gant.

Chapter Seven

1. The family group picture and the one showing Tom at seven, along with many other pictures, are reproduced in *Thomas Wolfe and His Family.* The college picture is in the University of North Carolina collection. The Harvard picture is reproduced in Elmer D. Johnson, *Of Time and Thomas Wolfe: A Bibliography* (New York, 1959). The 1929 picture appears in *Thomas Wolfe at Washington Square.* The picture showing Wolfe with his crate of manuscript illustrated the third installment of "The Story of a Novel," in *The Saturday Review,* December 28, 1935, p. 3. The 1937 family group is reproduced in *Thomas Wolfe and His Family.*
2. Cargill's "Introduction" to *Thomas Wolfe at Washington Square* (pp. 16-17, 70) collects conflicting testimony as to Wolfe's height. Aswell's statement, based on the undertaker's measurement of Wolfe's body, gives his height as six feet, six inches.
3. *Thomas Wolfe at Washington Square,* p. 88; Maxwell Perkins, "Thomas Wolfe," *Harvard Library Bulletin,* I (Autumn, 1947), 271.
4. *Thomas Wolfe,* pp. 12-13.
5. *Letters,* p. 55: *Letters to Mother,* pp. xxii-xxiii.
6. *Letters to Mother,* pp. 8, 83, 132.
7. *Letters,* pp. 80, 731-34.
8. *Letters,* p. 359.
9. Details of Aline Bernstein's life and of her career as stage and costume designer are summarized in *Who's Who in the Theatre,* 11th ed. (New York, 1952), pp. 339-40.
10. *Thomas Wolfe,* p. 166n.
11. *Ibid.,* p. 283.
12. *Letters,* pp. 391-97.
13. *Thomas Wolfe,* p. 375.
14. *Editor to Author,* pp. 30, 40, 116.
15. *Letters,* p. 213.
16. *Ibid.,* pp. 307, 398; *The Story of a Novel,* p. 80: *Thomas Wolfe,* p. 223.
17. *Editor to Author,* p. 99.

18. *Ibid.*, p. 100; *Thomas Wolfe*, p. 406.
19. For a detailed summary of the suit brought by Mrs. Boyd, see Miss Nowell's note, *Letters*, pp. 463-65.
20. Aswell, "Thomas Wolfe Did Not Kill Maxwell Perkins," *The Saturday Review of Literature*, XXXIV (Oct. 6, 1951), 16.
21. *Letters*, pp. 777-78. Previously published in *Editor to Author*, p. 141.
22. *Editor to Author*, p. 279.
23. *Letters*, p. 33.
24. *Letters to Mother*, p. 50.
25. *Letters*, pp. 118, 179, 215.
26. *Ibid.*, pp. 98, 121, 227-28.
27. *The Enigma of Thomas Wolfe*, pp. 36-37.
28. *Letters*, pp. 150, 179.
29. *Letters to Mother*, p. 211. See Kennedy, p. 370 for an unpublished note on Wolfe's views in 1938.
30. *Letters*, pp. 552-53.
31. *Editor to Author*, p. 180: *Letters*, p. 652.
32. *Letters*, pp. 72, 128.
33. Martha Dodd, *Through Embassy Eyes* (New York, 1939), pp. 89-95, 212.
34. *Letters*, pp. 735-36.
35. To Volkening, *The Enigma of Thomas Wolfe*, p. 49; *Letters* pp. 752-54.
36. *Letters to Mother*, pp. 58-59.
37. *Letters*, p. 61; *Thomas Wolfe at Washington Square*, pp. 72 (n.77), 88; *Letters*, pp. 476-77.
38. *The Web and the Rock*, p. 590.
39. *Thomas Wolfe*, pp. 107, 109.
40. *The Hills Beyond*, p. 196.
41. *Letters*, p. 757.
42. *Ibid.*, p. 268.

Chapter Eight

1. *The Story of a Novel* includes three errors of fact. Wolfe says (p. 27) "in February, 1930, about five months after the publication of *Look Homeward, Angel*, I found it possible to resign from the faculty of New York University. . . ." Since the novel was published October 18 and Wolfe resigned as of February 1, the lapse of time was little more than three months. Later (p. 85), Wolfe states that the manuscript of *Of Time and the River* was sent to the printer in October (1934) while he was on a trip to Chicago. In fact, the manuscript had gone to the printer early in July. Wolfe's letter to Robert Raynolds, July 8, 1934 (*Letters*, p. 416), makes it appear that

Wolfe was a willing collaborator at this point, for he says: "It seems unbelievable, but Perkins and I finished getting the manuscript ready for the printer last night." Wolfe may mean that he helped with the final ordering of manuscript, even though he opposed sending it off; but he seems in this letter to be relieved that it is off his hands. Finally, he says (p. 87) that "in January, 1935, I finished the last of my revisions on the proof," implying that he read proof in normal fashion. Much of the proof was read by Scribner's staff, and Wolfe later protested the charge of $1,100 for excessive corrections on the ground that he himself had not made the corrections. Kennedy (*Windows of Memory*, p. 269) accepts Wolfe's statement that the manuscript was sent to the printer in October, while Wolfe was in Chicago. Elizabeth Nowell (*Thomas Wolfe*, p. 239) is very specific that the manuscript went to the printer in July; by August, proof was coming through.

2. *The Story of a Novel*, p. 21. Hereafter referred to as *Story*.

3. *Ibid.*, p. 39.

4. *Ibid.*, p. 51.

5. *Ibid.*, pp. 74, 86.

6. Perkins, *Harvard Library Bulletin*, I, 270-72; *Letters*, pp. 187-90.

7. Maxwell Perkins, "Scribner's and Tom Wolfe," *The Enigma of Thomas Wolfe*, p. 59. Originally published in *The Carolina Magazine*, October, 1938.

8. Perkins, *Harvard Library Bulletin*, I, 272; *Story*, pp. 80-81.

9. *Ibid.*, I, 273.

10. *Story*, p. 81.

11. *Thomas Wolfe*, p. 227. Kennedy says, p. 269, that Wolfe himself added the chance meeting with Esther at the end of *Of Time and the River*.

12. *Editor to Author*, p. 91.

13. *Ibid.*, pp. 88, 91.

14. Perkins in *The Enigma of Thomas Wolfe*, p. 59.

15. *Letters*, pp. 413, 416, 418, 446, 490.

16. *Harvard Library Bulletin*, I, 272.

17. *Editor to Author*, pp. 229-30; *Letters*, p. 758.

18. *Thomas Wolfe*, pp. 133-34.

19. *Letters*, 445-46, 491.

20. *Editor to Author*, p. 106.

21. *The Hills Beyond*, pp. 355-56.

22. *Story*, p. 8.

23. Letters, pp. 254, 321-22; *Story*, p. 8. Kennedy adds from manuscript sources some details of Wolfe's interest in Joyce. See especially pp. 153, 156, 160 fn 26.

24. Nathan L. Rothman, "Thomas Wolfe and James Joyce: A

Study in Literary Influence," *The Enigma of Thomas Wolfe,* pp. 263-89. Originally published in *A Southern Vanguard,* ed. Allen Tate (New York, 1947), pp. 52-77.

25. William Braswell, "Thomas Wolfe Lectures and Takes a Holiday," *The Enigma of Thomas Wolfe,* p. 70. Originally published in *College English* (October, 1939).

26. *The Enigma of Thomas Wolfe,* p. 35.

27. *Letters,* pp. 324, 479-80.

28. *Letters,* p. 321.

29. *Letters,* p. 254.

30. May Cameron, "An Interview with Thomas Wolfe," *Press Time* (New York, 1936), p. 249. Reprinted from the New York *Post* of March 14, 1936, all but the first two paragraphs are quoted from Wolfe himself.

31. *Letters,* p. 29; *Wolfe at Washington Square,* p. 97; *Letters,* p. 656. Miss Cameron's "Interview" also alludes to Twain.

32. Letter to Volkening, *The Enigma of Thomas Wolfe,* p. 47. This paragraph is not given in *Letters,* pp. 289-93.

33. *Letters,* pp. 23-26.

34. *Ibid.,* pp. 248, 747, 703.

35. *Ibid.,* p. 468.

36. *Ibid.,* p. 495.

37. *Ibid.,* p. 275.

38. *Ibid.,* p. 254.

39. *Ibid.,* pp. 237-38.

40. *Ibid.,* pp. 250, 261-66.

41. *Ibid.,* p. 550.

42. *Ibid.,* p. 643.

43. *Ibid.,* pp. 449-50. The Rascoe comment is given in a footnote.

44. *Of Time and the River,* p. 867.

45. *Ibid.,* pp. 269-70.

46. *The Face of a Nation* (New York, 1939), p. vi.

47. *Ibid.,* p. 151; *Look Homeward, Angel,* p. 334.

48. *The Face of the Nation,* p. 163; *Of Time and the River,* p. 330.

49. *A Stone, A Leaf, A Door* (New York, 1954), p. vi.

50. *Ibid.,* pp. 87-89; *The Web and the Rock,* p. 441.

51. *Ibid.,* pp. 1, 29, 61, 109, 125, 135.

52. *Letters,* p. 368.

53. *The Hills Beyond,* pp. 362-63.

54. *Ibid.,* p. 363.

55. *Editor to Author,* p. 297.

56. This famous refrain has been little discussed. E. K. Brown, "Thomas Wolfe: Realist and Symbolist," *The Enigma of Thomas Wolfe,* pp. 219-20 (first published in *The University of Toronto*

Quarterly, January, 1941), interprets "stone" as the stone angel, symbolic of Gant's limitation; "leaf" derives from Coleridge's poem, and symbolic death; "door," the "chief of the three symbols, is the thin barrier between personalities." In the final scene of the novel, however, the symbols are repeated in Eugene's appeal to Ben: "And no leaf hangs for me in the forest; I shall lift no stone upon the hills; I shall find no door in any city." The clear implication is that all three symbols are positives—growth, building, opportunity?—which Eugene desires. Monroe M. Stearns ("Thomas Wolfe's Metaphysics," *Enigma*, p. 202) points out that the symbols parallel Wordsworth's line (*Prelude*, III, 160): "a tree, a stone, a withered leaf." In this line, however, Wordsworth is illustrating the stimulus to his imagination in the common sights of nature.

57. *Story*, p. 39.

58. *You Can't Go Home Again*, p. 731.

59. Vardis Fisher, "Thomas Wolfe and Maxwell Perkins," *Tomorrow*, X (July, 1951), 20-25.

60. *The Hills Beyond*, pp. 375-76.

61. Lavon Rascoe, "Interview with Mr. Faulkner," *Western Review*, XV (Summer, 1951), 304. Harvey Breit, "A Walk with Faulkner," New York *Times Book Review* (January 30, 1955), pp. 4, 12, elaborates Faulkner's earlier comment.

62. Mark Schorer, "Technique as Discovery," *Hudson Review*, I (Spring, 1948), 81. On October 25, 1929, Wolfe was "moved and honored" by what Mr. Schorer had written him in praise of *Look Homeward, Angel* (*Letters*, p. 206).

63. Pamela Hansford Johnson, "Thomas Wolfe and the Kicking Season," *Encounter*, XII (April, 1959), 77-80. Reprinted in part in C. Hugh Holman, *The World of Thomas Wolfe* (New York, 1962), pp. 60-62.

64. Mrs. Doris Lessing, quoted by Mrs. Johnson, p. 77.

Selected Bibliography

BIBLIOGRAPHIES

PRESTON, GEORGE R., JR. *Thomas Wolfe: a Bibliography* (New York: Charles S. Boesen, 1943). Data on first editions. Brief quotations from most critical articles listed.

Literary History of the United States, ed. by SPILLER, THORPE, JOHNSON, and CANBY (New York: The Macmillan Company, 1948), III, 784-86. *Id., Bibliography Supplement,* ed. by RICHARD M. LUDWIG (New York, 1959), pp. 213-15.

HOLMAN, C. HUGH. "Thomas Wolfe: A Bibliographical Study," University of Texas *Studies in Literature and Languages,* I (1959), 427-45. A comprehensive essay which groups and evaluates studies of Wolfe.

JOHNSON, ELMER D. *Of Time and Thomas Wolfe: A Bibliography with a Character Index of His Works* (New York: Scarecrow Press, Inc., 1959). For objections to some details of this work see Alexander D. Wainwright's review in *Papers of the Bibliographical Society of America,* LV (1961), 258-63. Johnson, however, gives the fullest list of Wolfe's periodical contributions and of critical articles about him.

PRIMARY SOURCES

The Correspondence of Thomas Wolfe and Homer Andrew Watt, ed. by Oscar Cargill and Thomas Clark Pollock. New York: New York University Press, 1954. Wolfe's letters were later included in the 1956 edition of his letters.

The Crisis in Industry. Chapel Hill, N.C.: The University of North Carolina, 1919. Not reprinted.

The Face of a Nation (poetical passages from the writings, selected by John Hall Wheelock). New York: Charles Scribner's Sons, 1939.

From Death to Morning. New York: Charles Scribner's Sons, 1935. Includes the following, all previously published in periodicals: "No Door," "Death the Proud Brother," "The Face of the War," "Only the Dead Know Brooklyn," "Dark in the Forest, Strange as Time," "The Four Lost Men," "Gulliver," "The Bums at Sunset," "One of the Girls in Our Party," "The Far and the Near," "In the Park," "The Men of Old Catawba," "Circus at Dawn," "The Web of Earth."

The Hills Beyond (with a Note on Thomas Wolfe by Edward C.

Aswell). New York: Harper and Brothers, 1941. Includes the following, previously published in periodicals: "The Lost Boy," "A Kinsman of His Blood" (previous title, "Arnold Pentland"), "Chickamauga," "Portrait of a Literary Critic," "The Lion at Morning," "God's Lonely Man." The following were previously unpublished: "No Cure for It," "Gentlemen of the Press," "The Return of the Prodigal," "On Leprechauns," and ten chapters of "The Hills Beyond."

The Letters of Thomas Wolfe, ed. Elizabeth Nowell. New York: Charles Scribner's Sons, 1956. Includes previously published letters by Wolfe to Margaret Roberts and to Professor Homer A. Watt; does not include Wolfe's letters to his mother, separately published and listed below. Includes several letters never mailed.

Look Homeward, Angel. New York: Charles Scribner's Sons, 1929.

Mannerhouse. New York: Harper and Brothers, 1948.

A Note on Experts: Dexter Vespasian Joyner. New York: House of Books, 1939.

Of Time and the River. New York: Charles Scribner's Sons, 1935.

The Portable Thomas Wolfe, ed. Maxwell Geismar. New York: Viking Press, 1946. Includes selections from Wolfe's four novels; *The Story of a Novel;* and the six short stories: "The Face of the War," "Only the Dead Know Brooklyn," "Dark in the Forest," "Circus at Dawn," "In the Park," and "Chickamauga."

The Short Novels of Thomas Wolfe, ed. C. Hugh Holman. New York: Charles Scribner's Sons, 1961. Includes, as originally published in magazines, "A Portrait of Bascom Hawke," "The Web of Earth," "I Have a Thing to Tell You," "The Party at Jack's"; and, as originally planned, the four-part story, "No Door."

A Stone, A Leaf, A Door (selected and arranged in verse by John S. Barnes). New York: Charles Scribner's Sons, 1945.

The Story of a Novel. New York: Charles Scribner's Sons, 1936. Previously published in *The Saturday Review of Literature,* December 14, 21, 28, 1935.

The Web and the Rock. New York: Harper and Brothers, 1939.

A Western Journal (A daily log of the Great Parks trip, June 20 to July 2, 1938). Pittsburg: The University of Pittsburg Press, 1951.

Thomas Wolfe's Letters to His Mother, Julia Elizabeth Wolfe, ed. by John Skally Terry. New York: Charles Scribner's Sons, 1943.

The Thomas Wolfe Reader, ed. by C. Hugh Holman. New York: Charles Scribner's Sons, 1962. Includes *The Story of a Novel,* episodes from the four novels, and the following short pieces: "The Face of the War," "Only the Dead Know Brooklyn," "Dark in the Forest, Strange as Time," "The Far and the Near," "In the Park," "The Lost Boy," "God's Lonely Man," and the last letter to Maxwell E. Perkins.

The Years of Wandering in Many Lands and Cities. New York: Charles S. Boesen, 1949. Reproduces six pages from Wolfe's notebooks.

You Can't Go Home Again. New York: Harper and Brothers, 1940.

Uncollected Writings

For Wolfe's student publications, see notes to chapters I and II. Later uncollected pieces are given in the order of their appearance:

"London Tower," *Sunday Citizen,* Asheville, N.C., July 19, 1925. Travel notes.

Letter to the editor, Asheville *Times,* May 4, 1930.

"The Grass Roof," New York *Evening Post,* April 4, 1931. Review of a novel by Younghill Kang.

CAMERON, MAY. "An Interview with Thomas Wolfe," New York *Post,* March 14, 1936. Reprinted in *Press Time.* All but the first two paragraphs are direct quotation.

"Fame and the Poet," *American Mercury,* XXXIX (October, 1936), 149-54.

"Return," Asheville *Citizen-Times,* May 16, 1937.

"The Man Who Lives with His Idea: Which Tells the Story of Frederick H. Koch and the Playmakers of Chapel Hill," *Carolina Play-Book,* XVI (March-June, 1943), 15-22.

"Old Man Rivers," *Atlantic Monthly,* CLXXX (December, 1947), 92-104.

"Something of My Life," *The Saturday Review of Literature,* XXXI February 7, 1948), 6-8. Original draft of a sketch previously published. *Enigma.*

"Justice is Blind," *The Enigma of Thomas Wolfe,* ed. Richard Walser (Cambridge, 1953), pp. 91-100. Excerpt from the Spangler novel.

"The Isle of Quisay," *Comparative Literature,* IX (Winter, 1957), 41-42. Hitherto unpublished fragment, imitative of Anatole France, ed. Daniel L. Delakas.

"Welcome to Our City," *Esquire,* October, 1957, pp. 58-83. See the November issue, p. 12, for retraction of a statement regarding the Theatre Guild in *Esquire's* introductory comment.

SECONDARY SOURCES

Books

ADAMS, AGATHA BOYD. *Thomas Wolfe: Carolina Student* ("Extension Publication," Vol. XV, No. 2, January, 1950). Chapel Hill: University of North Carolina Library, 1950. Based largely on student publications of 1916-20.

Selected Bibliography

BERNSTEIN, ALINE FRANKAU. *Three Blue Suits*. New York: Equinox Cooperative Press, 1935. The third sketch, "Eugene," fictionally portrays Wolfe. See his *Letters*, pp. 391-97.

—————. *The Journey Down*. New York: Alfred A. Knopf, 1938. A fictional treatment of the love story given in Wolfe's novels about George Webber.

—————. *An Actor's Daughter*. New York: Alfred A. Knopf, 1941. Autobiographical. It parallels and supplements Esther Jack's reminiscences as recorded in *The Web and the Rock*.

DELAKAS, DANIEL L. *Thomas Wolfe, la France, et les romanciers français*. Paris: Jouve, 1950. Points out parallels between Wolfe and Proust, Flaubert, and Balzac.

The Enigma of Thomas Wolfe, ed. Richard Walser. Cambridge: Harvard University Press, 1953. Includes twenty-four biographical and critical essays, individually listed in the next section of this bibliography; and two uncollected pieces by Wolfe (listed above): "Something of My Life," and "Justice Is Blind."

FRINGS, KETTI. *Look Homeward, Angel* (a Play based on the Novel by Thomas Wolfe). New York: Charles Scribner's Sons, 1958. Opened on Broadway, November 28, 1957. Won the Drama Circle Award and Pulitzer Prize for 1957-58. Broadway run: 564 performances.

HOLMAN, C. HUGH. *Thomas Wolfe*. University of Minnesota Pamphlets on American Writers, No. 6. Minneapolis: University of Minnesota Press, 1960. Sympathetic and discriminating.

—————. *The World of Thomas Wolfe* (A Scribner Research Anthology). New York: Charles Scribner's Sons, 1962. Reprints *The Story of a Novel*, and thirty-two critical comments, the chief of which are individually listed below.

JOHNSON, PAMELA HANSFORD. *Hungry Gulliver* (an English Critical Appraisal of Thomas Wolfe). New York: Charles Scribner's Sons, 1948. Deals only with the four novels. Sees Wolfe's primary appeal in his Whitmanesque style.

KENNEDY, RICHARD S. *The Window of Memory: The Literary Career of Thomas Wolfe*. Chapel Hill, N.C.: University of North Carolina Press, 1962. An important, detailed study of the great mass of manuscripts.

MULLER, HERBERT J. *Thomas Wolfe* (The Makers of Modern Literature). Norfolk, Conn.: New Directions, 1947. Deals chiefly with the novels. Emphasizes Wolfe's intellectual content in comparison with his contemporaries.

NORWOOD, HAYDEN. *The Marble Man's Wife: Thomas Wolfe's Mother*. New York: Charles Scribner's Sons, 1947. Records Mrs. Wolfe's conversations with Norwood about her early life, Tom's youth, and particularly "The Web of Earth."

NOWELL, ELIZABETH. *Thomas Wolfe: A Biography.* Garden City, N. Y.: Doubleday & Company, 1960. Detailed factual biography, based on Miss Nowell's careful editing of the *Letters* (1956), and her acquaintance with most of Wolfe's associates. Though Miss Nowell says (p. 11) that the novels "cannot be taken as straight autobiography," she does treat many quotations from them as factually reliable.

PERKINS, MAXWELL E. *Editor to Author: The Letters of Maxwell E. Perkins* (selected and edited with commentary and introduction by John Hall Wheelock). New York: Charles Scribner's Sons, 1950.

POLLOCK, THOMAS CLARK and OSCAR CARGILL. *Thomas Wolfe at Washington Square.* New York: New York University Press, 1954. Includes Cargill's elaborately documented essay of eighty pages, three reminiscences by students, and four by colleagues, individually listed below.

PFISTER, KARIN. *Zeit und Wirklichkeit bei Thomas Wolfe.* Heidelberg, Germany: Carl Winter Universitatsverlag, 1954. Examines the influence of Bergson and Spengler on Wolfe.

REEVES, GEORGE M., JR. *Thomas Wolfe et L'Europe.* Paris: Marcel Didier, 1955. Sees Europe as a catalyst for Wolfe.

RUBIN, LOUIS D., JR. *Thomas Wolfe: The Weather of His Youth.* Baton Rouge: Louisiana State University Press, 1955. Emphasizes that the novels should be read as novels.

WALSER, RICHARD. *Thomas Wolfe.* New York: Barnes and Noble, 1961. Appreciative. Illustrated.

WATKINS, FLOYD C. *Thomas Wolfe's Characters: Portraits from Life.* Norman, Okla.: University of Oklahoma Press, 1957. Elaborate examination of the factual basis for characters and episodes, especially in Asheville. Concludes that Wolfe made few changes, and was at his best in dealing with Southern life.

WHEATON, MABEL WOLFE, with LEGETTE BLYTHE. *Thomas Wolfe and His Family.* Garden City, N. Y.: Doubleday & Company, 1961. An informal chronicle seeking to establish that the Wolfes are not the Gants. Sixteen pages of photographs.

Biographical and Critical Essays

A few incidental references cited in the footnotes are not repeated here. Items reprinted in *The Enigma of Thomas Wolfe* (1953) or *The World of Thomas Wolfe* (1962), listed above, are indicated by the words *Enigma* or *World.*

ALBRECHT, W. P. "Time as Unity in the Novels of Thomas Wolfe," *New Mexico Quarterly Review,* XIX (Autumn, 1949), 320-29. *Enigma.* "The unity of each novel, and of the four novels as one, is clarified by the opposition of the linear and the cyclical concepts of time."

————. "The Title of *Look Homeward, Angel,*" *Modern Language Quarterly,* XI (March, 1950), 50-57.

ARMSTRONG, ANNE W. "As I Saw Thomas Wolfe," *Arizona Quarterly,* II (Spring, 1946), 5-15. Details of his reading in 1937.

ASWELL, E. C. "A Note on Thomas Wolfe," appended to *The Hills Beyond,* pp. 349-86. Emphasizes Wolfe's growth and sense of form.

————. "En Route to a Legend," *The Saturday Review of Literature,* XXXI (November 27, 1948), 7, 34-36. Later published as the "Introduction" to the Signet edition of *The Adventures of Young Gant. Enigma. Look Homeward, Angel* has outlasted most of the books of the 1920's.

————. "Thomas Wolfe Did Not Kill Maxwell Perkins," *The Saturday Review of Literature,* XXXIV (October 6, 1951), 16-17, 44-46. Reply to Struthers Burt; see below.

BAKER, CARLOS. "Thomas Wolfe's Apprenticeship," *Delphian Quarterly,* XXIII (January, 1940), 20-25. Wolfe was influenced by Carlyle, particularly *Sartor Resartus.*

BARBER, P. W. "Thomas Wolfe Writes a Play," *Harpers,* CCXVI (May, 1958), 71-76. Amusing reminiscence of Wolfe's difficulties at the 47 Workshop, by a classmate.

BASSO, HAMILTON. "Thomas Wolfe: A Summing Up," *New Republic,* CIII (September 23, 1940), 422-23. Review of *You Can't Go Home Again* by a Southern novelist who was a personal friend of Wolfe.

BEACH, JOSEPH WARREN. *American Fiction: 1920 to 1940.* New York: The Macmillan Company, 1941. Part in *World.* Wolfe is one of eight writers selected for treatment in this volume.

BENÉT, STEPHEN V. "Thomas Wolfe's Torrent of Recollection," *The Saturday Review of Literature,* XXII (September 21, 1940), 5. *Enigma.* Review of *You Can't Go Home Again.* "There is a line, and a mature line."

BISHOP, DON. "Thomas Wolfe," *The New Carolina Magazine* (March, 1942), pp. 28-29, 35, 47-48. *Enigma.* Anecdotes of Wolfe's days at Chapel Hill.

BISHOP, JOHN PEALE. "The Sorrows of Thomas Wolfe," *Kenyon Review,* I (Winter, 1939), 7-17. Part in *World.* Wolfe is a culmination of the romantic spirit. His work lacks structure, and therefore meaning.

————. "The Myth and Modern Literature," *The Saturday Review of Literature,* XX (July 22, 1939), 3-4, 14. Thomas Wolfe and Hart Crane as "the two most conspicuous failures in American letters of recent years."

BLACKMUR, R. P. "Notes on the Novel," *Southern Review* (Spring, 1936), 898-99. Unfavorable.

BLYTHE, LEGETTE. "The Thomas Wolfe I Knew," *The Saturday Review of Literature*, XXVIII (August 25, 1945), 18-19. Reminiscence of Wolfe at Chapel Hill.

BRASWELL, WILLIAM. "Thomas Wolfe Lectures and Takes a Holiday," *College English*, I (October, 1939), 11-22. *Enigma*. Account of Wolfe's visit to Purdue University, where he delivered a lecture on May, 19, 1938.

BRIDGERS, ANN P. "Thomas Wolfe," *The Saturday Review of Literature*, XI (April 6, 1935), 599, 609. Anecdotal.

BROWN, E. K. "Thomas Wolfe: Realist and Symbolist," *University of Toronto Quarterly*, X (January, 1941), 153-66. *Enigma*. Symbols enabled Wolfe to go beyond the realistic method.

BROWN, JOHN MASON. "Thomas Wolfe as a Dramatist," New York *Post*, September 21, 1938. Reprinted in the author's *Broadway in Review* (New York, 1940). Brown was a classmate in the 47 Workshop.

BURGUM, EDWIN B. "Thomas Wolfe's Discovery of America," *Virginia Quarterly Review*, XXII (Summer, 1946), 421-37. *Enigma* and part in *World*. Instinctively rather than intellectually, Wolfe turned from subjectivity to objectivity.

BURT, STRUTHERS. "Catalyst for Genius: Maxwell Perkins," *The Saturday Review of Literature*, XXXIV (June 9, 1951), 6-8, 36-39. Praises Perkins' editorial efforts, and accuses Wolfe of hastening Perkins' death by "betraying" him. Issues of *The Saturday Review* for August 11 and September 1 carried several letters on this matter, including two from Struthers Burt and one from Fred W. Wolfe, the novelist's brother. On October 6 a formal reply by Aswell appeared (listed above).

CANBY, HENRY SEIDEL. "The River of Youth," *The Saturday Review of Literature*, XI (March 9, 1935), 529-30. *Enigma*. Review of *Of Time and the River:* "one of the most American books of our time," yet "an artistic failure."

CARPENTER, FREDERIC I. "Thomas Wolfe: The Autobiography of an Idea," *University of Kansas City Review*, XII (Spring, 1946), 179-87. Wolfe's idea was the American dream of freedom and democracy.

CHURCH, MARGARET. "Thomas Wolfe: Dark Time," *Publications of the Modern Language Association*, LXIV (September, 1949), 629-38. *Enigma*. Wolfe often echoes Proust in handling time, but did not become involved in Proustian metaphysics.

COLLINS, THOMAS L. "Thomas Wolfe," *Sewanee Review*, L (October, 1942), 487-504. Titled "Wolfe's Genius vs. His Critics" in *Enigma*. Replies to the negative criticism of De Voto and Warren

Selected Bibliography

(see below). Wolfe has scope, greatness, significance, and effective form.

COUGHLAN, ROBERT. "Tom Wolfe's Surge to Greatness," *Life* (September 17, 1956), pp. 178-96.

──────. "Grand Vision, a Final Tragedy," *Life* (September 24, 1956), pp. 168-84.

COWLEY, MALCOLM. "Unshaken Friend," *The New Yorker* (April 1, 1944), pp. 28-36; (April 8), pp. 30-40. Profile of Maxwell E. Perkins, with emphasis on his association with Wolfe.

──────. "Thomas Wolfe," *Atlantic Monthly*, CC (November 1957), 202-12. Part in *World*. Wolfe's immaturity resulted from his literary policy of maintaining an uncritical flow of composition. His extremes of exuberance and despair suggest a manic-depressive psychosis.

DANIELS, JONATHAN. "A Native at Large," *Nation*, CLI (October 12, 1940), 332.

──────. "Poet of the Boom," *Tar Heels*. New York: Dodd, Mead and Company, 1941. *Enigma*. Reminiscences by a fellow student at Chapel Hill, with an account of Wolfe's funeral.

DAVIS, RUTH. "Look Homeward, Angel," *The Saturday Review of Literature*, XXXIX (January 5, 1946), 13-14, 31-32. Transcript of talk given by Wolfe's mother to a New York University class, November 30, 1935.

DELAKAS, DANIEL L. "Thomas Wolfe and Anatole France," *Comparative Literature*, IX (Winter, 1957), 33-50. Wolfe's interest in Anatole France led to imitations in the notebooks of 1925-30.

DE VOTO, BERNARD. "Genius is Not Enough," *The Saturday Review of Literature*, XIII (April 25, 1936), 3-4, 14-15. *Enigma*. *World*. Review of *The Story of a Novel*. Objects to "placental" material. Organization of Wolfe's novels was delegated to Wolfe's editor, Maxwell Perkins.

DODD, MARTHA. *Through Embassy Eyes*. New York: Harcourt, Brace and Company, 1939. Wolfe's visits to Germany in 1935 and 1936 described, pp. 89-95.

DOW, ROBERT. "And Gladly Teche." *Thomas Wolfe at Washington Square*. Dow knew Wolfe at Harvard, and was Wolfe's colleague at New York University.

DOYLE, A. GERALD. "Drunk With Words." *Thomas Wolfe at Washington Square*. Doyle was a student of Wolfe.

EHRSAM, T. G. "I Knew Thomas Wolfe," *Book Collector's Journal*, I (June, 1936), 1, 3.

FADIMAN, CLIFTON. "The Wolfe at the Door." *Party of One: The Selected Writings of Clifton Fadiman*. New York: The World Publishing Company, 1955. *World;* Parody of *Of Time and the River*.

————. "The Web and the Rock," *The New Yorker*, XV (June 24, 1939), 82-84. *Enigma*. Review: "this book shows no growth."

FAGIN, N. BRYLLION. "In Search of an American *Cherry Orchard*," *Texas Quarterly*, I (Summer--Autumn, 1958), 132-141.

FISHER, VARDIS. "My Experiences with Thomas Wolfe," *Tomorrow* X (April, 1951), 24-30. *Thomas Wolfe at Washington Square*. Wolfe, oversubmissive and feminine, was blind to his own nature.

————. "Thomas Wolfe–Maxwell Perkins," *Tomorrow*, X (July, 1951), 20-25. Perkins was a mother-substitute.

FORSYTHE, ROBERT. "Reminiscences of Wolfe," *New Masses*, September 27, 1938, p. 14.

FROHOCK, W. M. "Thomas Wolfe: Of Time and Neurosis," *Southwest Review*, XXXIII (Autumn, 1948), 349-60. Revised in the author's *The Novel of Violence*. Dallas, Texas: University Press, 1950. *Enigma*. Part in *World*. Wolfe's exaggerated feeling of man's loneliness prevents his vision from being truly tragic.

GEISMAR, MAXWELL. "Thomas Wolfe: The Hillman and the Furies," *Yale Review*, XXXV (Summer, 1946), 649-65. Condensed from "Introduction" to *The Portable Wolfe* (1946).

————. "A Cycle of Fiction." *The Literary History of the United States*. Vol. II. Ed. by ROBERT E. SPILLER, WILLARD THORP, THOMAS H. JOHNSON, and HENRY SEIDEL CANBY. New York: The Macmillan Company, 1948. *World*. "While Faulkner seems to work steadily backward, Wolfe's movement is continuously forward. . . . Perhaps no other American has done so well with the first enchantments and terrors of the city."

————. "Thomas Wolfe: The Unfound Door," *Writers in Crisis*. New York: Houghton Mifflin Company, 1942. Part in *Enigma*. "His novels are the diary . . . of the artist in America."

GELFANT, BLANCHE HOUSMAN. "The City as Symbol." *The American City Novel*. Norman, Okla.: University of Oklahoma Press, 1954. Part in *World*. The city is Wolfe's key symbol of youth's frustrations.

GIBBS, ROBERT COLEMAN. "Thomas Wolfe's Four years at Chapel Hill. A Study of Biographical Source Material," unpublished M.A. thesis, University of North Carolina, 1958.

GORDON, CAROLINE. "*Rooted in Adolescence*," New York *Times Book Review*, March 7, 1948, pp. 10, 12. Review of volumes by Johnson and Muller.

HALPERIN, IRVING. " 'Torrential Production': Thomas Wolfe's Writing Practices," *Arizona Quarterly*, XIV (1958), 29-34.

————. "Wolfe's *Of Time and the River*," *Explicator*, XVIII (November, 1959), Item 9. The novel has a three-part pattern: Eugene's sense of being lost, his search for roots, his discovery of the present.

Selected Bibliography

HEIDERSTADT, DOROTHY. "Studying under Thomas Wolfe," *Mark Twain Quarterly*, VIII (Winter, 1950), 7-8. Wolfe at the Colorado Writers' Conference, 1935.

HOLMAN, C. HUGH. "Loneliness at the Core," *New Republic*, CXXXIII (October 10, 1955), 16-17. *World. Look Homeward, Angel* is "saved from mawkishness by a persuasive comic spirit." *World*.

—————. "'The Dark Ruined Helen of His Blood': Thomas Wolfe and the South." *South: Modern Southern Literature*. Ed. by LOUIS D. RUBIN, JR. and ROBERT D. JACOBS. New York: Doubleday and Company, 1961. Wolfe "a Southerner, torn by the tensions and issues that thoughtful Southerners feel."

HUTSELL, JAMES K. "Thomas Wolfe and 'Altamont,'" *Southern Packet*, IV (April, 1948), 1-8.

JACK, PETER M. "Remembering Thomas Wolfe," New York *Times Book Review* (October 2, 1938), pp. 2, 28.

JOHNSON, EDGAR. "Thomas Wolfe and the American Dream." *A Treasury of Satire*. Ed. by E. JOHNSON. New York: Simon and Shuster, 1945. Part in *World*.

JOHNSON, ELMER D. "Thomas Wolfe Abroad," Louisiana Library Association *Bulletin*, XVIII (1955), 9-11.

—————. "On Translating Thomas Wolfe," *American Speech*, XXXII (May, 1957), 95-101.

JOHNSON, PAMELA. "Thomas Wolfe and the Kicking Season," *Encounter* (England), XII (April, 1959), 77-80. Part in *World*. Eventually "we must sort him down" remembering that at times "he writes like a great novelist."

JOHNSON, STEWART. "Mrs. Julia Wolfe," *The New Yorker*, XXXIV (April 12, 1958), 39-44.

KAZIN, ALFRED. *On Native Grounds: An Interpretation of Modern Prose Fiction*. New York: Reynal and Hitchcock, 1942. Wolfe "always a boy, a very remarkable boy . . . the most self-centered and most inclusive novelist of the day." Same opinion in 1956 revision of this book.

KENNEDY, RICHARD S. "Thomas Wolfe at Harvard, 1920-1923," *Harvard Library Bulletin*, IV (Spring, Autumn, 1950), 172-90, 304-19. Adapted as "Wolfe's Harvard Years" in *Enigma*.

—————. "Tom Wolfe's Don Quixote," *College English*, XXIII (December, 1961), 185-91. Describes Aswell's editorial task in publishing the Webber novels; points out in *The Web and the Rock* certain parallels to Cervantes.

KENNEDY, WILLIAM F. "Economic Ideas in Contemporary Literature: The Novels of Thomas Wolfe," *Southern Economic Journal*, XX (July, 1953), 35-50. Part in *World*. Wolfe's writings favored economic change but failed to convey a clear meaning of spiritual fulfillment.

KOFSKY, BERNARD W. "Overloaded Black Briefcase." *Thomas Wolfe at Washington Square*. One of Wolfe's students in the fall of 1929.

KRAUSS, RUSSELL. "Replacing Tom Wolfe." *Thomas Wolfe at Washington Square*. Krauss took over certain of Wolfe's classes early in 1930.

KUSSY, BELLA. "The Vitalist Trend and Thomas Wolfe," *Sewanee Review*, L (July-September, 1942), 306-24. *World*. Nazism showed Wolfe the dangers of unchecked vitalism, but he lacked the critical intelligence to conceive any clear alternative.

LEDIG-ROWOHLT, HEINRICH M. "Thomas Wolfe in Berlin," *Der Monat*, I (October, 1948), 69. Translation in *The American Scholar*, XXII (Spring, 1953), 185-201.

LESSING, DORIS. "Thomas Wolfe, Myth-maker," *Manchester Guardian Weekly* (October 9, 1958), p. 11.

LITTLE, THOMAS. "The Thomas Wolfe Collection of William B. Wisdom," *Harvard Library Bulletin*, I (Autumn, 1947), 280-87.

McCOY, GEORGE W. "Asheville and Thomas Wolfe," *North Carolina Historical Review*, XXX (April, 1953), 200-17.

McELDERRY, B. R., JR. "The Autobiographical Problem in Thomas Wolfe's Earlier Novels," *Arizona Quarterly*, IV (Winter, 1948), 315-24.

———. "The Durable Humor in *Look Homeward, Angel*," *Arizona Quarterly*, XI (Summer, 1955), 123-28.

———. "Thomas Wolfe: Dramatist," *Modern Drama*, VI (May, 1963), 1-11.

MANDEL, JAMES. "Thomas Wolfe, A Reminiscence." *Thomas Wolfe at Washington Square*. Mandel, then a student at New York University, worked for Wolfe as a typist.

MIDDLEBROOK, L. RUTH. "Reminiscences of Tom Wolfe," *American Mercury* LXIII (November, 1946), 544-49.

———. "Further Memories of Tom Wolfe," *American Mercury*, LXIV (April, 1947), 413-20. Mrs. Middlebrook was a colleague at Washington Square.

NATANSON, M. A. "Privileged Moment: A Study in the Rhetoric of Thomas Wolfe," *Quarterly Journal of Speech*, XLIII (April, 1957), 143-50. *World*. "Rhetoric gives to the privileged moment a privileged status."

PERKINS, MAXWELL E. "Scribner's and Thomas Wolfe," *Carolina* Magazine, XLVIII (October, 1938), 15-17. *Enigma*. General tribute.

———. "Thomas Wolfe," *Harvard Library Bulletin*, I (Autumn, 1947), 269-79. Part in *World*. More specific comment on editing of Wolfe's manuscript.

POLK, WILLIAM. "Thomas Wolfe," *Carolina Magazine*, LXVIII (October, 1938), 4-5. Polk was, for a time, Wolfe's roommate at Harvard.

Selected Bibliography

POWELL, DESMOND. "Of Thomas Wolfe," *Arizona Quarterly*, I (Spring, 1945), 28-36. Powell, a former colleague at Washington Square, took Wolfe by automobile from Denver to Santa Fe in 1935.

PRIESTLEY, J. B. *Literature and Western Man*. New York: Harper and Brothers, 1960, pp. 438-40. *World*. Wolfe is one of the small and invaluable company of essentially American creators."

PUSEY, WILLIAM W. III. "The German Vogue of Thomas Wolfe," *Germanic Review*, XXIII (April, 1948), 131-48.

REEVES, PASCHAL. "The Humor of Thomas Wolfe," *Southern Folklore Quarterly*, XXIV (June, 1960), 109-20. Emphasizes Wolfe's debt to humor of the Old Southwest.

RIBALOW, HAROLD U. "Of Jews and Thomas Wolfe," *Chicago Jewish Forum*, XIII (1954), 89-99.

ROTHMAN, NATHAN L. "Thomas Wolfe and James Joyce: A Study in Literary Influence." *A Southern Vanguard*. Ed. ALLEN TATE. New York: Prentice-Hall, Inc., 1947, pp. 52-77. *Enigma*. Influenced by Joyce, Wolfe "remained always free of purely derivative writing."

RUBIN, LOUIS D., JR. "Thomas Wolfe in Time and Place," *Southern Renascence*. Ed. LOUIS D. RUBIN, JR., and ROBERT D. JACOBS. Baltimore: Johns Hopkins Press, 1953, pp. 290-305.

SCHOENBERGER, FRANZ. "Wolfe's Genius Seen Afresh," New York *Times Book Review* (August 4, 1946), pp. 1, 25, Revised, *Enigma*. Editor of the anti-Nazi *Simplicissmus*, Schoenberner pays tribute to Wolfe, whom he did not discover until 1945.

SCHORER, MARK. "Technique as Discovery," *Hudson Review*, I (Spring, 1948), 67-87. "Thomas Wolfe never really knew what he was writing *about*."

SIMPSON, CLAUDE M., JR. "Thomas Wolfe: A Chapter in His Biography," *Southwest Review*, XXV (April, 1940), 308-21.

SLOANE, WILLIAM. "Literary Prospecting," *The Saturday Review of Literature*, XIII (December 3, 1938), 4. Sloane read part of the ms. of *Look Homeward, Angel* for Longmans, Green, and Company.

SMITH, HARRISON. "Midwife to Literature," *The Saturday Review of Literature*, XXX (July 12, 1947), 15-16. Perkins was "right" in his editing of Wolfe.

SPILLER, ROBERT E. "Full Circle." *The Cycle of American Literature: An Essay in Historical Criticism*. New York: The Macmillan Company, 1955. *World*. Wolfe "the spontaneous, organic artist."

STAHR, ALDEN. "Thomas Wolfe at Chapel Hill," *Carolina Magazine*, (April, 1932), pp. 1, 8.

STEARNS, MONROE M. "The Metaphysics of Thomas Wolfe," *College English*, VI (January, 1945), 193-99. Wolfe "preaches a return to the natural man, reaffirms man's divinity and purpose," in ways parallel to Coleridge and Wordsworth. *Enigma*.

STONEY, GEORGE. "Eugene Returns to Pulpit Hill," *Carolina Magazine*, LXVIII (October, 1938) 11-14. Reminiscence.

TAYLOR, WALTER F. "Thomas Wolfe and the Middle-class Tradition," *South Atlantic Quarterly*, LII (October, 1953), 543-54. *World*.

TERRY JOHN SKALLY. "En Route to a Legend," *The Saturday Review of Literature*, XXXI (November 27, 1948), 7-9. Re-titled "Wolfe and Perkins" in *Enigma*. "Perkins . . . never made any changes in words or style."

THOMPSON, BETTY. "Thomas Wolfe: Two Decades of Criticism," *South Atlantic Quarterly*, XLIX (July, 1950), 378-92. *Enigma*. Interpretive rather than comprehensive.

VINING, LOU MYRTIS. "I Cover a Writers' Conference," *Writer's Digest*, XV (September, 1935), 30-32. Wolfe's appearance at Boulder, Colorado.

VOLKENING, HENRY T. "Penance No More," *Virginia Quarterly Review*, XV (Spring, 1939), 196-215. *Enigma*. Also *Thomas Wolfe at Washington Square*. Wolfe's opinions and reading tastes; letters, not completely reprinted in *Letters* (1956).

WALSER, RICHARD. "Some Notes on Wolfe's Reputation Abroad," *Carolina Quarterly*, I (March, 1949), 37-41.

WARREN, ROBERT PENN. "A Note on the Hamlet of Thomas Wolfe," *American Review*, V (May, 1935), 191-208. *Enigma*. Review of *Of Time and the River*. Commends Wolfe's portraiture, notes his vagueness of intention and his mysticism, and condemns his lack of focus.

WATKINS, FLOYD C. "Thomas Wolfe and the Southern Mountaineer," *South Atlantic Quarterly*, L (1951), 58-71.

————. "Thomas Wolfe and the Nashville Agrarians," *Georgia Review*, VII (Winter, 1953), 410-23. Finds fundamental agreements.

————. "Thomas Wolfe's High Sinfulness of Poetry," *Modern Fiction Studies*, II (Winter, 1956), 197-206. Defends Wolfe's poetic style.

WATTS, GEORGIA. "An Afternoon with Thomas Wolfe," *Writer's Digest*, XXXIX (February, 1959), 30-34. Miss Watts worked for Wolfe as a typist.

WOLFE, FRED W. "To the Editor," *The Saturday Review of Literature*, XXXIV (August 11, 1951), 23-24. Reply to Struthers Burt (see above).

————. "To the Editor," New York *Times Book Review*, July 31, 1960.

WOLFE, JULIA E. "Look Homeward, Angel," *The Saturday Review of Literature*, XXIX (January 5, 1946), 13, 14, 31, 32. Interview with Mrs. Wolfe, transcribed by Ruth Davis (listed above). July 2, 1938). Pittsburg: The University of Pittsburg Press, 1951.

Index

Index

Names of characters, places and sections in Thomas Wolfe's works are followed by the title—in parentheses—of the book in which they appear.

A Stone, A Leaf, A Door, edited by John S. Barnes, 166
Abramson, Jake ("The Party at Jack's"), 118
Adams, Henry, 160
Adams, Léonie, 75
Adding Machine, The, by Elmer Rice, 40
Adventures of Huckleberry Finn by Mark Twain, 64
Adventures of Tom Sawyer, The, by Mark Twain, 64
Alone, Alone, see Look Homeward, Angel, 122
Alsop, Jerry (The Web and the Rock), 92, 97, 102, 163
Altamont, 115, 155; (Look Homeward, Angel), 50, 78, 90; (Of Time and the River), 69, 70, 81; ("Return of the Prodigal"), 114; (Welcome to Our City), 40
Ambush by Arthur Richman, 38
American Magazine, The, 146
American Mercury, The, 68, 104, 152
An Actor's Daughter by Aline Bernstein, 137
Ancient Mariner, The, by Samuel T. Coleridge, 122, 160
Anderson, Sherwood, 160, 170
Andreyev, Leonid, 38
Ann (Of Time and the River), 77, 80
"Anteus: Earth Again" (Of Time and the River), 70; (The October Fair), 123
Arms and the Man by George Bernard Shaw, 38
Arrowsmith by Sinclair Lewis, 168
Arrowsmith, Martin (Arrowsmith), 168, 169
Asheville, North Carolina, 18, 21, 22, 24, 25, 27, 30, 31, 32, 46, 47, 58, 85, 86, 101, 129, 136, 146, 151, 162
Aswell, Edward C., 19, 86, 88, 89, 98, 102, 113, 124, 152, 157, 158, 167, 168, 171
Atlantic Monthly, The, 83
Aunt Maw (The Web and the Rock), 91, 92; (You Can't Go Home Again), 98, 99

Baker, George Pierce, 18, 20, 21, 31, 32, 36, 37, 44, 71, 130, 132, 171
Baker's 47 Workshop, 31, 34, 36, 37, 38, 42, 130, 172
Bailey, Joe (Welcome to Our City), 41
Baldpate Mountain (The Mountains), 37
Barnes, John S., 166
Barrie, James M., 161
Barry, Philip, 36
Barton, Hugh (Look Homeward, Angel), 60
Basso, Hamilton, 162
Beals, Eller ("The Web of Earth"), 110
Beautiful and Damned, The, by Scott Fitzgerald, 139
Beerbohm, Max, 161
Behrman, S. N., 36
Belmont Prize, 32
Benchley, Robert, 36
Benét, Will (William Rose), 147
Berliner Tageblatt, 84
Bernstein, Aline, 19, 20, 33, 45, 46, 66, 67, 68, 71, 77, 83, 102, 115, 122, 128, 129, 130, 133, 134, 135, 136, 137, 138, 142, 145, 147, 151, 171
Bixby, Horace, 64

Index

Blake, William, 92
Bland, Judge Rumford (*You Can't Go Home Again*), 99, 103
Blythe, Legette, 62
Boulder, Colorado, 83
Boyd, Madeleine (Mrs. Ernest), 46, 83, 142
Boyd, James, 124, 139
Brandell, Richard (*The Web and the Rock*), 94
Bridges, Robert ("Old Man Rivers"), 117
Brooke, Rupert, 28, 29
Broun, Heywood, 36
Brownell, W. C., 138
Brown, John Mason, 36, 37
Burgum, E. B., 75

Capek, Karel, 38
Captain Richard Hawkins (*Third Night*), 35
Cargill, Oscar, 151
Carlton, Henry, 72
Carolina Folk Plays, 34
Carolina Magazine, The, 26, 28, 35
Carolina Playmakers, 26, 28, 34, 35, 36, 64
Cervantes Saavedra, Miguel de, 163
Chapel Hill (University of North Carolina), 18, 20, 25, 26, 28, 30, 32, 34, 35, 42, 62, 63, 85, 90, 131
Cherry Orchard, The, by Anton Chekhov, 39
Civil War, 39, 106, 107, 108, 109, 110
Clemens, Samuel, *see* Mark Twain
Coleridge, Samuel Taylor, 61, 120, 160, 163
Colliers Magazine, 146
Collins, Wilkie, 136
Common Clay by Cleves Kinkead, 137
Conroy, Hunt (*You Can't Go Home Again*), 101
Cosmopolitan Magazine, 104
Coulsons at "Hill-Top Farm," 120
Cowley, Malcolm, 102
Crane, Dr. Frank, 146
Crane, Nebraska (*The Web and the Rock*), 91, 92, 97; (*You Can't Go Home Again*), 99, 101, 102

Cullenden, Roger ("A Cullenden of Virginia"), 29

Daniels Jonathan, 30, 47, 62, 63
"Dark Messiah, The," (*You Can't Go Home Again*), 98 .
Darktown (*Welcome to Our City*), 40, 41, 42
Day, Frederic L., 72
"Death of Ben Gant, The," (*Thomas Wolfe Reader*), 120
De Voto, Bernard, 84, 141, 164
Dickens, Charles, 92, 118
Dixieland (*Look Homeward, Angel*), 50
Dodd, Martha, 149
Dodd, William E., 82, 148
Dostoevski, Fyodor, 92, 163
Doland, Father ("In the Park"), 117
Donne, John, 137
Don Quixote by Miguel de Cervantes Saavedra, 162
Dorman libel suit, 85, 142
Dos Passos, John, 170, 172
Dow, Robert, 72
Dows, Olin, 72
Dreiser, Theodore, 47, 170
Drumgoole, Emily (Mrs. Ted Joyner), 105

Edison, Thomas A., 146
Editor To Author (Letters of Maxwell E. Perkins), 21
Edwards, Foxhall (*You Can't Go Home Again*), 20, 90, 98, 100, 101, 102, 103, 117, 119, 144, 152, 163, 170, 173
Eliot, Thomas Stearns, 161
Emerson, Ralph W., 160
Ervine, St John, 38
Esquire, 104
Eugene (*Three Blue Suits*), 135, 136

Farewell to Arms, A, by Ernest Hemingway, 17
Fata Morgana by Ernest Vajda, 38
Faulkner, William, 43, 114, 115, 161, 170, 172
"Faust and Helen" (*Of Time and the River*), 70, 123

Field God, The, by Paul Green, 34
Fisher, Vardis, 75, 171
Fitzgerald, F. Scott, 20, 47, 67, 139, 161, 162, 163, 170
Flaubert, Gustave, 162, 163
"Flight Before Fury" (*Of Time and the River; Thomas Wolfe Reader*), 120
Ford, Ford Madox, 161
Ford, Henry, 146
Fox, John, Jr., 35
France, Anatole, 161
Frere, A. S., 82, 157
Froelich, Mr. (*Three Blue Suits* by Aline Bernstein), 135, 136

Galsworthy, John, 42, 162
Gant family, 20, 48, 78, 101, 102, 103, 104, 105, 112, 114, 115, 118, 122, 137, 165; Benjamin Harrison ("Gentlemen of the Press"), 113; (*Look Homeward, Angel*), 17, 24, 27, 43, 48, 49, 50, 51, 52, 53, 59, 61, 65; ("The Web of Earth"), 111; Daisy (*Look Homeward, Angel*), 24; Eliza (Mrs.), 54; (*Look Homeward, Angel*), 48, 50, 51, 52, 53, 55, 60, 65, 91; ("No Cure For It"), 112; (*Of Time and the River*), 69, 81, 91; ("The Return of the Prodigal"), 114; ("The Web of Earth"), 110, 111, 114; Eugene, 80, 89, 90, 96, 97, 101, 165, 168, 169; ("Face of the War"), 113; ("Kinsman of His Blood") 114; (*Look Homeward, Angel*), 17, 19, 20, 26, 27, 30, 47, 48, 49, 50, 51, 52, 53, 54, 59, 60, 61, 63, 77, 78, 91, 122, 146, 159, 169, 170; ("The Lost Boy"), 113, 114; ("No Cure For It"), 112; (*Of Time and the River*), 39, 69, 70, 71, 72, 73, 77, 78, 79, 81, 82, 91, 98, 119, 120, 134, 146, 148, 155, 164; ("A Portrait of Bascom Hawke"), 118; ("The Return of the Prodigal"), 114; Gilbert, (*Look Homeward, Angel*), 24, 50, 78; Grover Cleveland ("The Lost Boy"), 113, 114; ("The Web of Earth"), 111;

Helen, (*Look Homeward, Angel*), 24, 48, 49, 50, 51, 60; (*Of Time and the River*), 69, 81; Luke (*Look Homeward, Angel*), 24, 48, 49, 51, 60; Lydia (W. O. Gant's second wife, "The Web of Earth"), 110; Maggie Efird, ("The Web of Earth"), 110; Steve (*Look Homeward, Angel*), 24, 48, 49, 51, 61; William Oliver, ("Four Lost Men"), 112; (*Look Homeward, Angel*), 20, 43, 47, 48, 50, 51, 52, 54, 55, 60, 65, 66, 77, 78, 82, 155, 159, 163; (*Of Time and the River*), 81, 82, 93, 155, 156; ("No Cure For It"), 112; ("The Lost Boy"), 113; ("The Web of Earth"), 110, 111, 114
Gavin, Buck (*The Return of Buck Gavin*), 35
"Genius is Not Enough" by Bernard De Voto, 84, 141
Goethe, Johann Wolfgang von, 82
Gone With the Wind by Margaret Mitchell, 161
Gorewitz, Boris (*Of Time and the River*), 73
Gottlieb, Max (*Arrowsmith*), 168
Great Gatsby, The, by Scott Fitzgerald, 139
Great War, 27, 28, 29, 78
Green, C. (*You Can't Go Home Again*), 103
Green, Paul, 28, 34, 44
Greenlaw, Edwin, 26, 30, 64, 130
Greenough, Chester, 31
The Guardsman by Ferenc Molnár, 38
Guest, Edgar A., 146
Guggenheim Fellowship, 67, 76, 122, 131, 134, 135, 136, 153

Hamlet by William Shakespeare, 39
Hansen, Harry, 47
Harcourt, Alfred, 85
Harper's (publishers), 19, 86, 88, 124, 141
Harper's Magazine, 104
Harvard University, 18, 20, 21, 22, 30, 31, 32, 37, 42, 50, 63, 69, 70, 71, 72, 74, 76, 77, 78, 79, 91, 97,

126, 130, 131, 132, 138, 142, 144, 146, 153, 159

Hatcher, Professor (*Of Time and the River*), 20, 71, 80

Hauser, Otto (*You Can't Go Home Again*), 98

Hawke, Bascom ("The Portrait of Bascom Hawke"–changed to Bascom Pentland in *Of Time and the River*), 118, 157, 163

Hawke, David Monkey (*The October Fair*), 123

Hawke, Delia ("The Web of Earth" –changed to Eliza Gant in *From Death to Morning*), 124

He Who Gets Slapped by Leonid Andreyev, 38

Heartbreak House by George Bernard Shaw, 38

Heilprinn, Miss (*You Can't Go Home Again*), 118

Helburn, Theresa, 36

Hemingway, Ernest, 17, 119, 139, 156, 161, 170, 172

Henry, Lieutenant Frederick (*A Farewell to Arms*), 17

Hensley, Dock ("The Web of Earth"), 111

Heyward, Du Bose, 43

Hilltop Farm, 45, 120

Hirsch, Lawrence (*Of Time and the River*), 118

Holman, C. Hugh, 118, 119, 120

Hook, Stephen (*You Can't Go Home Again*), 118

Hoover, Herbert, 147

Home to Our Mountains (*You Can't Go Home Again*), 96, 98, 99

Houghton-Mifflin Company, 85

Howard, Sidney, 36, 38

Howells, William Dean, 95

Huxley, Aldous, 147, 161

Ibsen, Henrik, 38

In Abraham's Bosom by Paul Green, 34

Injun Joe (*Adventures of Huckleberry Finn*), 64

Innocents Abroad by Mark Twain, 64, 65

Irving, Washington, 160

Jack, Esther, 20, 102, 135, 151; (*Of Time and the River*), 19, 20, 70, 80, 134, 156; ("The Party at Jack's"), 137; (*The Web and the Rock*), 90, 93, 94, 95, 96, 97, 117, 163, 166, 170; (*You Can't Go Home Again*), 98, 99, 100, 120

James, Laura (*Look Homeward Angel*), 26, 27, 51

James Rodney Publishing Company (*You Can't Go Home Again*), 98, 122, 177

Jane Clegg by St. John Ervine, 38

"Jason's Voyage" (*Of Time and the River*), 70

Jelliffe, Mrs. Belinda, 143

John Ferguson by St. John Ervine, 38

Johnson, Annie (*Welcome to Our City*), 41

Johnson, Dr. (*Welcome to Our City*), 41, 42

Johnson, Pamela, 173

Jones, Abe (*Of Time and the River*), 69, 72, 73

Jordan, Mr. (*Welcome to Our City*), 41

Journey Down, The, by Aline Bernstein, 136, 137

Joyce, James, 111, 124, 155, 158, 159, 163

Joyner family, 104, 105, 107, 171 ("The Hills Beyond"), 164; (*The Web and the Rock*), 91; Dolph ("The Hills Beyond"), 106; Drumgoole ("The Hills Beyond"), 105; Edward ("The Hills Beyond"), 106, 107, 108; Emily (Mrs. Theodore), ("The Hills Beyond"), 106; Mag (*The Web and the Rock*), 91; Major (*The Web and the Rock*), 91; Mark (*The Web and the Rock*), 91, 93; Robert ("The Hills Beyond"), 106, 107; Theodore ("The Hills Beyond"), 105, 107; Virginia ("The Hills Beyond"), 106; William ("The Hills Beyond"), 105, 107; Zachariah ("The Hills Beyond"), 105, 106

Joyner Heights Academy ("The Hills Beyond"), 105

Katamoto, Mr. (*You Can't Go Home Again*), 102, 163
Kinkead, Cleves, 36
Kittredge, George Lyman, 31, 72
"Kronos and Rhea: The Dream of Time" (*Of Time and the River*), 70
Koch, Frederick H., 26, 31, 34, 35, 130

Lafayette Escadrille ("Gentlemen of the Press"), 113
Lardner, Ring, 139
Latimer, Margery, 47
Lawrence, D. H., 161
Ledig-Rowohlt, Heinz, 149
Leonard, Margaret (*Look Homeward, Angel*), 53, 59, 78; Private school, 51
Lewis, Sinclair, 20, 48, 68, 69, 117, 168, 169, 170
Libya Hill ("The Hills Beyond"), 105, 106; (*The Web and the Rock*), 90, 94; (*You Can't Go Home Again*), 98, 99, 100
Life of Pope by Leslie Stephen, 161
Life on the Mississippi by Mark Twain, 64
"Lion Hunters, The" (*You Can't Go Home Again*), 103
Logan, Piggy (*You Can't Go Home Again*), 99
Looky Thar ("The Hills Beyond"), 106, 107, 108
Lowes, John Livingston, 31, 72, 130, 160
Luther, Martin, 141, 145

MacGowan, Kenneth, 36
Madame Bovary by Gustave Flaubert, 162
"The Magic Year" (*The Web and the Rock*), 93
Malone, Mr. (*The Web and the Rock*), 95, 96
Mann, Thomas, 161
Maugham, Somerset, 80, 161

McGuire, Dr. (*Of Time and the River*), 81; ("No Cure for It"), 112
McHarg, Lloyd (*You Can't Go Home Again*), 68, 100, 102, 163
Mears, Ed ("The Web of Earth"), 111
Milton, John, 166
Modern Monthly, 104
Moderwell, Hiram, 36
Molnár, Ferenc, 38
Montreux, Switzerland, 67
Munn, James B., 75
Murphy family (*Of Time and the River*), 71

Nathan, Robert, 161
Nation, The, 149, 150
Nazis, 84, 86, 100, 102, 119, 148
Negro Dick ("The Child by Tiger"), 92; (*The Web and the Rock*), 91, 97, 101
Neely, Miss (*Welcome to Our City*), 41
Neighborhood Playhouse, 33, 38, 133
Nelson, Dr. ("The Web of Earth"), 111
New Republic, The, 84, 104
New Yorker, The, 104
New York *Herald-Tribune*, 47
New York *Times*, 47, 70, 135, 138
New York University, 18, 30, 32, 45, 46, 47, 67, 68, 71, 72, 74, 77, 101, 130, 132, 134, 144, 145, 151
New York *World*, 47
North American Review, The, 104
Nowell, Elizabeth, 21, 111, 117, 124, 128, 135, 140

Of Human Bondage by Somerset Maugham, 80, 169
"Oktoberfest" (*The Web and the Rock; Thomas Wolfe Reader*), 120, 149
Old Catawba ("Men of Old Catawba") 105; (*Of Time and the River*), 79; (*You Can't Go Home Again*), 98
Old Kentucky Home (*Look Homeward, Angel*), 22, 24, 26, 59, 60

Index

O'Neill, Eugene, 36, 48, 161, 170
"Orestes: Flight Before Fury" (*Of Time and the River*), 69
O'Rourke, Father ("In the Park"), 117

Patton, Martha ("Chickamauga"), 108, 109
Pearson, Norman Holmes, 40
Peer Gynt by Henrik Ibsen, 38
Pentland family, 23, 104, 105, 114, 121, 122, 124, 157, 171; (*Look Homeward, Angel*), 60; Arnold ("A Kinsman of His Blood"), 114; Bascom (*Of Time and the River*; Bascom Hawke in "The Portrait"), 71, 79; Eliza *see* Eliza Gant, 55; Jim (*Look Homeward, Angel*), 60; Will (*Look Homeward, Angel*), 60
Perkins, Maxwell E., 19, 20, 21, 47, 67, 68, 77, 82, 83, 84, 85, 86, 88, 102, 111, 117, 123, 124, 127, 130, 135, 138, 139, 140, 141, 142, 143, 144, 145, 148, 155, 156, 157, 161, 163, 169
Pierce, Joel (*Of Time and the River*), 39, 70, 79
Pine Rock College (*The Web and the Rock*), 90, 91; (*You Can't Go Home Again*), 101
Porter, Mel ("The Web of Earth"), 110
Powell, Desmond, 83
Philo Vance Stories by Willard Huntington Wright, 139
Pi Kappa Phi, 26
Pickerbaugh, Dr. (*Arrowsmith*), 168
Pickwick Papers by Charles Dickens, 162
Porgy by Du Bose Heyward, 43
Princeton University, 22
Prokosch, Frederic, 75
"Proteus: the City" (*Of Time and the River*), 69, 72
Proust, Marcel, 161
Provincetown Theatre, 38
Pulpit Hill, 20; (*Look Homeward, Angel*), 61, 90
Purdue Speech, 43, 173

Purdue University, 19, 43, 86, 152, 159, 173
Purvis, Daisy (*You Can't Go Home Again*), 103

"Queen" Elizabeth (*Look Homeward, Angel*), 66, 78
"Quest of the Fair Medusa, The" (*You Can't Go Home Again*), 98

R. U. R. by Karel Čapek, 38
Radcliffe Agassiz Theatre, 37
Raisbeck, Kenneth, 32, 72, 133
Raleigh News and Observer, 28
Ramsay family, 43; (*Mannerhouse*), 38; Eugene (*Mannerhouse*), 39; General (*Mannerhouse*), 39
Randolph, Jim (*The Web and the Rock*), 91, 92, 97, 102
Rascoe, Burton, 163
Rawlings, Marjorie Kinnan, 156-57
Rawng and Wright (*The Web and the Rock*), 96
Redbook, The, 68, 104
Rice, Elmer, 40
Richman, Arthur, 38
Road to Xanadu, The, by John Livingston Lowes, 72, 130
Roberts, J. M., 25
Roberts, Margaret, 21, 25, 27, 35, 47, 53, 54, 73, 74, 129, 132, 144, 146, 171
Roosevelt, Franklin Delano, 148
Rothman, Nathan L., 159
Roughing It by Mark Twain, 64, 65
Rowohlt, Ernest, 82
Rutledge family (*Welcome to Our City*), 41, 42, 43; Lee (*Welcome to Our City*), 41

Saint Joan by George Bernard Shaw, 38
Sartorises of William Faulkner, 114
Saturday Evening Post, The, 24, 49, 104, 109, 146
Saturday Review of Literature, The, 19, 84, 141
Sayler, Oliver M., 42
Schlauch, Margaret, 75
Schorer, Mark, 172

Scribner, Charles II ("The Lion at Morning"), 117
Scribner's (publishing house), 19, 46, 67, 83, 88, 127, 128, 131, 134, 135, 138, 139, 141, 142, 143, 145, 157
Scribner's Magazine, 18
Shakespeare, William, 39, 72, 74, 163
Shaw, George Bernard, 38, 161
Sheldon, Edward, 36
Shelley, Percy Bysshe, 127
Shepperton, Randy (You Can't Go Home Again), 99, 100
Short Novels of Thomas Wolfe, The, edited by C. Hugh Holman, 118
Simonson, Lee, 36
Simpson, Genevieve (Of Time and the River), 71
Six Characters in Search of an Author by Luigi Pirandello, 43
Smith, Al., 147
Snopeses of William Faulkner, 43
Sorrel, Mr. (Welcome to Our City), 41
Starwick, Francis (Of Time and the River), 70, 71, 72, 77, 80
Steinbeck, John, 170, 172
Stephen, Leslie, 161
Strife by John Galsworthy, 42
Swift, Jonathan, 54, 161
Tale of a Tub by Jonathan Swift, 161
Tar Baby (student magazine), 26
Tar Heel (student newspaper), 26, 27, 28, 62
"Telemachus" (Of Time and the River), 69, 72, 78
Ten Eyck, Oswald, 163
Tender is the Night by F. Scott Fitzgerald, 162
Terry, John, 75
Theatre Guild (New York), 18, 32, 36, 37, 38, 130, 151
They Knew What They Wanted by Sidney Howard, 38
Thomas, General ("Chickamauga"), 109
Thomas Wolfe Reader edited by C. Hugh Holman, 120

Three Blue Suits by Aline Bernstein, 135
Titans (Of Time and the River), 70
Tod (Mannerhouse), 39
Torrington, Dr. (Look Homeward, Angel), 53
Tristram Shandy by Laurence Sterne, 162
Troy, William, 75
Twain, Mark, 64, 65, 160, 164

Ulysses by James Joyce, 111, 124, 158
Undying Fire, The, by H. G. Wells, 161
University of North Carolina, 18, 34, 47, 63, 74, 90, 129, 131, 132, 144, 153
Untermeyer, Louis, 166

Vajda, Ernest, 38
Van Vechten, Carl, 147
Vanity Fair (magazine), 104
Virginia Quarterly Review, The, 104
Voelcker, Thea, 84
Volkening, Henry, 73, 75, 147, 159, 162

Walker, N. A., 31
Wallace, George, 72
Wallace, Margaret, 47
Walpole, Hugh, 161
Washington Square College (New York University), 32, 76, 77, 127
Wasserman, Jakob, 161
Watt, Homer A., 32, 45, 74, 75
Weaver, Jim ("Chickamauga"), 108, 109
Weaver, Richard (The Mountains), 37
Weaver, Robert (Of Time and the River), 69, 72, 78, 122
Webber, George "Monk," 88, 89, 102, 169; ("The Hills Beyond") 105, 106; ("I Have a Thing to Tell You"), 119; ("The Vision of Spangler's Paul"), 124; (The Web and the Rock), 90, 91, 93, 94, 95, 96, 97, 166; (You Can't Go Home

Again), 20, 77, 98, 99, 100, 101, 103, 120, 152, 170, 173
Webber, John, 106, 107
Webber novels, 88, 89, 98, 101, 103, 104, 114, 124, 135, 144, 169, 170
Weldon, Professor (dramatic manuscript), 42, 43
Wells, Herbert George, 161
Wertheim, Maurice, 36
Westall family; John, 108; Julia Elizabeth, *see* Julia Wolfe, 22, 107; Thomas Casey, 23
Wheaton, Mabel Wolfe, *see* Mabel Wolfe, 57
Wheelock, John Hall, 123, 157, 165
Whitman, Walt, 160, 168
Wilder, Thornton, 161
Williams, Horace, 26, 30, 42, 63, 64, 130
Wilson, Herbert (*Three Blue Suits*), 135, 136
Winter, Ella, 98
Wolfe family; Benjamin Harrison, 23, 24, 27, 28, 81, 126; Effie, 24, 58, 59, 126; Frank, 24, 58, 59, 61, 85, 126; Fred, 22, 23, 24, 27, 32, 60, 86, 126; Grover Cleveland, 24, 83, 126; Julia, (Mrs. W. O.), 20, 21, 22, 23, 24, 25, 30, 54, 55, 57, 58, 60, 65, 87, 107, 110, 126; Mabel (Wheaton), 21, 24, 25, 58, 59, 60, 86, 126, 132, 146, 147; William Oliver (Mr.), 20, 22, 23, 24, 31, 54, 55, 56, 58, 60, 87, 126
Wolfe, Thomas, *passim;* autobiography in fiction, 20, 21, 23-24, 27, 30, 47, 53-65, 68, 71-77, 80-81, 97, 101-2; career summarized, 18-19, 129-31; college teacher, 32, 45-47, 67, 72-76, 130, 134; dramatic works, 31-33, 34-44, 151; dramatic quality of fiction, 52-53, 77-82, 108; education, 25, 26, 28-31, 62-64, 130-132; European travel, 32, 45-46, 67-69, 82-84, 152, 153; family relationships, 22, 23, 25, 49-50, 85, 86, 131-32; humor, 65, 66, 79, 102, 103, 117, 163-64; letters of Wolfe quoted,

23, 25, 27, 32, 35, 36, 37, 62, 63, 68, 74, 76, 88-89, 124, 131, 136, 143-44, 146, 147, 148, 149, 150-51, 152, 161, 162, 163; love affair with Mrs. Bernstein, 19, 45-46, 67, 71, 83, 115, 130, 133-38, 171; plans for work not completed, 42-43, 86, 104-08, 121-25, 157; poetic style, 51-52, 117, 164-68; reading and literary influences, 158-62; rhetoric, 77-82, 92-93, 116, 164; social views, 29, 97-98, 145-52, 172; structure of his fiction, 20, 50-51, 69-71, 118-19, 120-21, 140, 154, 155-58, 169-72; temperament, 127-29, 131-32, 139-40, 143

Writings of:

Alone, Alone, see Look Homeward, Angel, 122
"An Appreciation," 29
"Anatomy of Loneliness, The," *see* "The Hills Beyond," 152
"Angel on the Porch, An," *see Look Homeward, Angel*, 18
"Batesons, The," 42
Book of the Night, The (planned), 122, 157
Building of a Wall, The, see Look Homeward, Angel, 122
"Chickamauga," 85, 108, 109
"Child by Tiger, The," 92, 109
"Challenge, The," 29
"Circus at Dawn," 112
Concerning Honest Bob, 35
"Creative Movement in Writing, The," 28
"Crisis in Industry, The," 26, 29
"Death the Proud Brother," 115, 116
Deferred Payment, 35
"Drammer, The," 29
Face of a Nation, The, 165
"Face of the War, The," 113
Family, The, (fragment), 42
Fast Express, see Of Time and the River, 122, 123
"Four Lost Men, The," 112

From Death to Morning, (collection), 19, 83, 104, 119, 157, 165

"Gentlemen of the Press," 113

"God's Lonely Man," *see The Hills Beyond*, 152

Good Child's River, The, (planned), 122

"The Hills Beyond" (sketch), 105, 107, 114, 164, 171

The Hills Beyond (volume), 19, 104, 137, 152

The Hills Beyond Pentland (planned), 122, 124

"How to Keep Out of War," 149

"I Have a Thing to Tell You," 84, 118, 119, 149

Immortal Earth, see *The October Fair*, 123

"In the Park," 117, 137

Interstellar Interlude, 43

K 19, 68, 122

"Kinsman of His Blood, A," 114

Letters, 102, 135

"Lion at Morning, The," 117

Look Homeward, Angel, 17, 18, 19, 22, 26, 27, 33, 45, 47, 48, 50, 51, 53, 54, 58, 63, 64, 66, 67, 68, 70, 71, 75, 76, 78, 80, 82, 87, 91, 93, 102, 113, 114, 120, 121, 122, 129, 130, 131, 133, 138, 139, 142, 144, 146, 151, 155, 157, 158, 159, 160, 162, 164, 168, 169, 170

"Lost Boy, The," 113

Man on the Wheel, The, (planned), 122

Mannerhouse, 32, 37, 38, 39, 40, 43, 108, 133

Marble Man's Wife, The, 54

"Men of Old Catawba, The," 105, 143

Mountains, The, 31, 36, 42, 107

Mycerinus, 43

Niggertown, see *Welcome to Our City*, 32

"No Cure For It," 112, 114

"No Door," 84, 116, 118, 119, 120, 142

"No More Rivers," 84, 117

Note on Experts, A, 118

O Lost, see *Look Homeward, Angel*, 122

October Fair, The, 68, 83, 84, 121, 122, 123, 124, 140, 142, 154, 156, 169

Of Time and the River, 18, 39, 69, 71, 75, 76, 77, 78, 79, 80, 82, 83, 84, 90, 91, 92, 97, 98, 103, 114, 115, 118, 119, 120, 121, 122, 123, 124, 132, 134, 138, 140, 141, 142, 144, 146, 148, 149, 154, 155, 156, 157, 158, 163, 164, 166, 169, 170

"Old Man Rivers," 117

"Only the Dead Know Brooklyn," 116

Ordeal of Bondsman Doaks, The, (planned), 124

Pacific End (planned), 122

"Party at Jack's, The," 85, 118, 137, 148, 169

"Portrait of a Literary Critic, The," 118

"Portrait of Abe Jones" (*Thomas Wolfe Reader*), 120

"Portrait of Bascom Hawke, The," 68, 118, 122, 139

"Professor Hatcher's Celebrated Course" (*Thomas Wolfe Reader*), 120

Return of Buck Gavin, The, 35

"Return of the Prodigal, The," 114

"Russian Folksong," 29

Story of a Novel, The, 19, 54, 84, 121, 133, 140, 141, 153, 155, 158, 170, 171

Strikers, The, 42

Third Night, The, 35

"Universe of Daisy Purvis, The," 163

Vision of Paul Spangler, The, (planned), 86

Vision of Spangler's Paul, The, see *The Ordeal of Bondsman Doaks* (planned), 124

Web and the Rock, The, 19, 87, 89, 90, 92, 93, 95, 96, 97, 98, 109, 115, 117, 120, 137, 140, 163, 166, 170

"Web of Earth, The," 110, 111, 113, 114, 118, 122, 124

Welcome to Our City, 32, 33, 37, 38, 40, 42, 43, 71, 133, 151

Western Journal, The, 173

You Can't Go Home Again, 19, 77, 84, 85, 88, 89, 98, 102, 103, 117, 118, 120, 148, 163-64, 167, 170, 173

Woodfin Street, 24, 56, 58, 126, 131

Wordsworth, William, 166

Worth Prize, 26, 29, 145

Wright, Willard Huntington, 139

Wright, Miller ("The Web of Earth"), 111

Wylie, Elinor, 147

Yale Daily News, 40

Yale Dramatic Society, 40

Yale Review, The, 109

"Young Faustus" (*Of Time and the River*), 69, 71, 72

"Young Icarus" (*You Can't Go Home Again*), 98

Young, Stark, 161

Zola, Émile, 162